Evenings at Donaldson Manor

Or, The Christmas Guest

Maria J. McIntosh

Evenings at Donaldson Manor Or, The Christmas Guest

Copyright © 2022 Indo-European Publishing

All rights reserved

The present edition is a reproduction of previous publication of this classic work. Minor typographical errors may have been corrected without note; however, for an authentic reading experience the spelling, punctuation, and capitalization have been retained from the original text.

ISBN: 978-1-64439-896-8

CHAPTER I

The largest and the most picturesque country-house of all I know in America, is the mansion house of my friends, the Donaldsons. I would gladly inform the reader of its locality, but this Colonel Donaldson has positively prohibited, for a reason too flattering to my self-love to be resisted.

"You know, my dear Madam," I give his own words, by which I hope the courteous reader will understand that I am really too modest even to seem to adopt the flattering sentiment they convey "You know, my dear madam, that your description will be read by every body who is any body, and that through it my simple home will become classic ground. If I permit you to direct the tourist tribe to it, I shall be pestered out of my life when summer comes, by travelling artists, would-be poets, and romantic young ladies."

I may not therefore, dear reader, tell you whether this pleasant abode be washed by the waves of the Atlantic or by the turbid current of the Mississippi; whether it be fanned by the flower-laden zéphyrs of the South, or by the health-inspiring breezes of the North. The exterior must indeed have been left wholly to your imagination, had I not fortunately obtained a sketch from a young friend, an amateur artist, of whom I shall have more to say presently. As I could not in honor present you with even this poor substitute, as I trust you will consider it, for my word-painting, without Colonel Donaldson's consent, I have been compelled, in deference to his wish, to divest the picture of every thing that would mark the geographical position of the place represented. The shape of its noble old trees we have been permitted to retain; but their foliage we have been obliged to render so indistinctly, that even Linnaeus himself would find it impossible to decide whether it belonged to the elm of the North when clothed in all its summer luxuriance, or to the gigantic live-oak of the South. Even of the house itself we have been permitted to give but a rear view, lest the more marked features of the landscape in front should hint of its whereabouts. As to the figures which appear in the foreground of the picture, they are but figments of my young artist friend's imagination. One of them you may observe carries under the arm a sheaf of wheat, not a stalk of which I assure you ever grew on the Donaldson lands.

Even from this imperfect picture of the exterior, you will perceive that the house is, as I have said, both large and picturesque. Within, the rooms go rambling about in such a strange fashion, that an unaccustomed guest attempting to make his way without a guide to the chambre de nuit in which he had slept only the night before, would be very apt to find himself in the condition of a certain bird celebrated in nursery rhymes as wandering,

Up stairs and down stairs
And in the ladies' chambers.

In this house have the Donaldsons lived and died for nearly two hundred years, and during all that time they have never failed to observe the Christmas with right genuine, old English hospitality. Then, their sons and their daughters, their men-servants and their maid-servants, and the stranger within their gates, felt the genial influence of their gratitude to Him who added year after year almost unbroken temporal prosperity to the priceless gift commemorated by that festival. At many of these reunions it has been my good fortune to be present. Indeed, though only "AUNT Nancy," by that courtesy which so often accords to the single sisterhood some endearing title, as a consolation, I presume, for the more honorable one of MRS. which their good or evil fortune has denied them, I have been ever received at Donaldson Manor as at my own familiar home; nor was it matter of surprise to myself or to our mutual friends, when the Col. and Mrs. Donaldson named their fourth daughter after me, modifying the old-fashioned Nancy, however, into its more agreeable synonyme of Annie.

This daughter has been, of course, my peculiar pet. In truth, however, she has been scarcely less the peculiar pet of father and mother, brothers and sisters, friends and neighbors sweet Annie Donaldson, as all unite in calling her, and certainly a sweeter, fresher bud of beauty never opened to the light than my name-child. And yet, reader, it may be that could I faithfully stamp her portrait on my page, you would exclaim at my taste, and declare there was no beauty in it. I will even acknowledge that you may be right, and that there is nothing artistically beautiful in the dark-gray eyes, the clear and healthy yet not dazzlingly fair complexion, the straight though glossy dark-brown hair, and the form, rounded and buoyant, but neither tall enough to be dignified nor petite enough to be fairy-like. But sure I am that you could not know the spirit, gentle and playful yet lofty and earnest, which looks out from her eyes and speaks in her clear, silvery tones and graceful gestures, without feeling that Annie Donaldson is beautiful. Nor am I alone in this opinion. My friend Mr. Arlington fully agrees with me, as you would be convinced if you could see the admiring expression with which he gazes on her. As this gentleman cannot plead the Colonel's reason for any reserve respecting his place of residence, I shall not hesitate to inform the reader that he is a young lawyer of New-York, who has preserved, amidst much study and some business, the natural taste necessary to the enjoyment of country scenes and country sports. During those weeks of summer when New-York is deserted, alike by the wearied man of business and the ennuye idler, Mr. Arlington, instead of rushing with the latter to the overcrowded hotels of Saratoga and Newport, takes his gun and dog, his pencil and sketch-book, and with an agreeable companion, or, if this may not be, some choice books, as a resource against a rainy day, he goes to some wild spot the wilder the better where he roves at will from point to point of interest and beauty, and spends his time in reading, sketching, and alas, for human imperfection! shooting. These vagrant habits first brought him into the neighborhood of Donaldson Manor, and he had for two successive summers hunted with the Colonel and sketched with the young ladies, when he was invited to join their Christmas party in 18 . Here I was introduced to him, and in a few days we were the best friends in the world.

Mr. Arlington's sketch-book, of which I have already spoken, served to elicit one of our points of sympathy. Bound down by the iron chain of necessity to that point of space occupied by my own land, and that point of time filled by my own life, yet with a heart longing for acquaintance with the beautiful distant and the noble past, I have ever loved the creations of that art which furnished food to these longings; and as my fortune has denied me the possession of fine paintings, I have become somewhat noted in my own little circle for my collection of fine engravings. Many of these have peculiar charms for me, from their association, fancied or real, with some place or person that does interest or has interested me. In the leisure of a solitary life, it has amused me to append to these engravings a description of the scenes or a narrative of the incidents which they suggested to my mind, and for their association with which I particularly valued them. Annie was well aware of the existence of these descriptions and narratives, and, with a pretty despotism which she often exercises over those she loves, she insisted that I should surrender them to her for the gratification of the assembled party. One condition only was I permitted to make in this surrender, and this was, that Mr. Arlington should also bring forth his portfolio for inspection, and should describe the locale of the scene sketched, or relate the circumstances under which the sketches were made. A pretty ruse this, my gentle Annie, by which you furnished the artist with an opportunity to display to others the talents which had charmed yourself. In accordance with this compact, the drawings, with their accompanying narratives, were produced, and received with such approbation, that by the same sweet tyranny which drew them from their hiding-places, we have been ordered to send this Christmas Guest to bear the simple stories to other houses, with the hope that they may give equal pleasure to their inmates.

CHAPTER II

Merrily blazed the wood fire in the huge old chimney of the large parlor in which we were accustomed to assemble in the evening, at Donaldson Manor, and its light was thrown upon faces bright with good-humored merriment, yet not without some touch of deeper and more earnest feeling. That party would of itself have made an interesting picture. There was Col. Donaldson, tall, gaunt, his figure slightly bent, yet evincing no feebleness, his curling snow-white locks, his broad bold forehead, and shaggy brows overhanging eyes beaming with kindness. Beside him sat Mrs. Donaldson, still beautiful in her green old age. Her face was usually pale, yet her clear complexion, and the bright eyes that looked out from beneath the rich Valenciennes border of her cap, redeemed it from the appearance of ill health. Her form, stately yet inclining to embonpoint, was shown to advantage by the soft folds of the rich and glossy satin dress which ordinarily, at mid-day, took the place in summer of her cambric morning-dress, and in winter of her cashmere robe de chambre. Mrs. Donaldson has a piece of fancy netting which she reserves for her evening work, because, she says, it does not make much demand upon her eyes. This the mischievous and privileged Annie calls "Penelope's Web," declaring, that whatever is done on it in the evening is undone the next morning. Around the table, on which the brightest lights were placed for the convenience of those who would read or sew, clustered the two married daughters of the house who always return to their "home," as they still continue to call Donaldson Manor, for the Christmas holidays Annie, Mr. Arlington, and myself. Miss Donaldson, the eldest daughter of my worthy friends, is the housekeeper of the family, and usually sits quietly beside her mother, somewhat fatigued probably by the active employments of her day. The two sons of Col. Donaldson, the elder of whom is only twenty-three, his sons-in-law, and his grandson, Robert Dudley, a fine lad of twelve, give animation to the scene by moving hither and thither, now joining our group at the table, now discussing in a corner the amusements of to-morrow, and now entertaining us with a graphic account of to-day's adventures, of the sleighs upset, or the skating-matches won.

Such was the party assembled little more than a week before Christmas the last year, when Annie called upon Mr. Arlington and myself to redeem the pledges we had given, and surrender our portfolios to her. Some slight contention arose between us on the question who should first contribute to the entertainment of the company; Mr. Arlington exclaiming "Place aux Dames," and I contending that there was great want of chivalry in thus putting a woman into the front of the battle. This little dispute was terminated by the proposal that Annie having been blindfolded to secure impartial justice, the two portfolios should be placed on the table, and she should choose, not only from which of them our entertainment should be drawn, but the very subject that should furnish it. Mr. Arlington vehemently applauded this proposal, and then urged that he must himself tie the handkerchief, as no one else, he feared, would make it an effectual blind. Annie submitted to his demand, though she professed to feel great indignation at his implied doubt of her honesty. No one else, we believe, would have taken so much time for the disposal of this screen, or been so careful in the arrangement of the bands of hair over which, or through which, the handkerchief was passed; and the touch of no other hand, perhaps, would have called up so bright a color to the cheeks, and even to the brow, of our sweet Annie. When permitted to exercise her office, Annie, to my great pleasure, without an instant's hesitation, while a mischievous little smile played at the corners of her mouth, placed her hand on Mr. Arlington's portfolio, and drew from it a paper, which, on being exhibited, was found to contain the pencilled outline of many heads grouped together in various positions, some being apparently elevated considerably above the others.

"Ah, Miss Annie!" exclaimed Mr. Arlington, with considerable satisfaction apparent in his voice and manner, "you must try again, and I think I must trouble you, ladies, for another handkerchief. This seems to me to have been scarcely thick enough."

"I appeal to the company," cried Annie, "whether this is in accordance with Mr. Arlington's engagement. Was he not to accept any thing I should draw from his portfolio as the foundation of his sketch?"

"Ay, ay," was responded from every part of the room.

"But pray, my good friends," persisted Mr. Arlington, "observe the impossibility of compliance with your demand. How can I possibly hope to entertain you by any thing based upon that memento of an idle hour in court, which I should long ago have destroyed, had I not fancied that I could detect in those sketchy outlines those mere profiles very accurate likenesses of the heads for which they were taken?"

"Those heads look as though they might have histories attached to them," said Annie, as she bent to examine them more narrowly.

"Histories indeed they have," said Mr. Arlington.

"Give them to us," suggested Col. Donaldson.

"You have them already. These are all men whose histories are as well known to the public as to their own families. There is the elder K , at once so simple in heart and so acute in mind. Cannot you read both in his face? There is his son; and there is D. B. O , and O. H , and G , and J . What can I tell you of any of them that you do not know already?"

"Who are these?" asked Annie, pointing to two heads, placed somewhat aloof from the rest, and near each other. "That older face is so benevolent in its expression, and the younger has so noble a physiognomy, and looks with such reverence on his companion, that I am persuaded they have a history beyond that which belongs to the world. Is it not so?"

"It is. Those are Mr. Cavendish and Herbert Latimer. They have a history, and I will give it you if you desire it, though, thus impromptu, I must do it very imperfectly I fear."

"No apologies," said Col. Donaldson. "Begin, and do your best; no one can do more."

"Than my best," said Mr. Arlington, with a smile, "thank you. My narrative will have at least one recommendation truth as I have received its incidents from Latimer himself."

Without further preliminary, Mr. Arlington commenced the relation of the following circumstances, which he has since written out, by Annie's request, at somewhat greater length for insertion here, giving it the title of

THE MAIN CHANCE

Herbert Latimer was only twenty when, having passed the usual examination, he was admitted, by a special act of the legislative assembly of his native State, to practise at the bar. Young as he was, he had already experienced some of the severest vicissitudes of life. His father had been a bold, and for many years a successful merchant, and the young Herbert, his only child, had been born and nurtured in the lap of wealth and luxury. He was only sixteen a boy but a boy full of the noble aspirations and lofty hopes that make manhood honorable, when his father died. Mr. Latimer's last illness had been probably rendered fatal by the intense anxiety of mind he endured while awaiting intelligence of the result of a mercantile operation, on which, contrary to the cautious habits of his earlier years, he had risked well nigh all he possessed. He did not live to learn that it had completely failed, and that his wife and child were left with what would have seemed to him the merest pittance for their support.

The character and talents of young Latimer were well known to his father's friends, and more than one among them offered him a clerkship on what could not but be considered as very advantageous terms. To these offers Herbert listened with painful indecision. For himself, he would have suffered cheerfully any privation, rather than relinquish the career which his inclinations had prompted, and with which were connected all his glowing visions of the future but his mother had he a right to refuse what would enable her to preserve all her accustomed elegances and indulgences?

"You must be aware, Master Latimer," said he who had made him the most liberal offers, and who saw him hesitating on their acceptance, "you must be aware that only my friendship for your father could induce me to offer such terms to so young a man, howsoever capable. Three hundred dollars this year, five hundred the next, if you give satisfaction in the performance of your duties, a thousand dollars after that till you are of age, and then a share in the business equal to one-fourth of its profits these are terms, sir, which I would offer to no one else. Your father was a friend to me, sir, and I would be a friend to his son."

"I feel your kindness and liberality, sir."

"And yet you hesitate?"

"Will you permit me, sir, to ask till to-morrow for consideration? I must consult my mother."

"That is right, young man; that is right. She knows something of life, and will, I doubt not, advise you to close with so unexceptionable an offer."

"Whatever she may advise, sir, be assured I will do."

"I have no doubt then, sir, that I shall see you to-morrow prepared to take your place in my store. Good morning."

Assuming as cheerful an air as he could, Herbert went from this interview to his mother's sitting room. Mrs. Latimer raised her eyes to his as he entered, and reading with a mother's quick perception the disturbance of his mind, she asked him in a tone of alarm, "What is the matter, Herbert?"

"Only a very pleasant matter, mother," said Herbert, with forced cheerfulness, which he endeavored to preserve while relating the offer just received.

"And would you relinquish the study of the law, Herbert?" inquired Mrs. Latimer.

"Not if I could help it, mother; but you know Mr. Woodleigh told you that five hundred dollars a year was the utmost that he could hope to save for you. If I study law, it must be several years before I can add any thing to this sum I may even be compelled " The features of Herbert worked, tears rushed to his eyes, and he turned away, unable to speak the thought that distressed him.

"You speak of what can be saved for me, Herbert of what you may be compelled to do. Do you suppose that we can have separate interests in this question? are not your hopes my hopes will not your success, your triumph, be mine too? The only consideration for us, it seems to me, is whether the profession you have chosen and the prospects open to you in it, are worth some present sacrifice."

"They are worth every sacrifice on my part but you, mother "

"Have no separate interest from my child I have shared all your hopes, all your aspirations, Herbert, and it would cost me less to live on bread and water, to dress coarsely, and lodge hardly for the next five years, than to yield my anticipations of your future success."

Others had felt for Herbert, and had offered to aid him, and he had turned from them with a deeper sense of his need and diminished confidence in his own powers his mother felt with him, and he was cheered and strengthened. The offers of the friendly merchant were gratefully declined. By the sale of her jewels, Mrs. Latimer obtained the sum necessary to meet the expenses incident to her son's first entrance on his professional studies. She then appropriated three hundred dollars of their little income to his support in the city, and withdrew herself to the country, where, she said, the remaining two hundred would supply all her wants. When Herbert would have remonstrated against these arrangements, she reminded him that they were intended to accomplish her own wishes no less than his. He ceased to remonstrate, but he did what was better he acted and the very first year, by self-denying economy and industry, he was enabled to return to her fifty dollars of the amount she had allotted to him. The second year he did better, and the third year Mrs. Latimer was able to return to the city and board at the same house with her son. It was only by the joy she expressed at their re-union that Herbert learned how painful the separation had been to her. She would not waste his strength and her own in vain lamentation over a necessary evil. Four years sufficed to prepare Herbert Latimer for his profession, and through the influence of some of his mother's early friends, exerted at her earnest request, the legislative act which permitted his entrance on its duties, was passed. The knowledge of his circumstances had excited a warm interest for him in many minds, and they who heard his name for the first time, when he stood before them for examination, could not but feel prepossessed in favor of the youth, on whose bold brow deep and lofty thoughts had left their impress, and in whose grave, earnest eyes the spirit seer might have read the history of a life of endurance and silent struggle. All were interested in him all evinced that interest by gentle courtesy of manner and almost all seemed desirous to make his examination as light as possible all save one one usually as remarkable for his indulgence to young aspirants, as for the legal acumen and extensive knowledge, which had won for him a large share of the profits and honors of his profession. His associates now wondered to find him so rigidly exact in his trial of young Latimer's acquirements.

"You were very severe on our young tyro to-day," said a brother lawyer, and one on whom early associations and similarity of pursuits, rather than of tastes, had conferred the privileges of a friend on Mr. Cavendish, as they walked together from the court-house.

"I saw that he did not need indulgence, and I gave him an opportunity of proving to others that he did not but I had another and more selfish reason for my rigid test of his powers."

Mr. Cavendish spoke smilingly, and his friend was emboldened to ask "And pray what selfish motive could you have for it!"

"I wished to see whether he would suit me as a partner."

"A partner!"

"Yes when a man has lived for half a century, he begins to think that he may possibly grow old some day, and I would provide myself with a young partner, who may take the laboring oar in my business when age compels me to lay it aside."

"All that may do very well I have some thought of doing the same myself; but I shall look out for a young man who is well connected. Connections do a great deal for us, you know, and we must always have an eye to the main chance."

"I agree with you, but we should probably differ about what constitutes the main chance."

"There surely can be no difference about that; it means with every one the one thing needful."

"And what is, in your opinion, the one thing needful?"

"Why this, to be sure," and Mr. Duffield drew his purse from his pocket, and shook it playfully.

"A somewhat different use of the term from that which the Bible makes," said Mr. Cavendish.

"Oh! let the Bible alone, and let me hear what you think of it."

"Pardon me, I cannot let the Bible alone if I tell you my own opinions, for from the Bible I learned them."

"It seems a strange book, I must say, to consult for a law of partnerships."

"Had you a better acquaintance with it, Duffield, you would learn that its principles apply to all the relations of life. The difference between us is, that when you estimate man's chief object, or as you call it, his 'main chance,' you take only the present into view, you leave out of sight altogether the interminable future, with its higher hopes and deeper interests, and relations of immeasurably greater importance."

"I find it enough for one poor brain to calculate for the present."

"A great deal too much you will find it, if you leave out of your sum so important an item as the relations of that present to the future. Depend on it, Duffield, that he makes the most for this life, as well as for the next, of his time, his talents, and his wealth, who uses them as God's steward, for the happiness of his fellow-creatures, as well as for his own."

"And so, for the happiness of your fellow-creatures, you are going to give away half of the best practice in the State?"

"I am going to do no such thing. In the first place, I did not tell you that I was going to offer young Latimer an equal division of the profits of my practice; and for what I may offer him I have already taken care to ascertain that he can return a full equivalent. His talents need only a vantage-ground on which to act, and I rejoice to be able to give him that which my own early experience taught me to value."

"Well we shall see ten years hence how your rule and mine work. I think I shall offer a partnership to young Conway he is already rising in his profession, and is connected with some of our wealthiest families."

"Very well we shall see."

Herbert Latimer had nerved himself to endure five, or it might be ten more years of profitless toil, ere he should gain a position which would make his talents available for more than the mere essentials of existence. Let those who have looked on so dreary a prospect who have buckled on their armor for such a combat judge of the grateful emotion with which he received the generous proposal of Mr. Cavendish. This proposal, while it gave him at once an opportunity for the exercise of his powers, secured to him for the first year one-fifth, for the two following years one-fourth, and after that, if neither partner chose to withdraw from the connection, one-half of the profits of a business, the receipts of which had for several years averaged over ten thousand dollars. Mr. Cavendish soon found that he had done well to trust to the gratitude of his young partner for inducing the most active exercise of his powers. Stimulated by the desire to prove himself not unworthy of such kindness, and to secure his generous friend from any loss, Herbert never overlooked aught that could advance the interests, nor grew weary of any task that could lighten the toil of Mr. Cavendish.

"Herbert, you really make me ashamed of myself, you are so constantly busy that I seem idle in comparison," said Mr. Cavendish, as he prepared one day to lay by his papers and leave the office at three o'clock. "Pray put away those musty books, and bring Mrs. Latimer to dine with us this is a fête day with us. My daughter, who has been for two months with her uncle and aunt in Washington, has returned, and I want to introduce her to Mrs. Latimer."

"My mother will come to you with pleasure, I am sure."

"And you?"

"Will come too, if I possibly can. You dine at five?"

"Yes and remember punctuality is the soul of dinner as well as of business. So do not let the charms of Coke upon Lyttleton make you forget that fair ladies and hungry gentlemen are expecting you." Mr. Cavendish closed the door with a smiling face, and Herbert Latimer turned for another hour to his books and papers. At a quarter before five he stood with his mother in the drawing-room of Mr. Cavendish, and received his first introduction to one who soon became the star of his life.

Mary Cavendish was not beautiful far less could the word pretty have been applied to her but she was lovely. All that we most love in woman, all pure and peaceful thoughts, all sweet and gentle affections, seemed to beam from her eyes, or to sit throned upon her fair and open brow. She had enjoyed all the advantages, as it is termed, of a fashionable education, but the influences of her home had been more powerful than those of her school, and she remained what nature had made her a warm-hearted, truthful, generous, and gentle girl too ingenuous for the pretty affectations, too generous for the heartless coquetries which too often teach us that the accomplished young lady has sacrificed, for her external refinement, qualities of a nobler stamp and more delicate beauty. The only daughter among several children, she was an idol in her home, and every movement of her life seemed impelled by the desire to repay the wealth of affection that was lavished upon her. It was impossible to see such a being daily in the intimacy of her home associations the sphere in which her gentle spirit shone most brightly without loving her; and Herbert soon felt that he loved her, yet he added in his thoughts "in all honor," and to him it would have seemed little honorable to attempt to win this priceless treasure from him to whose generosity he had owed his place in her circle. Mrs. Latimer, though she did not fear for her son's honor, trembled for his future peace as she marked the sadness which often stole over him, after spending an hour in the society of this lovely girl; but Mrs. Latimer was a wise woman she knew that speech is to such emotions often as the lighted match to a magazine, and she kept silence.

For almost a year after his introduction, Herbert continued in daily intercourse with Mary Cavendish to drink fresh draughts of love, yet so carefully did he guard his manner, that no suspicion of his warmer emotions threw a shadow over her friendship, or checked the frankness with which she unveiled to him the rich treasures of her mind and heart. It was in the autumn succeeding their first acquaintance that Mr. and Mrs. Cavendish issued cards for a large party at their house. It would be too gay a scene for the quiet taste of Mrs. Latimer, but Herbert would be there, and at the request of Mrs. Cavendish he promised to come early. The promise was kept. He arrived half an hour at least before any other guest, bringing with him a bouquet of rare and beautiful flowers for Mary. As he entered the hall he heard a slight scream from the parlor beside whose open door he stood. The scream was in a voice to whose lightest tone his heart responded, and in an instant, he was beside Mary Cavendish, had clasped her in his arms, and pressing her closely to his person, was endeavoring to extinguish with his hands the flames that enveloped her. The evening was cold: there was a fire in the stove, before which Mary stood arranging some flowers on the mantel-piece, when the door was opened for him. The sudden rush of air had wafted her light, floating drapery of gauze and lace into the fire, and in a moment all was in a blaze. Fortunate was it for her, that under this light, flimsy drapery, was worn a dress of stouter texture and less combustible material a rich satin. After the slight scream which had brought him to her side, Mary uttered no sound, and with his whole soul concentrated on action, he had been equally silent till the last spark was smothered. Then gazing wildly in her pallid face he exclaimed, "In mercy speak to me! Did I come too late? Are you burned?"

"I scarcely know I think not," she faltered out. Then, as she made an effort to withdraw from his arms, added quickly "no not at all."

Completely overpowered by the revulsion of feeling which those words occasioned, Herbert clasped her again in his arms, and fervently ejaculating, "Thank God!" pressed his lips to her cheek. At that moment, the voice of Mr. Cavendish was heard in the next room, and breaking from him, Mary rushed to her astonished father, and burying her face in his bosom, burst into tears. Aroused to full consciousness by the presence of another, Herbert stood trembling and dismayed at the remembrance of his own rashness. Agitated as she was, Mary was compelled to answer her father's questions, for he seemed wholly unable to speak.

"Latimer, I owe my child's life probably to you. How shall I repay the debt?" cried Mr. Cavendish, attempting, as he spoke, to clasp Herbert's hand. He winced at the touch, and a sudden contraction passed over his face.

"You are burned," said Mr. Cavendish, and would have examined his hand, but throwing his handkerchief over it, Herbert declared it was not worth mentioning, though at the same time he confessed that the pain was sufficient to make him desirous to return home, and have some soothing application made to it. Mr. Cavendish parted from him with regret, with earnest charges that he should take care of himself, and equally earnest hopes that he might be sufficiently relieved to return to them before the evening was passed; but Mary still lay in her father's arms, with her face hidden, and noticed Herbert's departure neither by word nor look.

"I have outraged her delicacy, and she cannot bear even to see me," he said to himself.

In passing out he accidentally trod on the flowers which he had selected with such care "Crushed like my own heart!" he ejaculated mentally.

A fortnight passed before Herbert Latimer could take his accustomed place in the office of Mr. Cavendish. His hand had been deeply burned so deeply that the pain had produced fever. During this period of suffering, Mr. Cavendish had often visited him, and Mrs. Cavendish had more than once taken his mother's place at his bedside; but Herbert found little pleasure in their attentions, for he said to himself, "If they knew all my presumption, they would be less kind."

His illness passed away, his hand healed, and he resumed his accustomed avocations; but no invitation, however urgent, could win him again to the house of Mr. Cavendish. "I have proved my own weakness I will not place myself again in the way of temptation," was the language of his heart. Apologies became awkward. He felt that he must seem to his friend ungracious if not ungrateful; and one day observing unusual seriousness in the countenance of Mr. Cavendish on his declining an invitation to dine with him, he exclaimed, "You look displeased, and I can hardly wonder at it; but could you know my reason for denying myself the pleasure of visiting you, I am sure you would think me right."

"Perhaps so; but as I do not know it, you cannot be surprised that your determined withdrawal from our circle should wound both my feelings and those of my family."

Herbert covered his eyes with his hand for a moment, and then turning them with a grave and even sad expression on Mr. Cavendish, said, "I have declined your invitations only because I could not accept them with honor: I love your daughter I have loved her almost from the first hour of my acquaintance with her."

"And why have you not told me so before, Herbert?" asked Mr. Cavendish, with no anger in his tones.

"Because I believed myself capable of loving in silence, and while I wronged no one, I was willing to indulge in the sweet poison of her society; but a moment of danger to her destroyed my self-control. What has been may be again I have learned to distrust myself I cannot tamper with temptation, lest I should one day use the position in which you have placed me, and the advantages which you have bestowed on me, in endeavoring to win from you a treasure which you may well be reluctant to yield to me."

"Herbert, I only blame you for not having spoken to me sooner of this."

"I feel now that I should have done so it was a want of self-knowledge, the rash confidence of one untried which kept me silent."

"No, Herbert it was a want of knowledge of me of confidence in my justice I will not say my kindness. What higher views do you suppose I can entertain for my daughter, than to make her the wife of one who has a prospect of obtaining the most distinguished eminence in my own profession."

"If that prospect be mine, to you I owe it could I make it a plea for asking more?"

"You owe what I did for you to the interest and esteem excited by your own qualities, and all I did has only given you a place for the exercise of those qualities I do not know how you will win Mary's forgiveness for refraining from her society on such slight grounds."

"Dare I hope for your permission to seek that forgiveness?"

"Dare I hope for your company to dinner to-day?"

"Now that you know all, nothing could give so much pleasure though I fear "

"What, fearing again!"

"I fear that Miss Cavendish is very much displeased with me."

"For saving her life?"

"No not exactly that."

Herbert Latimer did not confide the cause of his fear to Mr. Cavendish, neither did he suffer it to interfere with his visit on that day. He went to dinner, but stayed to tea, and long after, and as Mary was his companion for much, if not all of this time, we presume that her displeasure could not have been manifested in any very serious manner.

It was about six weeks after this renewal of his visits that Mr. Duffield meeting his friend Mr. Cavendish one morning, accosted him with, "I hear that your daughter is going to be married to young Latimer is it true?"

"Yes, and I heartily wish the affair were over, for I hope Herbert will recover his senses when he is actually married, as now I am obliged to attend to his business and my own too."

"Not much profit in that, I should think I manage somewhat differently."

"Did you not tell me that you intended forming a partnership with young Conway?"

"Yes but before I had done so, I heard that Sprague, who is as well connected as Conway, and a great deal more industrious, would go into business with me on less exacting terms. He has been associated with me for some time. He does all the drudgery of the business, and is content with one-eighth of the profits for five years."

"Those are low terms with talent and connection too, I should think he could have done better."

"Why, you see his connections were of little use to him while he was alone, for he was so desperately poor that they did not like to acknowledge him, but I knew as soon as he began to rise they would all notice him, and so it has proved. I have no doubt I shall gain through them more than the thousand dollars a-year which Sprague will draw, while I shall be saved every thing that is really disagreeable or laborious in my practice; and you give two thousand dollars a-year, and are to have your daughter married to a gentleman who leaves all the business on your hands which of us, do you think, has attended most successfully to the main chance?"

"According to my views of the main chance, it is not to be determined by such data but even in your own view we may have a very different account to render nine years hence?"

"Ah, well! Ten years from the day that Latimer passed we will compare notes."

Ten years are long in prospective, but it seemed to both parties only a short time when the appointed anniversary came. On that day Mr. Cavendish invited several of his brother lawyers, and amongst them Mr. Duffield, to dinner. Herbert Latimer, his wife and mother, his two noble boys, and though last, not least in importance, if in size, his little girl, her grandfather's especial pet, were of the party. It was a well assorted party. The guests found good cheer and social converse the cherished friends of the house, food for deeper and higher enjoyment When the ladies had withdrawn, calling Herbert Latimer to the head of the table, Mr. Cavendish seated himself beside Mr. Duffield.

"Well, Duffield!" he exclaimed, "do you know that it is ten years to-day since Herbert Latimer stood before us for examination?"

"Ah!" ejaculated Mr. Duffield, in the tone of one who did not care to pursue the subject further.

"You remember our agreement are you still willing to make our success in that time a test of the truth of our respective principles?"

"It may afford a more conclusive proof of your better judgment in the selection of an associate."

"Sprague stands very high in his profession."

"Yes I knew he would, for he has talent and connection therefore I chose him; but he left me just at the time these were beginning to be available, as soon as the five years for which our agreement was made, had expired."

"What occasioned his leaving you?"

"Why, Duval offered him better terms than I had done I should not have cared so much for his going, but he carried off many of my clients, with whom he had ingratiated himself during his connection with me. My practice has scarcely recovered yet from the injury which he did it."

"He seems to have acted on your own principle, and to have considered the main chance to mean the most money."

"And do you suppose Latimer would have remained with you if he could have made better terms for himself?"

"I know that during my long illness he was offered double what he was receiving, or could then hope ever to receive from my practice, and his reply to the offer was that the bonds forged by gratitude and affection, no interest could break. He has now built up the business again to far more than it was when he joined me I know that I owe most of it to him, yet he will not listen to any advice to dissolve our partnership. Gentlemen," he said, "I have a sentiment to propose to you, which you may drink in wine or water as you like best. 'THE MAIN CHANCE always best secured by obedience to the golden rule as ye would that others should do unto you, do ye even so to them.'"

CHAPTER III

The morning after Mr. Arlington had commenced our Christmas entertainments with the sketch of his friend Herbert Latimer's life, was dark and gloomy. At least, such was its aspect abroad, where leaden clouds covered the sky, and a cold, sleety rain fell fast; but within, all was bright, and warm, and cheerful. Immediately after breakfast we separated, each in search of amusement suited to his or her own tastes: some to the music room, some to the library, and Robert Dudley and Annie Donaldson to a game of battledore and shuttlecock in the wide hall, with Mr. Arlington for a spectator. As the storm increased, however, all seemed to feel the want of companionship, and without any preconcerted plan, we found ourselves, about two hours after breakfast, again assembled in the room in which quiet, patient Mrs. Donaldson sat, ravelling the netting of the last evening.

"Now for Aunt Nancy's portfolio," cried Annie, as soon as conversation began to flag.

The proposal was seconded so warmly that, as I could urge nothing against it, the portfolio was immediately produced, and Annie, taking possession of it, commissioned Robert Dudley to draw forth an engraving: "Scene, a chamber by night, a sleeping baby and a sleepy mother, a basket of needle-work I am sure it is needle-work on the floor, and a cross suspended from the wall," said Annie, describing the engraving which she had taken from Robert.

"That cross looks promising," said Colonel Donaldson, who likes a little romance as well as any of his daughters. "Let us have the fair lady's history, Aunt Nancy."

"I know nothing about her," said I, with a smile at his eagerness.

"Then why, dear Aunt Nancy, did you keep the engraving?" asked Annie.

"I might answer, because of my interest in the scene it depicts a scene in which religion seems to shed its sanctifying influence over the tenderest affection and the homeliest duties of our common life; but I had another reason."

"Ah! I knew it," exclaimed Annie.

"I first saw this print in company with a very cultivated and interesting German lady, to whose memory the sleeping baby recalled a cradle song written by her countryman, the brave Koerner. She sang it for me, and as the German is, I am grieved to say, a sealed book to me, she gave me a literal translation of the words, which "

"Which you have put into English verse, and written here at the back of the engraving in the finest of all fine writing, and which papa will put on his spectacles and read for us."

"No; I commission Mr. Arlington to do that," said the Colonel, "without his spectacles."

"First," said I, "let me assure you that the original is full of a simple, natural tenderness, which I fear, in the double process of translating and versifying, has entirely escaped."

Mr. Arlington, taking the paper from Annie, now read,

THE CRADLE SONG;
A FREE TRANSLATION FROM KOERNER.

I.
Slumberer! to thy mother's breast,
So fondly folded, sweetly rest!

Within that fair and quiet world,
With downy pinions scarce unfurl'd,
Life gently passes, nor doth bring
One dream of sorrow on its wing.

II.

Pleasant our dreams in early hours,
When Mother-love our life embowers;
Ah! Mother-love! thy tender light
Hath vanished from my sky of night,
Scarce leaving there one fading ray
To thrill me with, remember'd day.

III.

Thrice, by the smiles of fav'ring Heaven,
To man this holiest joy is given;
Thrice, circled by the arms of love,
With glowing spirit he may prove
The highest rapture heart can feel,
The noblest hopes our lives reveal.

IV.

The earliest blessings that enwreathed
His infant days, 'twas Love that breathed.
In Love's warm smile the nursling blooms,
Nor fears one shade that o'er him glooms,
While flowers unfold and waters dance
In joy, beneath his first, fresh glance.

V.

And when around the youth's bold course
Clouds gather tempests spend their force
When his soul darkens with his sky,
Again the Love-God hovers nigh;
And on some gentle maiden's breast
Lulls him, once more, to blissful rest.

VI.

But when his heart bends to the power
Of storm, as bends the summer flower,
'Tis Love that, as the Angel-Death
Wooes from his lips the ling'ring breath,
And gently bears his soul above,
To the bright skies the home of Love.

"Poor Koerner!" said Mr. Arlington, as he concluded reading this song if indeed it may claim that name in its English dress "I can sympathize, as few can do, with his mournful memory of mother-love."

This was said in a tone of such genuine emotion, that I looked at him with even more pleasure than I had hitherto done.

"Such tenderness touches us particularly when found, as in Koerner, in union with manly and vigorous qualities perhaps, because it is a rare combination," said Mrs. Dudley.

"Is it rare?" I asked doubtfully. "The results of my own observation have led me to believe that it is precisely in manly, vigorous, independent minds that we see the fullest development of our simple, natural, home-affections."

"You are right, Aunt Nancy," said Col. Donaldson; "it is only boys striving to seem manly and men of boyish minds, who fail to acknowledge with reverence and tenderness the value of a mother's love."

"So convinced am I of this," I replied, "that I would ask for no more certain indication of a man's nobility of nature, than his manner to his mother. I remember a striking illustration of the fidelity of such an indication in two brothers of the name of Manning, with whom I was once acquainted. The one was quite a petit-maitre a dandy; the other, a fine creature large-minded and large-hearted. The first betrayed in every look and movement, that he considered himself greatly his mother's superior, and feared every moment that she should detract from his dignity by some sin against the dicta of fashion; the other did honor at once to her and to himself, by his reverent devotion to her. They were a contrast, and a contrast which circumstances brought out most strikingly. Ah, Mr. Arlington! I wish you could have seen them a sketch of them from your pencil would have been a picture indeed."

"We will take your word-painting instead," said Mr. Arlington.

"A mere description in words could not present them to you in all their strongly marked diversity of character. To do this, I must give you a history of their lives."

"And why not?" and "Oh, yes, Aunt Nancy, that is just what we want," was echoed from one to another. They consented to delay their gratification till the evening, that I might have a little time to arrange my reminiscences; and when "the hours of long uninterrupted evening" came, and we had

" stirr'd the fire and closed the shutters fast,
Let fall the curtains, wheeled the sofa round,"

and disposed ourselves in comfort for talking and for listening, I gave them the relation which you will find below under the title of

THE BROTHERS;
OR, IN THE FASHION AND ABOVE THE FASHION

"Some men are born to greatness some achieve greatness and some have greatness thrust upon them." Henry Manning belonged to the second of these three great classes. The son of a mercantile adventurer, who won and lost a fortune by speculation, he found himself at sixteen years of age called on to choose between the life of a Western farmer, with its vigorous action, stirring incident and rough usage and the life of a clerk in one of the most noted establishments in Broadway, the great source and centre of fashion in New-York. Mr. Morgan, the brother of Mrs. Manning, who had been recalled from the distant West by the death of her husband, and the embarrassments into which that event had plunged her, had obtained the offer of the latter situation for one of his two nephews, and would take the other with him to his prairie-home.

"I do not ask you to go with me, Matilda," he said to his sister, "because our life is yet too wild and rough to suit a delicate woman, reared, as you have been, in the midst of luxurious refinements. The difficulties and privations of life in the West fall most heavily upon woman, while she has little of that sustaining power which man's more adventurous spirit finds in overcoming difficulty and coping with danger. But let me have one of your boys; and by the time he has arrived at manhood, he will be able, I doubt not, to offer you in his home all the comforts, if not all the elegances of your present abode."

Mrs. Manning consented; and now the question was, which of her sons should remain with her, and which should accompany Mr. Morgan. To Henry Manning, older by two years than his brother George, the choice of situations was submitted. He went with his uncle to the Broadway establishment, heard the duties which would be demanded from him, the salary which would be given, saw the grace with which the elegants behind the counter displayed their silks, and satins, and velvets, to the elegantes before the counter, and the decision with which they promulgated the decrees of fashion; and with that just sense of his own powers, which is the accompaniment of true genius, he decided at once that there lay his vocation. George, who had not been without difficulty kept quiet, while his brother was forming his decision, as soon as it was announced, sprang forward with a whoop that would have suited a Western forest better than a New-York drawing-room, threw the Horace he was reading across the table, clasped first his mother and then his uncle in his arms, and exclaimed, "I am the boy for the West. I will help you fell forests and build cities there, uncle. Why should not we build cities as well as Romulus and Remus?"

"I will supply your cities with all their silks, and satins, and velvets, and laces, and charge them nothing, George," said Henry Manning, with that air of superiority with which the worldly-wise often look on the sallies of the enthusiast.

"You make my head ache, my son," complained Mrs. Manning, shrinking from his boisterous gratulation; but Mr. Morgan returned his hearty embrace, and as he gazed into his bold, bright face, with an eye as bright as his own, replied to his burst of enthusiasm, "You are the very boy for the West, George. It is out of such brave stuff that pioneers and city-builders are always made."

Henry Manning soon bowed himself into the favor of the ladies who formed the principal customers of his employer. By his careful and really correct habits, and his elegant taste in the selection and arrangement of goods, he became also a favorite with his employers themselves. They needed an agent for the selection of goods abroad, and they sent him. He purchased cloths for them in England, and silks in France, and came home with the reputation of a travelled man. Having persuaded his mother to advance a capital for him by selling out the bank stock in which Mr. Morgan had founded her little fortune, at twenty-four years of age he commenced business for himself as a French importer. Leaving a partner to attend to the sales at home, he went abroad for the selection of goods, and the further enhancement of his social reputation. He returned in two years with a fashionable figure, a most recherche style of dress, moustachios of the most approved cut, and whiskers of faultless curl a finished gentleman in his own conceit. With such attractions, the prestige which he derived from his reported travels and long residence abroad, and the savoir faire of one who had made the conventional arrangements of society his study, he quickly arose to the summit of his wishes, to the point which it had been his life's ambition to attain. He became the umpire of taste, and his word was received as the fiat of fashion. He continued to reside with his mother, and paid great attention to her style of dress, and the arrangements of her house, for it was important that his mother should appear properly. Poor Mrs. Manning! she sometimes thought that proud title dearly purchased by listening to his daily criticisms on appearance, language, manners, which had been esteemed stylish enough in their day.

George Manning had visited his mother only once since he left her with all the bright imaginings and boundless confidence of fourteen, and then Henry was in Europe. It was during the first winter after his return, and when the brothers had been separated for nearly twelve years, that Mrs. Manning informed him she had received a letter from George, announcing his intention to be in New-York in December, and to remain with them through most if not all of the winter. Henry Manning was evidently annoyed at the announcement.

"I wish," he said, "that George had chosen to make his visit in the summer, when most of the people to whom I should hesitate to introduce him would have been absent. I should be sorry to hurt his feelings, but really, to introduce a Western farmer into polished society " Henry Manning shuddered, and was silent. "And then to choose this winter of all winters for his visit, and to come in December, just at the very time that I heard yesterday Miss Harcourt was coming from Washington to spend a few weeks with her friend, Mrs. Duffield!"

"And what has Miss Harcourt's visit to Mrs. Duffield to do with George's visit to us?" asked Mrs. Manning.

"A great deal at least it has a great deal to do with my regret that he should come just now. I told you how I became acquainted with Emma Harcourt in Europe, and what a splendid creature she is. Even in Paris, she bore the palm for wit and beauty and fashion too that is in English and American society. But I did not tell you that she received me with such distinguished favor, and evinced so much pretty consciousness at my attentions, that had not her father, having been chosen one of the electors of President and Vice-President, hurried from Paris in order to be in this country in time for his vote, I should probably have been induced to marry her. Her father is in Congress this year, and you see, she no sooner learns that I am here, than she comes to spend part of the winter with a friend in New-York."

Henry arose at this, walked to a glass, surveyed his elegant figure, and continuing to cast occasional glances at it as he walked backwards and forwards through the room, resumed the conversation, or rather his own communication.

"All this is very encouraging, doubtless; but Emma Harcourt is so perfectly elegant, so thoroughly refined, that I dread the effect upon her of any outre association by the by, mother, if I obtain her permission to introduce you to her, you will not wear that brown hat in visiting her a brown hat is my aversion it is positively vulgar but to return to George how can I introduce him, with his rough, boisterous, Western manner, to this courtly lady? the very thought chills me" and Henry Manning shivered "and yet, how can I avoid it, if we should be engaged?"

With December came the beautiful Emma Harcourt, and Mrs. Duffield's house was thronged with her admirers. Hers was the form and movement of the Huntress Queen rather than of one trained in the halls of fashion. There was a joyous freedom in her air, her step, her glance, which, had she been less beautiful, less talented, less fortunate in social position or in wealth, would have placed her under the ban of fashion; but, as it was, she commanded fashion, and even Henry Manning, the very slave of conventionalism, had no criticism for her. He had been among the first to call on her, and the blush that flitted across her cheek, the smile that played upon her lips, as he was announced, might well have flattered one even of less vanity.

The very next day, before Henry had had time to improve these symptoms in her favor, on returning home, at five o'clock, to his dinner, he found a stranger in the parlor with his mother. The gentleman arose on his entrance, and he had scarcely time to glance at the tall, manly form, the lofty air, the commanding brow, ere he found himself clasped in his arms, with the exclamation, "Dear Henry! how rejoiced I am to see you again."

In George Manning the physical and intellectual man had been developed in rare harmony. He was taller and larger every way than his brother Henry, and the self-reliance which the latter had laboriously attained from the mastery of all conventional rules, was his by virtue of a courageous soul, which held itself above all rules but those prescribed by its own high sense of the right. There was a singular contrast, rendered yet more striking by some points of resemblance, between the pupil of society, and the child of the forest between the Parisian elegance of Henry, and the proud, free grace of George. His were the step and bearing which we have seen in an Indian chief; but thought had left its impress on his brow, and there was in his countenance that indescribable air of refinement which marks a polished mind. In a very few minutes Henry became reconciled to his brother's arrival, and satisfied with him in all respects but one his dress. This was of the finest cloth, but made into large, loose trowsers, and a species of hunting-shirt, trimmed with fur, belted around the waist, and descending to the knee, instead of the tight pantaloons and closely fitting body coat prescribed by fashion. The little party lingered long over the table it was seven o'clock before they arose from it.

"Dear mother," said George Manning, "I am sorry to leave you this evening, but I will make you rich amends to-morrow by introducing to you the friend I am going to visit, if you will permit me. Henry, it is so long since I was in New-York that I need some direction in finding my way must I turn up or down Broadway for Number , in going from this street?"

"Number ," exclaimed Henry in surprise; "you must be mistaken that is Mrs. Duffield's."

"Then I am quite right, for it is at Mrs. Duffield's that I expect to meet my friend this evening."

With some curiosity to know what friend of George could have so completely the entree of the fashionable Mrs. Duffield's house as to make an appointment there, Henry proposed to go with him and show him the way. There was a momentary hesitation in George's manner before he replied, "Very well, I shall be obliged to you."

"But excuse me George you are not surely going in that dress this is one of Mrs. Duffield's reception evenings, and, early as it is, you will find company there."

George laughed as he replied; "They must take me as I am, Henry. We do not receive our fashions from Paris at the West."

Henry almost repented his offer to accompany his brother; but it was too late to withdraw, for George, unconscious of this feeling, had taken his cloak and cap, and was awaiting his escort. As they approached Mrs. Duffield's house, George, who had hitherto led the conversation, became silent, or answered his brother only in monosyllables, and then not always to the purpose. As they entered the hall, the hats and cloaks displayed there showed that, as Henry supposed, they were not the earliest visitors. George paused for a moment and said, "You must go in without me, Henry. Show me to a room where there is no company," he continued, turning to a servant "and take this card in to Mrs. Duffield be sure to give it to Mrs. Duffield herself."

The servant bowed low to the commanding stranger; and Henry, almost mechanically, obeyed his direction, muttering to himself, "Free and easy, upon my honor." He had scarcely entered the usual reception-room and made his bow to Mrs. Duffield, when the servant presented his brother's card. He watched her closely, and saw a smile playing over her lips as her eyes rested on it. She glanced anxiously at Miss Harcourt, and crossing the room to a group in which she stood, she drew her aside. After a few whispered words, Mrs. Duffield placed the card in Miss Harcourt's hand. A sudden flash of joy irradiated every feature of her beautiful face, and Henry Manning saw that, but for Mrs. Duffield's restraining hand, she would have rushed from the room. Recalled thus to a recollection of others, she looked around her, and her eyes met his. In an instant, her face was covered with blushes, and she drew back with embarrassed consciousness almost immediately, however, she raised her head with a proud, bright expression, and though she did not look at Henry Manning, he felt that she was conscious of his observation, as she passed with a composed yet joyous step from the room.

Henry Manning was awaking from a dream. It was not a very pleasant awakening, but as his vanity rather than his heart was touched, he was able to conceal his chagrin, and appear as interesting and agreeable as usual. He now expected with some impatience the denouement of the comedy. An hour passed away, and Mrs. Duffield's eye began to consult the marble clock on her mantel-piece. The chime for another half-hour rang out; and she left the room and returned in a few minutes, leaning on the arm of George Manning.

"Who is that? What noble-looking man is that?" were questions Henry Manning heard from many from a very few only the exclamation, "How oddly he is dressed!" Before the evening was over Henry began to feel that he was eclipsed on his own theatre that George, if not in the fashion, was yet more the fashion than he.

Following the proud, happy glance of his brother's eye, a quarter of an hour later, Henry saw Miss Harcourt entering the room in an opposite direction from that in which she had lately come. If this was a ruse on her part to veil the connection between their movements, it was a fruitless caution. None who had seen her before could fail now to observe the softened character of her beauty, and those who saw

"A thousand blushing apparitions start

Into her face"

whenever his eyes rested on her, could scarcely doubt his influence over her.

The next morning George Manning brought Miss Harcourt to visit his mother; and Mrs. Manning rose greatly in her son Henry's estimation, when he saw the affectionate deference evinced towards her by the proud beauty.

"How strange my manner must have seemed to you sometimes!" said Miss Harcourt to Henry one day. "I was engaged to George long before I met you in Europe; and though I never had courage to mention him to you, I wondered a little that you never spoke of him. I never doubted for a moment that you were acquainted with our engagement."

"I do not even yet understand where and how you and George met."

"We met at home my father was Governor of the Territory State now in which your uncle lives: our homes were very near each other's, and so we met almost daily while I was still a child. We have had all sorts of adventures together; for George was a great favorite with my father, and I was permitted to go with him anywhere. He has saved my life twice once at the imminent peril of his own, when with the wilfulness of a spoiled child I would ride a horse which he told me I could not manage. Oh! you know not half his nobleness," and tears moistened the bright eyes of the happy girl.

Henry Manning was touched through all his conventionalism, yet the moment after he said, "George is a fine fellow, certainly; but I wish you could persuade him to dress a little more like other people."

"I would not if I could," exclaimed Emma Harcourt, while the blood rushed to her temples; "fashions and all such conventional regulations are made for those who have no innate perception of the right, the noble, the beautiful not for such as he he is above fashion."

What Emma would not ask, she yet did not fail to recognize as another proof of correct judgment, when George Manning laid aside his Western costume and assumed one less remarkable.

Henry Manning had received a new idea that there are those who are above the fashion. Allied to this was another thought, which in time found entrance to his mind, that it would be at least as profitable to devote our energies to the acquisition of true nobility of soul, pure and high thought and refined taste, as to the study of those conventionalisms which are but their outer garment, and can at best only conceal for a short time their absence.

CHAPTER IV

The next day was brilliant. Snow had fallen during the night, and the sun, which arose without a cloud, was reflected back from it with dazzling brightness, while every branch and spray glittered in its casing of ice as though it had been a huge diamond. Before we met at breakfast, the younger members of the party had decided on a sleigh-ride. Even Col. Donaldson malgré old age and rheumatism, found himself unable to resist the cheerful morning and their gay solicitations, and accompanied them. Mrs. Donaldson and I were left alone, a circumstance which did not afflict either of us. Mrs. Donaldson was never at a loss for pleasant occupation for her hours, and Annie had given me something to do in parting.

"Remember, Aunt Nancy, we shall look to you for our entertainment this evening; you shall be permitted to choose your subject. Is not that gracious?" she added, with a laugh at her own style of command, springing at the same moment from the sleigh in which Mr. Arlington had already placed himself at her side, and running up the steps to the piazza, where I stood, that she might give me another kiss, and satisfy herself that she had not wounded the amour propre of her old friend, by speaking so much en reine. I was, in truth, pleased to be reminded of the demand which might be made on me in the evening, while I had time to glance over sketches intended only for myself, and ascertain whether they contained any thing likely to interest others.

A late dinner re-united us, and the fatigues of the morning having been repaired by an hour's rest in the afternoon, our party was more than usually fresh and ready for enjoyment when we met in the evening. I had availed myself of Annie's permission, and selected my subject. It was a crayon sketch of a lovely lake, taken by Philip Oswald, the son of one of my most valued friends. The sketch was made while all around remained in the wilderness of uncultivated nature. Since that day, the stillness has been disturbed by the sound of the axe and the hammer. Upon the borders of that sweet lake, a fair home has risen, from which the incense of grateful and loving hearts has gone up to the Creator of so much beauty. The associations which made this scene peculiarly interesting to me I had long since written out, and now give to the reader under the title of

LOSS AND GAIN;
OR, HEARTS VERSUS DIAMONDS

Winter had thrown its icy fetters over the Hudson, and stilled even the stormier waves of the East River, as the inhabitants of New-York designate that portion of the Harbor which lies between their city and Brooklyn. The city itself its streets its houses all wore the livery of this "ruler of the inverted year" while in many a garret and cellar of its crowded streets, ragged children huddled together, seeking to warm their frozen limbs beneath the scanty covering of their beds, or cowering over the few half-dying embers, which they misnamed a fire. Yet the social affections were not chilled rather did they seem to glow more warmly, as though rejoicing in their triumph over the mighty conqueror of the physical world. Christian charity went forth unchecked through the frosty air and over the snow-clad streets, to shelter the houseless, to clothe the naked, to warm the freezing. Human sympathies awoke to new-life, the dying hopes and failing energies of man; and the sleigh-bells, ringing out their joyous peals through the day, and far, far into the night, told that the young and fair were abroad braving all the severities of the season, in their eager search after pleasure. In the neighborhood of Waverley Place, especially, on the evening of the 16th of December, did this merry music "wake the silent air" to respond to the quick beatings of the gay young hearts anticipating the fête of fêtes, the most brilliant party of the season, which was that evening to be given at the house of the ruler of fashion the elegant Mrs. Bruton.

Instead of introducing our readers to the gay assemblage of this lady's guests, we will take them to the dressing-room of the fairest among them, the beautiful, the gay, the brilliant Caroline Danby. As the door of this inner temple of beauty opens at the touch of our magic wand, its inmate is seen standing before a mirror, and her eye beams, and her lip is smiling with anticipated triumph. Does there seem vanity in the gaze she fastens there? Look on that form of graceful symmetry, on those large black eyes with their jetty fringes, on the rich coloring of her rounded cheeks, and the dewy freshness of her red lip, and you will forget to censure. But see, the mirror reflects another form a form so slender that it seems scarcely to have attained the full proportions of womanhood, and a face whose soft gray eyes and fair complexion, and hair of the palest gold, present a singular contrast to the dark yet glowing beauty beside her. This is Mary Grayson, the orphan cousin of Caroline Danby, who has grown up in her father's house. She has glided in with her usual gentle movement, and light, noiseless step, and Caroline first perceives her in the glass.

"Ah, Mary!" she exclaims, "I sent for you to put this diamond spray in my hair; you arrange it with so much more taste than any one else."

Mary smilingly receives the expensive ornament, and fastens it amidst the dark, glossy tresses. At this moment the doorbell gives forth a hasty peal, and going to the head of the stairs, Mary remains listening till the door is opened, and then comes back to say, "Mrs. Oswald, Caroline, and Philip."

"Pray, go down and entertain them till I come, Mary" and seemingly nothing loth, Mary complies with the request.

In the drawing-room to which Mary Grayson directed her steps stood a stately looking lady, who advanced to meet her as she entered, and kissing her affectionately, asked, "Are you not going with us this evening?"

"No; my sore throat has increased, and the Doctor is positive; there is no appeal from him, you know; I am very sorry, for I wished to see some of Philip's foreign graces," she said playfully, as she turned to give her hand to a gentleman who had entered while she was speaking. He received it with the frank kindness of a brother, but before he could reply the door of the drawing-room opened, and Caroline Danby appeared within it. Philip Oswald sprang forward to greet her, and from that moment seemed forgetful that there was any other thing in life deserving his attention, save her radiant beauty. Perhaps there was some little regard to the effect of his first glance at that beauty, in her presenting herself in the drawing-room with her cloak and hood upon her arm, the diamond sparkling in her uncovered tresses, and the soft, rich folds of her satin dress and its flowing lace draperies, shading without concealing the graceful outline of her form. The gentleman who gazed so admiringly upon her, who wrapped her cloak around her with such tender care, and even insisted, kneeling gracefully before her, on fastening himself the warm, furred overshoes upon her slender foot, seemed a fit attendant at the shrine of beauty. Philip Oswald had been only a few weeks at home, after an absence of four years spent in European travel. The quality in his appearance and manners, which first impressed the observer, was refinement perfect elegance, without the least touch of coxcombry. It had been said of him, that he had brought home the taste in dress of a Parisian, the imaginativeness of a German, and the voice and passion for music of an Italian. Few were admitted to such intimacy with him as to look into the deeper qualities of the mind but those who were, saw there the sturdy honesty of John Bull, and the courageous heart and independent spirit of his own America. Some of those who knew him best, regretted that the possession of a fortune, which placed him among the wealthiest in America, would most probably consign him to a life of indolence, in which his highest qualities would languish for want of exercise.

By nine o'clock Caroline Danby's preparations were completed, and leaning on one of Philip Oswald's arms, while the other was given to his mother, she was led out, and placed in the most splendid sleigh in New York, and wrapped in the most costly furs. Philip followed, the weary coachman touched his spirited horses with the whip, the sleigh-bells rang merrily out, and Mary Grayson was left in solitude.

The last stroke of three had ceased to vibrate on the air when Caroline Danby again stood beside her cousin. Mary was sleeping, and a painter might have hesitated whether to give the palm of beauty to the soft, fair face, which looked so angel-like in its placid sleep, or to that which bent above her in undimmed brilliancy.

"Is it you, Caroline? What time is it?" asked Mary, as she aroused at her cousin's call.

"Three o'clock; but wake up, Mary; I have something to tell you, which must not be heard by sleepy ears."

"How fresh you look!" exclaimed Mary, sitting up in bed and looking at her cousin admiringly. "Who would believe you had been dancing all night!"

"I have not been dancing all night, nor half the night."

"Why what have you been doing then?"

"Listening to Philip Oswald. Oh Mary! I am certainly the most fortunate woman in the world. He is mine at last he, the most elegant, the most brilliant man in New-York, and with such a splendid fortune. I was so happy, so excited, that I could not sleep, and therefore I awoke you to talk."

"I am glad you did, for I am almost as much pleased as you can be such joy is better than sleep; but all the bells in the city seem to be ringing did you see any thing of the fire?"

"Oh yes! the whole sky at the southeast is glowing from the flames the largest fire, they say, that has ever been known in the city but it is far enough from us down in Wall-street and who can think of fires with such joy before them? Only think, Mary, with Philip's fortune and Philip's taste, what an establishment I shall have."

"And what a mother in dear, good Mrs. Oswald!"

"Yes but I hope she will not wish to live with us mother-in-laws, you know, always want to manage every thing in their sons' houses."

Thus the cousins sat talking till the fire-bells ceased their monotonous and ominous clang, and the late dawn of a winter morning reddened the eastern sky. It was half-past nine o'clock when they met again at their breakfast; yet late as it was, Mr. Danby, usually a very early riser, was not quite ready for it. He had spent most of the night at the scene of the fire, and had with great difficulty and labor saved his valuable stock of French goods from the destroyer. When he joined his daughter and niece, his mind was still under the influence of last night's excitement, and he could talk of nothing but the fire.

"Rather expensive fireworks, I am afraid," said Caroline flippantly, as her father described the lurid grandeur of the scene.

"Do not speak lightly, my daughter, of that which must reduce many from affluence to beggary. Millions of property were lost last night. The 16th of December, 1835, will long be remembered in the annals of New-York, I fear."

"It will long be remembered in my annals," whispered Caroline to her cousin, with a bright smile, despite her father's chiding.

"Not at home to any but Mr. Philip Oswald," had been Caroline Danby's order to the servant this morning; and thus when she was told, at twelve o'clock, that that gentleman awaited her in the drawing-room, she had heard nothing more of the fire than her father and the morning paper had communicated. As she entered, Philip arose to greet her, but though he strove to smile as his eyes met hers, the effort was vain; and throwing himself back on the sofa, he covered his face with his hand, as though to hide his pallor and the convulsive quivering of his lips from her whom he was reluctant to grieve. Emboldened by her fears, Caroline advanced, and laying her hand on his, exclaimed, "What is the matter? Are you ill? your mother? pray do not keep me in suspense, but tell me what has happened."

He seemed to have mastered his emotion, from whatever cause it had proceeded; for removing his hand, he looked earnestly upon her, and drawing her to a seat beside him, said in firm, though sad tones, "That has happened, Caroline, which would not move me thus, but for your dear sake I asked you last night to share my fortune to-day I have none to offer you."

"Gracious heaven!" exclaimed Caroline, turning as pale as he, "what do you mean?"

"That in the fire last night, or the failures which the most sanguine assure me it must produce, my whole fortune is involved. If I can recover from the wreck what will secure to my poor mother the continuance of her accustomed comforts, it will be beyond my hopes; for me the luxuries, the comforts, the very necessaries of life must be the produce of my own exertion. I do not ask you to share my poverty, Caroline; I cannot be so selfish; had I not spoken of my love last night, you should never have heard it though it had been like a burning fire, I would have shut it up within my heart but it is too late for this; you have heard it, and I have heard the remembrance brings with it a wild delirious joy, even in this hour of darkness " and the pale face of Philip Oswald flushed, and his dimmed eye beamed brightly again as he spoke: "I have heard your sweet confession of reciprocal regard. Months, perhaps years may pass before I attain the goal at which I last night thought myself to have already arrived before I can dare to call you mine but in our land, manly determination and perseverance ever command success, and I fear not to promise you, dearest, one day a happy home though not a splendid one if you will promise me to share it. Look on me, Caroline give me one smile to light me on my way with such a hope before me, I cannot say my dreary way."

He ceased, yet Caroline neither looked upon him, nor spoke. Her cheek had grown pale at his words, and she sat down with downcast eyes, cold, still, statue-like at his side. Yet did not Philip Oswald doubt her love. Had not her eye kindled and her cheek flushed at his whispered vows had not her hand rested lovingly in his, and her lip been yielded to the first kiss of love how, then, could he dare to doubt her? She was grieved for his sake he had been selfishly abrupt in his first communication of his sorrow, and now he the stronger must struggle to bear and to speak cheerfully for her sake. And with this feeling he had been able to conclude far more cheerfully than he commenced. As she still continued silent, he bent forward, and would have pressed his lip to her cheek, saying, "Not one word for me, dear one," but, drawing hastily back, Caroline said with great effort,

"I think, Mr. Oswald it seems to me that that an engagement must be a heavy burden to one who has to make his own way in life I I should be sorry to be a disadvantage to you."

It was a crushing blow, and for an instant he sat stunned into almost death-like stillness by it: but he rallied; he would leave no loop on which hope or fancy might hereafter hang a doubt. "Caroline," he said, in a voice whose change spoke the intensity of his feelings, "do not speak of disadvantage to me your love was the one star left in my sky but that matters not what I would know is, whether you desire that the record of last evening should be blotted from the history of our lives?"

"I I think it had better be I am sure I wish you well, Mr. Oswald."

It was well for her, perhaps, that she did not venture to meet his eye that look of withering scorn could hardly ever have vanished from her memory it was enough to hear his bitter laugh, and the accents in which he said, "Thank you, Miss Danby your wishes are fully reciprocated may you never know a love less prudent than your own."

The door closed on him, and she was alone left to the companionship of her own heart evil companionship in such an hour! She hastened to relate all that had passed to Mary, but Mary had no assurances for her she had only sympathy for Philip "dear Philip" as she called him over and over again. "I think it would better become one so young as you are, to say, Mr. Oswald, Mary," said Caroline, pettishly.

"I have called him Philip from my childhood, Caroline I shall not begin to say Mr. Oswald now." Mary did not mean a reproach, but to Caroline's accusing conscience it sounded like one, and she turned away indignantly. She soon, however, sought her cousin again with a note in her hand.

"I have been writing to Mrs. Oswald, Mary," she said; "you are perhaps too young, and Mr. Oswald too much absorbed in his own disappointment, to estimate the propriety of my conduct; but she will, I am sure, agree with me, that one expensively reared as I have been, accustomed to every luxury, and perfectly ignorant of economy, would make the worst possible wife to a poor man; and she has so much influence over Mr. Oswald, that, should she accord with me in opinion on this point, she can easily convince him of its justice. Will you take my note to her? I do not like to send it by a servant it might fall into Philip's hands."

Nothing could have pleased Mary more than this commission, for her affectionate heart was longing to offer its sympathy to her friends. Mrs. Oswald assumed perhaps a little more than her usual stateliness when she heard her announced, but it vanished instantly before Mary's tearful eye, as she kissed the hand that was extended to her. Mrs. Oswald folded her arms around her, and Mary sank sobbing upon the bosom of her whom she had come to console. And Mrs. Oswald was consoled by such true and tender sympathy. It was long before Mary could prevail on herself to disturb the flow of gentler affections by delivering Caroline's note. Mrs. Oswald received it with an almost contemptuous smile, which remained unchanged while she read. It was a labored effort to make her conduct seem a generous determination not to obstruct Philip's course in life, by binding him to a companion so unsuitable to his present prospects as herself. In reply, Mrs. Oswald assured Caroline Danby of her perfect agreement with her in the conviction that she would make a very unsuitable wife for Philip Oswald. "This," she added, "was always my opinion, though I was unwilling to oppose my son's wishes. I thank you for having convinced him I was right in the only point on which we ever differed."

It cannot be supposed that this note was very pleasing to Caroline Danby; but, whatever were her dissatisfaction, she did not complain, and probably soon lost all remembrance of her chagrin in the gayeties which a few men of fortune still remained, amidst the almost universal ruin, to promote and to partake.

In the mean time, Philip Oswald was experiencing that restlessness, that burning desire to free himself from all his present associations, to begin, as it were, a new life, which the first pressure of sorrow so often arouses in the ardent spirit. Had not his will been "bound down by the iron chain of necessity," he would probably have returned to Europe, and wasted his energies amidst aimless wanderings. As it was, he chose among those modes of life demanded by his new circumstances, that which would take him farthest from New-York, and place him in a condition the most foreign to all his past experience, and demanding the most active and most incessant exertion. Out of that which the fire, the failure of Insurance Companies and of private individuals, had left him remained, after the purchase of a liberal annuity for his mother, a few thousands to be devoted either to merchandise, to his support while pursuing the studies necessary for the acquirement of a profession, or to any mode of gaining a living, which he might prefer to these. The very hour which ascertained this fact, saw his resolution taken and his course marked out.

"I must have new scenery for this new act in the drama of my life," he said to his mother. "I must away away from all the artificialities and trivialities of my present world, to the rich prairies, the wide streams, the boundless expanse of the West. I go to make a new home for you dear mother you shall be the queen of my kingdom."

This was not the choice that would have pleased an ambitious, or an over-fond mother. The former would have preferred a profession, as conferring higher social distinction; the latter would have shrunk from seeing one nursed in the lap of luxury go forth to encounter the hardships of a pioneer. But Mrs. Oswald possessed an intelligence which recognized in that life of bold adventure, and physical endurance, and persevering labor, that awaited her son in the prosecution of his plans, the best school for the development of that decision and force of character which she had desired as the crowning seal to Philip's intellectual endowments, warm affections, and just principles; and, holding his excellence as the better part of her own happiness, she sanctioned his designs, and did all in her power to promote their execution. He waited, therefore, only to see her leave the house whose rent now exceeded her whole annual income, for pleasant rooms in a boarding-house, agreeably situated, before he set out from New-York.

It is not our intention minutely to trace his course, to describe the "local habitation" which he acquired, or detail the difficulties which arose in his progress, the strength with which he combated, or the means by which he overcame them. For his course, suffice it that it was westward; for his habitation, that it was on the slope of a hill crowned with the gigantic trees of that fertile soil, and beside a lake, "a sheet of silver" well fitted to be

"A mirror and a bath for beauty's youngest daughters;"

and that the house, which he at length succeeded in raising and furnishing there, united somewhat the refinement of his past life to the simplicity of his present; for his difficulties, we can only say, he met them and conquered them, and gained from each encounter knowledge and power. For two years, letters were the only medium of intercourse between his mother and himself, but those letters were a history a history not only of his stirring, outer life, but of that inner life which yet more deeply interested her. Feeling proud herself of the daring spirit, the iron will, the ready invention which these letters displayed, yet prouder of the affectionate heart, the true and generous nature, it is not wonderful that Mrs. Oswald should have often read them, or at least parts of them, to her constant friend and very frequent visitor, Mary Grayson. Nor is it more strange that Mary, thus made to recognize in the most interesting man she had yet known, far more lofty claims to her admiration, should have enshrined him in her young and pure imagination as some "bright, particular star."

Two years in the future! How almost interminable seems the prospect to our hopes or our affections! but let Time turn his perspective glass let us look at it in the past, and how it shrinks and becomes as a day in the history of our lives! So was it with Philip Oswald's two years of absence, when he found himself, in the earliest dawn of the spring of 1838, once more in New-York. Yet that time had not passed without leaving traces of its passage traces in the changes affecting those around him yet deeper traces in himself. He arrived in the afternoon of an earlier day than that on which he had been expected. In the evening Mrs. Oswald persuaded him to assume, for the gratification of her curiosity, the picturesque costume worn by him in his western home. He had just re-entered her room, and she was yet engaged in animated observation of the hunting-shirt, strapped around the waist with a belt of buckskin, the open collar, and loosely knotted cravat, which, as the mother's heart whispered, so well became that tall and manly form, when there was a slight tap at the door, and before she could speak, it opened, and Mary Grayson stood within it. She gazed in silence for a moment on the striking figure before her, and her mind rapidly scanned the changes which time and new modes of life had made in the Philip Oswald of her memory. As she did so, she acknowledged that the embrowned face and hands, the broader and more vigorous proportions, and even the easy freedom of his dress, were more in harmony with the bold and independent aspect which his character had assumed, than the delicacy and elegance by which he had formerly been distinguished. His outer man was now the true index of a noble, free, and energetic spirit a spirit which, having conquered itself, was victor over all and as such, it attracted from Mary a deeper and more reverent admiration, than she had felt for him when adorned with all the trappings of wealth and luxurious refinement. The very depth of this sentiment destroyed the ease of her manner towards him, and as Philip Oswald took the hand formerly so freely offered him, and heard from her lips the respectful Mr. Oswald, instead of the frank, sisterly Philip, he said to himself "She looks down upon the backwoodsman, and would have him know his place." So much for man's boasted penetration!

Notwithstanding the barrier of reserve thus erected between them, Philip Oswald could not but admire the rare loveliness into which Mary Grayson's girlish prettiness had expanded, and again, and yet again, while she was speaking to his mother, and could not therefore perceive him, he turned to gaze on her, fascinated not by the finely turned form or beautiful features, but by the countenance beaming with gentle and refined intelligence. Here was none of the brilliancy which had dazzled his senses in Caroline Danby, but an expression of mind and heart far more captivating to him who had entered into the inner mysteries of life.

A fortnight was the limit of Philip Oswald's stay in the city. He had come not for his mother, but for the house in which she was to live, and he carried it back with him. We do not mean that his house, with all its conveniences of kitchen and pantry, its elegances of parlor and drawing-room, and its decorations of pillar and cornice fitly joined together, travelled off with him to the far West. We do not despair of seeing such a feat performed some day, but we believe it has not yet been done, and Philip Oswald, at least, did not attempt it; he took with him, however, all those useful and ornamental contrivances in their several parts, accompanied by workmen skilled in putting the whole together. Again in his western home, for another year, his head and his hands were fully occupied with building and planting. For the first two years of his forest life, he had thought only of the substantial produce of the field the rye, the barley, the Indian corn, which were to be exchanged for the "omnipotent dollar" but woman was coming, and beauty and grace must be the herald of her steps. For his mother, he planted fruits and flowers, opened views of the lake, made a gravelled walk to its shore bordered with flowering shrubs, and wreathed the woodbine, the honeysuckle, and the multiflora rose around the columns of his piazza. For his mother this was done, and yet, when the labors of the day were over, and he looked forth upon them in the cool, still evening hour, it was not his mother's face, but one younger and fairer which peered out upon him from the vine-leaves, or with tender smiles wooed him to the lake. Young, fair, and tender as it was, its wooings generally sent him in an opposite direction, with a sneer at his own folly, to stifle his fancies with a book, or to mark out the plan of the morrow's operations.

More than a year had passed away and Philip Oswald was again in New-York, just as spring was gliding into the ardent embraces of summer. This time he had come for his mother, and with all the force of his resolute will, he shut his ears to the flattering suggestions of fancy, that a dearer pleasure than even that mother's presence might be won. He had looked steadily upon his lot in life, and he accepted it, and determined to make the best of it and to be happy in it; yet he felt that it was after all a rugged lot. Without considering all women as mercenary as Caroline Danby, which his knowledge of his mother forbade him to do, even in his most woman-scorning mood, he yet doubted whether any of those who had been reared amidst the refinements of cultivated life, could be won to leave them all for love in the western wilds; and as the unrefined could have no charms for him, he deliberately embraced bachelordom as a part of his portion, and, not without a sigh, yielded himself to the conviction that all the wealth of woman's love within his power to attain, was locked within a mother's heart.

A fortnight was again the allotted time of Philip Oswald's stay; but when that had expired, he was persuaded to delay his departure for yet another week. He had been drawn, by accompanying his mother in her farewell visits, once more within the vortex of society, and his manly independence and energy, his knowledge of what was to his companions a new world, and his spirit-stirring descriptions of its varied beauty and inexhaustible fertility, made him more the fashion than he had ever been. He had often met Caroline Danby now Mrs. Randall and Mary more than once delicately turned her eyes away from her cousin's face, lest she should read there somewhat of chagrin as Mr. Randall, with his meaningless face and dapper-looking form insignificant in all save the reputation of being the wealthiest banker in Wall-street, and possessing the most elegant house and furniture, the best appointed equipage, and the handsomest wife in the city stood beside Philip Oswald with

" a form indeed
Where every god did seem to set his seal,
To give the world assurance of a man,"

and a face radiant with intelligence, while circled by an attentive auditory of that which was noblest and best in their world, his eloquent enthusiasm made them hear the rushing waters, see the boundless prairies, and feel for a time all the wild freedom of the untamed West. Such enthusiasm was gladly welcomed as a breeze in the still air, a ruffle in the stagnant waters of fashionable life.

Within two or three days of their intended departure, Mrs. Oswald proposed to Philip that they should visit a friend residing near Fort Lee, and invited Mary to accompany them. Among the acquaintances whom they found on board was an invalid lady, who could not bear the fresh air upon deck; and Mary, pitying her loneliness and seclusion, remained for awhile conversing with her in the cabin. Mrs. Oswald and Philip were on deck, and near them was a young and giddy girl, to whose care a mother had intrusted a bold, active, joyous infant, seemingly about eight months old.

"That is a dangerous position for so lively a child," said Philip Oswald to the young nurse, as he saw her place him on the side of the boat; "he may spring from your arms overboard."

With that foolish tempting of the danger pointed out by another, which we sometimes see even in women, the girl removed her arms from around the child, sustaining only a slight hold of its frock. At this moment the flag of the boat floated within view of the little fellow, and he sprang towards it. A splash in the water told the rest but even before that was heard, Philip Oswald had dashed off his boots and coat, and the poor child had scarcely touched the waves when he was beside it, and held it encircled in his arm.

"Oh, Mary! Mr. Oswald! Mr. Oswald!" cried one of Mary's young acquaintances, rushing into the cabin with a face blanched with terror.

"What of him?" questioned Mary, starting eagerly forward.

"He is in the water. Oh, Mary! he will be drowned."

Mary did not utter a sound, yet she felt in that moment, for the first time, how important to her was Philip Oswald's life. Tottering towards the door, she leaned against it for a moment while all around grew dark, and strange sounds were buzzing in her ears. The next instant she sank into a chair and lost her terrors in unconsciousness. The same young lady who had played the alarmist to her, as she saw the paleness of death settle on Mary's face and her eyes close, ran again upon the deck, exclaiming, "Mary Grayson is fainting, pray come to Mary Grayson."

Philip Oswald was already on deck, dripping indeed, but unharmed and looking nobler than ever, as he held the recovered child in his arms. As that cry, "Mary Grayson is fainting," reached his ears, he threw the infant to a bystander, and hastened to the cabin followed by Mrs. Oswald.

"What has caused this?" cried Mrs. Oswald, as she saw Mary still insensible, supported on the bosom of her invalid friend.

"Miss Ladson's precipitation," said the invalid, looking not very pleasantly on that young lady; "she told her Mr. Oswald was drowning."

"Well, I am sure I thought he was drowning."

"If he had been, it would have been a pity to give such information so abruptly," said Mrs. Oswald, as she took off Mary's bonnet, and loosened the scarf which was tied around her neck.

"I am sure," exclaimed Miss Ladson, anxious only to secure herself from blame, "I am sure I did not suppose Mary would faint; for when her uncle's horse threw him, and every body thought he was killed, instead of fainting she ran out in the street, and did for him more than any body else could do. I am sure I could not think she would care more for Mr. Oswald's danger than for her own uncle's."

No one replied to this insinuation; but that Philip Oswald heard it, might have been surmised from the sudden flush that rose to his temples, and from his closer clasp of the unconscious form, which at his mother's desire he was bearing to a settee. Whether it were the water which oozed from his saturated garments over her face and neck, or some subtle magnetic fluid conveyed in that tender clasp, that aroused her, we cannot tell; but a faint tinge of color revisited her cheeks and lips, and as Philip laid her tenderly down, while his arms were still around her, and his face was bending over her, she opened her eyes. What there was in that first look which called such a sudden flash of joy into Philip Oswald's eyes, we know not; nor what were the whispered words which, as he bowed his head yet lower, sent a crimson glow into Mary's pale cheeks. This however we do know, that Mrs. Oswald and her son delayed their journey for yet another week; and that the day before their departure Philip Oswald stood with Mary Grayson at his side before God's holy altar, and there, in the presence of his mother, Mr. Danby, Mr. and Mrs. Randall, and a few friends, they took those vows which made them one for ever.

Does some starched prude, or some lady interested in the bride's trousseau, exclaim against such unseemly haste? We have but one excuse for them. They were so unfashionable as to prefer the gratification of a true affection to the ceremonies so dear to vanity, and to think more of the earnest claims of life than of its gilded pomps.

Mr. Danby had been unable to pay down the bride's small dower of 8000 dollars; and when he called on his son-in-law, Mr. Randall, to assist him, he could only offer to indorse his note to Mr. Oswald for the amount, acknowledging that it would be perilous at that time to abstract even half that amount from his business. It probably would have been perilous indeed, as in little more than a month after he failed for an enormous amount; but fear not, reader, for the gentle Caroline: she still retained her elegant house and furniture, her handsome equipage and splendid jewels. These were only a small part of what the indignant creditors found had been made over to her by her grateful husband.

Six years have passed away since the occurrence of the events we have been recording. Caroline Randall, weary of the sameness of splendor in her home, has been abroad for two years, travelling with a party of friends. It is said convenient phrase that that her husband had declared she must and shall return, and that to enforce his will he has resolved to send her no more remittances, to honor no more of her drafts, as she has already almost beggared him by her extravagance abroad. Verily, she has her reward!

One farewell glance at our favorite, Mary Grayson, and we have done.

Beside a lovely lake, over whose margin light graceful shrubs are bending, and on whose transparent waters lie the dense forest shadows, though here and there the golden rays of the declining sun flash through the tangled boughs upon its dancing waves, a noble-looking boy of four years old is sailing his mimic fleet, while a lovely girl, two years younger, toddles about, picking "pitty flowers," and bringing them to "papa, mamma, or grandmamma," as her capricious fancy prompts. Near by, papa, mamma, grandmamma, and one pleased and honored guest, are grouped beneath the bending boughs of a magnificent black walnut, and around a table on which strawberries and cream, butter sweet as the breath of the cows that yielded it, biscuits light and white, and bread as good as Humbert himself could make, are served in a style of elegant simplicity, while the silver urn in which the water hisses, and the small china cups into which the fragrant tea is poured, if they are somewhat antique in fashion, are none the less beautiful or the less valued by those who still prize the slightest object associated with the affections beyond the gratification of the vanity.

The evening meal is over. The shadows grow darker on the lake. Agreeable conversation has given place to silent enjoyment, which Mrs. Oswald interrupts to say, "Philip, this is the hour for music; let us have some before Mary leaves us with the children."

Full, deep-toned was the manly voice that swelled upon that evening air, and soft and clear its sweet accompaniment, while the words, full of adoring gratitude and love, seemed incense due to the heaven which had so blessed them.

The last sweet notes had died away, and Mary, calling the children, leads them to their quiet repose, after they have bestowed their good-night kisses. Philip Oswald follows her with his eyes, as, with a child on each hand, she advances with gentle grace upon the easy slope, to the house on its summit. She enters the piazza, and is screened from his view by its lattice-work of vines, but he knows that soon his children will be lisping their evening prayer at her knee, and the thought calls a tender expression to his eyes as he turns them away from his "sweet home."

Contrast this picture with that of Caroline Randall's heartless splendor, and say whether thou wilt choose for thy portion the gratification of the true and pure household affections which Heaven has planted in thy nature, or that of a selfish vanity?

CHAPTER V

This morning, as I sat in the library writing a letter, Annie came in and seated herself at a table on the opposite side of the room. Her unusual stillness caused me to look up after some minutes, and I found that Mr. Arlington's portfolio having been left upon the table, she had drawn from it one of his pencilings, and was gazing steadfastly upon it, as I could not but think, with something troubled in the expression of her usually open and cheerful face. While I was still observing her, the door behind her opened, and Mr. Arlington himself entered. A blush arose to Annie's cheeks as she saw him; a blush which had its origin, I thought, in some deeper feeling than a mere girlish shame at being found so engrossed by one of his productions.

"What have you there?" he asked, as seating himself beside her, he took the paper from what seemed to me her somewhat reluctant hand. No sooner had he looked on it, than his own bright face became shadowed, as hers had been, and yet he smiled, too, as he said, "That portfolio is really an omnium gatherum. I had no idea this had found its way there. When I first read Mrs. Hemans' poem of 'The Bird's Release,' it reminded me of this scene of my boyhood, though if I have never spoken to you of my darling Grace, you will not be able to understand why."

"You never have," said Annie, answering his looks rather than his words, while a slight increase of color was again perceptible in her fair cheek.

"She was my sister, my only sister; we were but two, the petted darlings of a widowed mother. I told you, that few could sympathize as I could with Koerner's memory of Mother-love. I was but six years old, and just such a chubby, broad-shouldered little varlet, I fancy, as I have sketched here, when Grace, who was two years older, and the loveliest, merriest little creature in the world, died. My mother was already beginning to feel the influence of that disease, which, two years later, terminated her life, and, I have no doubt, the death of Grace, who was her idol, increased the rapidity of its progress."

There was silence for some minutes, and then Annie said softly, "But what of the bird?"

"It was a thrush which had been given to Grace some time before her death, and which she was trying to tame for me. My mother could not bear to see it after her death, and with some difficulty persuaded me to give it its liberty. You will now see why I should have dedicated this sketch to Grace, and why these lines should have brought the scene to my mind, and caused me indeed to make this drawing of it."

"Will you read the lines for me?" asked Annie, "I had not finished them when you took the paper from me."

To tell you a secret, reader, I do not believe she had seen any thing on the paper except the few words in German text written at its head, "To my darling Grace."

Mr. Arlington read in a tone of feeling and interest,

THE BIRD'S RELEASE.
BY MRS. HEMANS.

Go forth, for she is gone!
With the golden light of her wavy hair
She is gone to the fields of the viewless air:

She hath left her dwelling lone!
Her voice hath pass'd away!
It hath passed away like a summer breeze,
When it leaves the hills for the for blue seas,
Where we may not trace its way.
Go forth, and like her be free:
With thy radiant wing, and thy glancing eye,
Thou hast all the range of the sunny sky,
And what is our grief to thee?
Is it aught even to her we mourn?
Doth she look on the tears by her kindred shed?
Doth she rest with the flowers o'er her gentle head?
Or float on the light wind borne?
We know not but she is gone!
Her step from the dance, her voice from the song,
And the smile of her eye from the festal throng;
She hath loft her dwelling lone!
When the waves at sunset shine,
We may hear thy voice amidst thousands more,
In the scented woods of our glowing shore;
But we shall not know 'tis thine!
Even so with the loved one flown!
Her smile in the starlight may wander by,
Her breath may be near in the wind's low sigh
Around us but all unknown.
Go forth, we have loosed thy chains!
We may deck thy cage with the richest flowers
Which the bright day rears in our eastern bowers;
But thou wilt not be lured again.
Even thus may the summer pour
All fragrant things on the land's green breast,
And the glorious earth like a bride be dress'd;
But it wins her back no more!

I was doubtful whether either Mr. Arlington or Annie were aware of my presence, and was just debating with myself whether I should make them aware of it by addressing them, or quietly steal away, when Col. Donaldson decided the point by entering the library and speaking to me. He came to ask that I would come to the parlor and see a boy who had just been sent from one of our charitable institutions, to which he had applied for a lad to act as a helper to his old waiter, John, who was now old enough to require some indulgence, and had always been trustworthy enough to deserve some. The boy looked intelligent and honest he was neat in his person and active in his movements.

"He is an orphan," said Col. Donaldson, "and the managers of the institution have offered to bind him to me for seven years, or till he is of age. What do you think of it!"

"If the boy himself be willing, I should be glad to know he was so well provided for," I replied; "though in general, no abolitionist can be more vehemently opposed to negro slavery than I am to this apprenticeship business. What is it but a slavery of the worst description? The master is endowed with irresponsible power, without the interest in the well-being of his slave, which the planter, the actual owner of slaves, ordinarily feels."

"You speak strongly," said Col. Donaldson.

"I feel strongly on this subject," I answered. "I knew one instance of the effects of this system which I have often thought of publishing to the world, as speaking more powerfully against it than a thousand addresses could do."

"Tell it to us, Aunt Nancy," said Robert Dudley.

"It is too long to tell now," said I, as the dinner-bell sounded.

"Then let us have it this evening," urged Col. Donaldson "for it is a subject in which I am much interested."

Accordingly, in the evening, I gave them the "o'er true tale" of

THE YOUNG MISANTHROPE

"In the blue summer ocean, far off and alone," lies a little island, known to mariners in the Pacific only for the fine water with which it supplies them, and for the bold shore which makes it possible for ships of considerable tonnage to lie in quiet near the land. Discovered at first by accident, it has been long, for these reasons, visited both by English and American whalers. A few years since, and no trace of man's presence could be found there beyond the belt of rocks, amidst which arose the springs that were the chief, and indeed only attraction the island presented to the rough, hardy men by whom it had been visited. But within that stony girdle lay a landscape soft and lovely as any that arose within the tropical seas. There the plantain waved its leafy crown, the orange shed its rich perfume, and bore its golden fruit aloft upon the desert air, and the light, feathery foliage of the tamarind moved gracefully to the touch of the dallying breeze. All was green, and soft, and fair, for there no winter chills the life of nature, but,

"The bee banquets on through a whole year of flowers."

It was a scene which might have seemed created for the abode of some being too bright and good for the common earth of common men, or for some Hinda and Hafed, who, driven from a world all too harsh and evil for their nobler natures, might have found in it a refuge,

"Where the bright eyes of angels only
Should come around them to behold
A paradise so pure and lonely."

Alas for the dream of the poet! This beautiful island became the refuge, not of pure and loving hearts, but of one from whose nature cruel tyranny seemed to have blotted out every feeling and every faculty save hatred and fear; and he who first introduced into its yet untainted solitudes the bitter sorrows and dark passions of humanity, was a child, who, but ten years before, had lain in all the loveliness of sinless infancy upon a mother's bosom. Of that mother's history he knew nothing whether her sin or only her sorrows had thrown him fatherless upon the world, he was ignorant he had only a dim memory of gentle eyes, which had looked on him as no others had ever looked, and of a low, sweet voice, speak to him such words as he had never heard from any other. He had been loved, and that love had made his life of penury in an humble hovel in England, bright and beautiful; but his mother had passed away from earth, and with her all the light of his existence. Child as he was, the succeeding darkness preserved long in brightness the memory of the last look from her fast glazing eyes, the last words from her dying lips, the last touch of her already death-cold hand. She died, and the same reluctant charity which consigned her to a pauper's grave, gave to her boy a dwelling in the parish poor-house. With the tender mercies of such institutions the author of Oliver Twist has made the world acquainted. They were such in the present case, that the poor little Edward Hallett welcomed as the first glad words that had fallen on his ears for two long, weary years, the news that he was to be bound apprentice to a captain sailing from Portsmouth in a whaling ship. He learned rather from what was said near him, than to him, that this man wanted a cabin boy, but would not have one who was not bound to him, or to use the more expressive language in which it reached the ears of his destined victim, "one with whom he could not do as he pleased."

He who had come within the poor-house walls at six years old, a glad, rosy-cheeked, chubby child, went from them at eight, thin, and pale, and grave, with a frame broken by want and labor, a mind clouded, and a heart repressed by unkindness. But, sad as was the history of those years, the succeeding two taught the poor boy to regard them as the vanished brightness of a dream. The man we should more justly say, the fiend to whom the next fourteen years of his life were by bond devoted, was a savage by nature, and had been rendered yet more brutal by habits of intoxication. In his drunken orgies, his favorite pastime was to torture the unfortunate being whom the "guardians of the poor" of an English parish had placed in his power. It would make the heart of the reader sick, were we to attempt a detail of the many horrible inventions by which this modern Caligula amused his leisure hours, and made life hideous to his victim. Nor was it only from this arch-fiend that the poor boy suffered. Mate, cook, and sailors, soon found in him a butt for their jokes, an object on which they might safely vent their ill-humor, and a convenient cover for their own delinquencies.

He was beaten for and by them. The evil qualities which man had himself elicited from his nature, if not implanted there the sullenness, and hardiness, and cunning he evinced, were made an excuse for further injury. During his first voyage of eighteen months, spite of all this, hope was not entirely dead in his heart. The ship was to return to England, and he determined to run away from her, and find his way back to the poor-house. It was a miserable refuge, but it was his only one. He escaped he found his way thither through many dangers he told his story. It was heard with incredulity, and he was returned to his tormentors, to learn that there is even in hell "a deeper hell."

Again he went on a whaling voyage. Day after day the fathomless, the seemingly illimitable sea, the image of the Infinite was around him but his darkened mind saw in it only a prison, which shut him in with his persecutors. Night after night the stars beamed peacefully above him, luring his thoughts upward, but he saw in them only the signals of drunken revelry to others, and of deeper woe to himself. There was but one wish in his heart it had almost ceased to be a hope to escape from man; to live and die where he should never see his form, never hear his voice. The ship encountered a severe storm. She was driven from her course, her voyage lengthened, and some of her water-casks were stove in. They made for an island, not far distant, by the chart, to take in a fresh supply of water. Edward Hallett heard the sailors say to each other that this island was uninhabited, and his wish grew into a passionate desire a hope. For the completion of this hope, he had but one resource the sword and the shield of the feeble cunning; and well he exercised his weapon.

The ship lay within a quarter of a mile of the shore, and a boat was sent to procure water one man remaining always to fill the empty vessels while the others returned to the ship with those already filled. The best means of accomplishing his purpose that occurred to the poor boy was to feign the utmost degree of terror at the lonely and unprotected situation of this man during the absence of his comrades. He spoke his terrors where he knew they would be heard by the prime author of his miseries. The result was what he had anticipated.

"Ye're afraid, are ye, of being left there by yerself! Ye'd rather be whipped, or tied up by the thumbs, or be kept at the mast-head all night, would ye? Then, dam'me, that's just what I'll do to you. Here, hold on with that boat take this youngster with you, and you can bring back Tom, and leave him to fill the casks for you."

Well did the object of his tyranny act his part. He entreated, he adjured all around him to save him from so dreaded a fate in vain, of course for his affected agonies only riveted the determination of his tyrant. It was a new delight to see him writhe in agony, and strive to draw back from those who were urging him to the boat. He was forced in, borne to the island, and left to his task. But this was not enough. He could not escape in the broad light of day, from a spot directly under the eyes of his tormentors, while between him and the ship a boat was ever coming and going. Through the day he must persist in the part he had assumed. He did not fail to continue it, and when the day approached its close, he sent to the ship the most urgent entreaties that he might be allowed to return there before it was night. The sailors, rough and hard as they generally were to him, sympathized with his agony of fear, and asked that he might return; but his demon was now inflamed by drink, and every word in favor of his petition insured its rejection. He even made the unusual exertion of going up himself in the last boat, that he might see the victim of his malice, and feast his ears with the cries and objurgations which terror would wring from him.

"If we should forget you in the morning, you can take the next homeward bound ship that stops here, but don't tell your friends at the poor-house too bad a tale of us," were the parting words of this wretch.

Darkness and silence were around the desolate boy, but they brought no fear with them. Man, his enemy, was not there. He saw not the beauty of the heavens, from which the stars looked down on him in their unchanged serenity, or of the earth, where flowers were springing at his feet, and graceful shrubs were waving over him. He heard not the deep-toned sea uttering its solemn music, or the breeze whispering its softer notes in his ear. He only saw the ship, the abode of men, fading into indistinctness, as the darkness threw its veil over it; he only heard the voice in his heart, proclaiming ever and again, "I am free." Before the morrow dawned, he had surmounted the rocks at the landing place, and wandered on with no aim, but to put as great a distance as possible between him and the ship. Two hours' walking brought him again to the sea, in an opposite direction to that by which he had approached the island. Here he crawled into a hiding-place among the rocks, and lay down to rest. The day was again declining before he ventured forth from his covert, and cautiously approached the distant shore, whence he might see the ship. He reached the spring by which he had stood yester eve, when his companions parted from him, with something like pity stirring in the hearts of all but one among them. Fearfully he looked around before him but no shadow on the earth, no sail upon the pathless sea, told of man's presence. He was alone alone indeed, for the beauty of Nature aroused no emotion in his withered heart, and he held no communion with Nature's God. He was indeed an orphaned soul. Could he have loved, had it been but a simple flower, he would have felt something of the joy of life; but the very power of love seemed to have been crushed from his heart, by years of cold neglect and harsh unkindness.

Weeks, months passed, without any event that might awaken the young solitary from his torpor. By day, he roved through the island, or lay listlessly under the shadow of a tree; by night, he slept beneath the rocks which had first sheltered him; while the fruits, that grew and ripened without his care, gave him food. Thus he lived a merely animal life, his strongest sensation one of satisfaction for his relief from positive suffering, but with nothing that could be called joy in the present, and with no hope for the future; one to whom God had given an immortal spirit, capable of infinite elevation in the scale of intelligence and happiness, and whom man had pressed down to ay, below the level of the brutes, which sported away their brief existence at his side. Such tyranny as he had experienced, is rare; but its results may well give an impressive, a fearful lesson, to those to whom are committed the destinies of a being unconnected with them by any of those ties which awaken tenderness, and call forth indulgence in the sternest minds. Let them beware, lest the "iron rule" crush out the life of the young heart, and darken the intellect by extinguishing the light of hope.

Terrible was the retribution which his crimes wrought out for the author of our young hero's miseries. When he received the intelligence from the men whom he had sent in the morning to bring him from the island, that he was nowhere to be found, he read in their countenance what his own heart was ready to repeat to him, that he was his murderer; for neither they nor he doubted that the terrified boy had rushed into the sea, and been drowned in the effort to escape the horrors raised by his wild and superstitious fancy. From that hour his persecutor suffered tortures as great as his bitterest enemies could have desired to inflict on him. The images which drove him with increased eagerness to the bottle, became more vivid and terrific under the influence of intoxication. He drank deeper and deeper, in the vain hope to banish them, and died ere many months had passed, shouting, in his last moments, alternate prayers and curses to the imagined form of him whom he supposed the hope of revenge had conjured from the ocean grave to which his cruelties had consigned him.

Five months passed over Edward Hallett, in the dead calm of an existence agitated by neither hope nor fear. The calm was broken one evening by the sight of a seaman, drawing water from the spring which had brought his former companions to the island. As he came in sight, the man turned his head, and stood for an instant spell-bound by the unexpected vision of a human being on that island, whose matted locks and tattered garments spoke the extreme of misery. There was only one hope for the sad wild boy it was in flight and turning, he ran swiftly back; but the path was strewn with rocks, and, in his haste, he stumbled and fell. In a moment his pursuer stood beside him, acclaiming in a coarse, but kindly meant language:

"What the devil are you runnin' away from me for, youngster? I'm sure I wouldn't hurt ye but get up, and tell us what you're doing here, and where ye've come from."

The speaker attempted, while addressing the boy, to raise him from the ground, but he resisted all his efforts, and met all his questioning with sullen silence.

"By the powers, I'm thinking I've caught a wild man. I wonder if there's any more of 'em. If I can only get this one aboard, he'll make my fortune. I'll try for it, any how, and offer the capting to go shares with my bargain;" and he proceeded to lift the slight form of the pauper boy in his brawny arms, and bear him to the boat, which, during the scene, had approached the shore. One who had had less experience of the iron nature of man, would have endeavored, in Edward Hallett's circumstances, to move his captor by entreaties to leave him to his dearly prized freedom; but he had long believed, with the poet,

"There is no pulse in man's obdurate heart
It does not feel for man;"

and after the first wild struggle, which had only served to show that he was an infant in the hands of the strong seaman, he abandoned himself to his fate, in silent despair. With closed eyes and lips, he suffered himself, without a movement, to be borne to the boat, and deposited in it, amidst the many uncouth and characteristic exclamations of his captor and his companions, who would not be convinced that it was really a child of the human race, thus strangely found on this isolated spot. Hastily they bore him to the ship, which the providence of God had sent, under the guidance of a kind and noble spirit, for the salvation of this, his not forgotten, though long tried creature.

Captain Durbin, of the barque Good Intent, was one who combined, in no usual degree, the qualities of boldness and energy with the kindest, the tenderest, and most generous feelings. These were wrought into beautiful harmony, by the Christian principles which had long governed his life, and from which he had learned to be, at the same time, "diligent in business" and "kindly affectioned" to have no fear of man, and to love his brother, whom he had seen, as the best manifestation of devotion to God, whom he had not seen. Perhaps he had escaped the usual effect of his rough trade, in hardening the manners, at least, by the influence on him of his only child, a little girl, now six years old, who was his constant companion, even in his voyages. Little Emily Durbin had lost her mother when she was only two years old. The circumstances of her own childhood had wrought into the mind of the dying Mrs. Durbin, the conviction that only a parent is a fitting guardian for a child. To all argument on this subject she would reply, "It seems to me that God has put so much love into a parent's heart, only that he may bear with all a child's waywardness, which other people can't be expected to bear with."

True to her principles, she had exacted a promise from her husband, in her dying hour, that he would never part from their Emily. The promise had been sacredly kept.

"I will retire from sea as soon as I have enough to buy a place on shore, for Emily's sake; but till then, her home must be in my cabin. She is under God's care there, as well as on shore, and perhaps it would be better for her, should I be lost at sea, to share my fate." Such were the remarks of Captain Durbin, in reply to the well-meant remonstrances of his friends.

Emily had a little hammock slung beside his own the books in which he taught her made a large part of his library; and he who had seen her kneel beside her father to lisp her childish prayer, or who had heard the simple, beautiful faith with which she commended herself to the care of her Father in Heaven, when the waves roared and the winds howled around her floating home, would have felt, perhaps, that the most important end of life, the cultivation of those affections that connect us with God and with our fellow-creatures, might be attained as perfectly there as elsewhere.

The astonishment of Captain Durbin and the pity of his gentle child may be conceived, at the sight of the poor boy, who was brought up from the boat by his captor and owner, as he considered himself, and laid at their feet, while they sat together in their cabin he writing in his log-book, and she conning her evening lesson. To the proposition that he should give the prize so strangely obtained a free passage, and share in the advantages to be gained by its exhibition in America, Captain Durbin replied by showing the disappointed seaman the impossibility of the object of these speculations being some product of Nature's freaks some hitherto unknown animal, with the form, but without the faculties of man.

"Do you not see that he has clothes "

"Clothes do ye call them!" interrupted the blunt sailor, touching the pieces of cloth that hung around, but no longer covered the thin limbs.

"Rags, perhaps I had better say but the rags have been clothes, woven and sewn by man's hands so he must have lived among men civilized men and he has grown but little, as you may perceive, since those clothes were made therefore, he cannot have been long on the island."

"But how did he get there? Who'd leave a baby like this there by himself?"

"That we may never know, for the boy must either be an idiot which he does not look like, however or insane, or dumb but let that be as it will, we will do our duty by him, and I thank God for having sent us here in time to save him."

The master of the ship usually gives the tone to those whom he commands, and Captain Durbin found no difficulty in obtaining the help of his men in his kind intentions to the boy so strangely brought amongst them. By kind, yet rough hands, he was washed, his hair was cut and combed, and a suit of clean, though coarse garments, hastily fitted to him by the best tailor among them fitted, not with the precision of Stultz certainly, but sufficiently well to enable him to walk in them without danger of walking on them or of leaving them behind. But he showed no intention of availing himself of these capabilities. Wherever they carried him he went without resistance wherever they placed him he remained he ate the food that was offered him but no word escaped his lips, no voluntary movement was made by him, no look marked his consciousness of aught that passed before him. He had again assumed his only shield from violence cunning. He could account in no way for his being left unmolested, except from the belief, freely expressed before him, that nature, by depriving him of intelligence, or of speech, had unfitted him for labor, and he resolved to do nothing that should unsettle that belief. But he found it more difficult than he had supposed it would be to preserve this resolution, for he was subjected to the action of a more potent influence than any he had yet encountered kindness. All were ready to show him this in its common forms, but none so touchingly or so tenderly as the little Emily Durbin. It was a beautiful sight to see that gentle child, with eyes blue as the heavens, whose pure and lovely spirit they seemed to mirror, gazing up at the dark boy as though she hoped to catch some ray of the awakening spirit flitting over the handsome but stolid features. Sometimes she would sit beside him, take his hand in hers, or stroke gently the dark locks that began again to hang in neglected curls around his face, and speak to him in the tenderest accents, saying, "I love you very much, pretty boy, and my father loves you too, and we all love you don't you love us? but you can't tell me I forgot that never mind, I'll ask our Heavenly Father to make you talk. Don't you know Jesus made the dumb to speak when he was here on earth? Did you ever hear about it? Poor boy! you can't answer me but I'll tell you all about it:" and then in her sweet words and pitying voice she would tell of the Saviour of men how he had made the deaf to hear and the dumb to speak, and she would repeat his lessons of love, dwelling often on her favorite text, "This is my commandment, that ye love one another even as I have loved you, that ye also love one another."

Thus by this babe, God was in his love leading the chilled heart of that poor, desolate boy, back to himself to hope to heaven. It was impossible that the dew of mercy should thus, day by day and hour by hour, distil upon a spirit indurated by man's cruelties, without softening it. Edward Hallett began to love that sweet child, to listen to her step and voice, to gaze upon her fair face, to return her loving looks, and to long to tell her all his story. Emily became aware of the new expression in his face, and redoubled her manifestations of interest. She entreated that he should be brought in when her father read the Bible and prayed with her, night and morning. "Who knows, it may be that our Heavenly Father will make him hear us," was her simple and pathetic response to Captain Durbin's assurance that it was useless, as he either could not or would not understand them. Never had Edward Hallett's resolution been more severely tried than when he saw her kneel, with clasped hands and uplifted face, at her father's knee, and heard her pray in her own simple words that "God would bless the poor little dumb boy whom he had sent to them, and that he would make him speak, and give him a good heart, that he might love them." Captain Durbin turned his eyes upon the object of her prayer at that moment, and he almost thought that his lips moved, and was quite certain that his eyes glistened with emotion. From this time he was as anxious as Emily herself for the attendance of the strange boy at their devotions.

For many weeks the ship had sped across that southern sea with light and favoring breezes, but at length there came a storm. The heavens were black with clouds the wind swept furiously over the ocean, and drove its wild waves in tremendous masses against the reeling ship. Captain Durbin was a bold sailor, as we have said, and he had weathered many a storm in his trim barque; but Emily knew by the way in which he pressed her to his heart this night, before he laid her, not in her hammock, but on the narrow floor of his state-room, and by the tone in which he ejaculated, "God bless you, and take care of you, my beloved child!" that there was more danger tonight than they had ever before encountered together; and as he was leaving her she drew him back and said, "Father, I can't sleep, and I should like to talk to the little dumb boy; won't you bring him here, and let him sit on my mattress with me?"

Captain Durbin brought Edward Hallett and placed him beside Emily, where, by bracing themselves against the wall of the state-room, they might prevent their being dashed about by the rolling of the vessel.

Emily welcomed him with an affectionate smile, and taking his hand, which now sometimes answered the clasp of hers, told him that he must not be afraid, though there was a great storm, for their Father in Heaven could deliver them out of it if it were His will, and if it were not, He would take them to himself, if they loved Him, and loved one another as the blessed Saviour had commanded them. "And you know we must die some way," continued the sweet young preacher, "and father says it is just as easy to go to Heaven from the sea as from any other place." She paused a moment, and then added in a low tone, "But I think I had rather die on shore, and be buried by my mother in the green, shady church-yard it is so quiet there."

Emily crept nearer and nearer to her young companion as she spoke, with that clinging to human love and care which is felt by the hardest breast in moments of dread. His heart was beating high with the tenderest and the happiest emotions he had ever known, when a wave sweeping over the deck of the ship, and breaking through the skylight, came tumbling in upon them. It forced them asunder, and the falling of their lantern at the same moment left them in darkness amidst the tossing of the ship, the rolling of the furniture, and the noise of the many waters. Edward Hallett's first thought was for Emily; he felt for her on every side, but she was not in the state-room; he groped his way into the cabin, but he could not find her, and he heard no sound that told of her existence. In terror for her, self was forgotten love conquered fear, as it had already obtained the empire over hate, and he called her "Emily dear Emily! hear me answer me, Emily?"

He listened in vain for the faint voice for which he thirsted. Suddenly he bounded up the cabin steps and rushed to the post at which he knew Captain Durbin was most likely to be found in such a scene, crying as he went, "Emily! Emily! oh bring a light and look for Emily!"

The shrill cry of a human heart in agony was heard above the bellowing of the winds and the rush of the waves, and without waiting for a question, without heeding even the miracle that the dumb had spoken, Captain Durbin hastened below, followed by his agitated summoner. As quickly as his trembling hands permitted, he struck a light and looked around for his child. She had been dashed against a chest, and lay pale and seemingly lifeless, with the red blood oozing slowly from a cut in the temple. Edward Hallett had lifted her before Captain Durbin could lay aside his light, and as he approached him, looking up with a face almost as pale as that which lay upon his arm, he exclaimed, "Oh, sir, surely she is not dead!"

It was not till Emily had again opened her soft eyes and assured her father that she was not much hurt, that any notice was taken of the very unusual fact of Edward Hallett's speaking.

"Father, how did you know I was hurt?"

"He whom we have thought a dumb boy called me, and told me he could not find you," said Captain Durbin, looking earnestly, almost sternly at Edward, who colored as he felt that eyes he dared not meet were upon him. But the gentle, loving Emily took his hand, and said, "Did our good Heavenly Father make you speak? I am so glad please speak to me!"

Edward could not raise his eyes to hers, but covering his face with his other hand, he fell on his knees, saying to her and Captain Durbin, "I am afraid it was very wicked, but indeed I couldn't help it. I could speak all the time, Emily, but I was afraid of being beaten as I used to be, if I seemed like other people now if they beat me I must bear it better for me to be beaten than to have Emily lie there with no one to help her."

"But who is going to beat you? Nobody will beat you we all love you don't we, father?" cried Emily, bending forward and putting her arm around the neck of her protege.

"We must hear first whether he is worthy of our love, my dear," said Captain Durbin, as he attempted to withdraw his daughter's arm, and to make her lie down again but Edward had seized the little hand and held it around his neck, while he exclaimed in the most imploring tones, "Oh, sir I let Emily love me nobody else except my poor mother ever loved me. Beat me as much as you please, and I will not say a word, but oh! pray, sir! don't tell Emily she must not love me."

"And, father, if he were wicked, you know you told me once that we must love the wicked and try to do them good, because our Father in Heaven loved us while we were yet sinners," urged Emily.

That gentle voice could not be unheeded, and as Captain Durbin kissed her, he laid his hand kindly on the boy's head, saying in more friendly tones, "I hope he has not been wicked, but we will hear more about it to-morrow I cannot stay longer with you now, and you must lie still just where I have put you, or you may roll out and get hurt. We shall have a rough sea most of the night, though, thank God! no danger, for the wind had shifted and slackened a little before that great wave swept you away!"

"May I not stay by Emily, sir, and tell her what made me not speak? I will not let her sit up again."

"Oh, yes! do, father, let him stay till you come down again."

Captain Durbin consented, and when he came down again at midnight from the deck, the children had both fallen asleep, but their hands were clasped in each other's, and the flushed cheeks and dewy lashes of both showed that they had been weeping. The next morning Captain Durbin heard the story of the orphan boy. Emily Durbin stood beside him while he told it, and he needed the courage which her presence gave him, for his cowed spirit could not yet rise to confidence in man. The mingled indignation and pity with which Captain Durbin heard the simple but touching narrative of his life the earnest kindness with which, at the conclusion, he drew him to his side, and told him that he would be his father, and Emily his sister, adding, "God gave you to me, and as His gift I will love you and care for you," first taught him that his friend Emily was not the one only angel of mercy in our world. As time passed on, and Captain Durbin kept well the promise of those words, instructing him with care and guarding him with tenderness as well as with fidelity, his faith became firm, not only in his fellow-men, but in Him who had brought such great good for him out of the darkest evil. His long repressed affections sprang into vigorous growth, his intellect expanded rapidly in their glow, his eye grew bright, his step elastic, and his whole air redolent of a joy which none but those who have suffered as he had done can conceive. In the handsome youth who returned two years afterwards with Captain Durbin to Boston, and who walked so proudly at his side, leading Emily by the hand, few could have recognized the wild boy of that western Island.

Such was the transformation which the spirit of love, breathing itself through the lips of a little child, had effected. "Verily, of such" children "is the kingdom of heaven."

CHAPTER VI

The entertainment of the evening gave its character to our conversation on the following morning. It was a conversation too grave for introduction into a work intended only to aid in the entertainment of festive hours: it commenced with the English "poor-laws," and ended with a discussion of the tenure of property in that land, and the wisdom of our own republican fathers in abolishing entails a subject affording a fair opportunity to us Americans, to indulge a little in that self-glorification which we are accused of loving so well.

"What a curious book would a 'History of Entails' be!" exclaimed Mr. Arlington, "how full of the romance of life!"

"Romance!" ejaculated Annie.

"Yes, romance; for under this system, the poor man, whose life seemed doomed to one unbroken struggle with fortune, for the necessaries of existence, finds himself, by some unexpected casualty, the possessor of rank, and of what seems to him boundless wealth."

"Ah, yes!" said I, "but you have given us only the bright side of the picture. To make room for this stranger, whose only connection with the house of which he has so unexpectedly become the head is probably that preserved in genealogical tables, the daughters of the house, or their children it may be, reared in luxury, must go forth to a life of comparative privation. I met, some years ago, in one of my visits to the Far West, a young Englishman, who but I will read you the story of his life, as I wrote it out soon after parting with him."

"Have you a picture of him, Aunt Nancy?" asked Robert Dudley.

"Yes, Robert," I replied with a smile, "but you must have patience, for I shall neither show the picture nor tell the story till evening."

When we were assembled in the evening, Annie, with much ceremony, led me to the high-backed arm-chair, which she called the Speaker's Chair, and placed before me the small travelling desk, in which she knew my manuscripts were kept. I unlocked it, and soon found the scroll of which I was in search.

"But the picture, Aunt Nancy where is the picture?" cried the eager Robert.

"Here it is," I cried, as I loosened the ribbon with which the manuscript was bound together, and produced a small engraving; a fancy subject, however, rather than an actual portrait, and of no general interest. The print was eagerly caught by Robert, and handed around the circle, with exclamations of, "How handsome!" "What an exquisite picture!" Mr. Arlington looked at it a moment, then, with a smiling glance at me, handed it, without a word of comment, to Col. Donaldson.

"The impertinent puppy!" ejaculated the Colonel, "engrossed with his hawk and his hound, and wearing such an insolent air of self-absorption in the presence of a lady" (for the artist had introduced a lovely young maiden in the scene). "Poor girl!" continued the Colonel; "if she were in any way connected with him, I am not surprised that she should look so sad and reproachful."

Mr. Arlington's smiling glance was again turned on me; and I met it with a hearty laugh.

"Indeed, Aunt Nancy," said the Colonel, who seemed strangely annoyed at my laughter, "I think your friend does you little credit, and I can only hope that he had some of these lordly airs drubbed out of him at the West."

As Col. Donaldson spoke he threw down the engraving which he had held, and pushed his chair from the table.

"I assure you, sir," I replied, "my friend has as few lordly airs as it is possible to conceive in one born to such lordly circumstances. It was not my intention to impose on you that picture as an actual likeness of him though had you ever seen him I might easily have done so, as it really resembles him very much in his personal traits."

"Well, I am glad he did not sit for this picture," said Col. Donaldson; "now I can listen to your story with some pleasure."

"Thank you; you must first take some reflections suggested to me by the incidents I have here narrated. Of the character of these reflections, you will form some conception from the title I have given to the tale into which I have interwoven them. I have called it

"LIFE IN AMERICA."

"Men and Manners in America" was the comprehensive title of a book issued some fifteen or twenty years ago, by a gentleman from Scotland, to whom, we fear, Americans have never tendered the grateful acknowledgments he deserved for his disinterested efforts to teach them to eat eggs properly, and to give due time to the mastication of their food. This benevolently instructive work was the precursor of a host of others on the same topics, and others of a kindred character. America has been the standard subject for the trial essays of European tyros in philosophy, political economy, and book-making in general. Society in America has been presented, it would seem, in all its aspects religious, educational, industrial, political, commercial, and fashionable. Our schools and our prisons, our churches and our theatres, have been in turn the subject of investigation, of unqualified censure, and of scarcely less unqualified laudation.

The subject thus dissected, put together, and dissected again, has not been able to restrain some wincing and an occasional outcry, when the scalpel has been held by a more than usually unskilful hand demonstrations of sensibility which have occasioned apparently as much disapprobation as surprise in the anatomists. We flatter ourselves that there is peculiar fitness in the metaphor just used, for the outer form only of American life has been touched by these various writers. Its spirit, that which gives to it its peculiar organization, has evaded them as completely as the soul of man evades the keenest investigations of the dissecting room. Even of the seat of the spirit of the point whence it sends forth its subtle influences, giving activity and direction to every member of the HOMES of America, they have little real knowledge. The anatomist the reader will pardon the continuation of a figure so illustrative of our meaning the anatomist knows that not only can he never hope to lay his finger upon the principle of life, but that ere he can pry into those cells in which its mysterious processes are evolved, they must have been dismantled of all that could have guided him to any certain deductions respecting its nature and mode of action. And seldom is the eye of the stranger, never that of the professed bookmaker, suffered to rest upon our homes till they have undergone changes that will as completely baffle his penetration. Nor is this always designedly. It is from a delicate instinct which shrinks from subjecting its most sacred and touching emotions to the rude gaze and ruder comment of the world.

We have been led to these observations by certain events of which we have lately become informed, and which we would here record, as illustrative of some peculiarities of social life in America, and especially of the new development of character manifested by women under the influence of these peculiarities.

The ringing of bells, the firing of cannon, the huzzaing of the assembling multitude on the announcement in London of the victory of Waterloo, must have seemed a bitter mockery to many a heart, mad with the first sharp agony of bereavement. "The few must suffer that the many may rejoice," say the statesman and the warrior while they plan new conquests. It may be so, but we have at present to do with the sufferings of the few.

On the list of the killed in that battle appeared the name of Horace Danforth, Captain in the 41st Regiment of Infantry. It was a name of little note, but there was one to whom it was the synonyme of all that gave beauty or gladness to life; and ere the bells had ceased to sound, or the eager crowd to huzza, her heart was still. With her last quivering sigh had mingled the wail of a new-born infant.

Thus was Horace Maitland Danforth ushered into life. He had been born at the house of his maternal uncle, Sir Thomas Maitland, and as his mother had been wholly dependent on this gentleman, and his father had been a soldier of fortune, leaving to his son no heritage but his name, he continued there, as carefully reared and tenderly regarded as though he had been the heir to Maitland Park and to all its dependencies. Though Sir Thomas had, for many years after the birth of his nephew intended to marry, it was an intention never executed, and when Horace attained his twenty-first birthday, his majority was celebrated as that of his uncle's heir, and as such he was presented by Sir Thomas Maitland to his assembled tenantry. Soon after this event, the Baronet obtained for his nephew a right to the name and arms of Maitland a measure to which, knowing little of his father's family, Horace readily consented. Sir Thomas Maitland died suddenly while yet in the prime of life, and was succeeded by Sir Horace, then twenty-four years of age. In the enjoyments of society, of travel, and of those thousand luxuries, mental and physical, which fortune secures, three years passed rapidly away with the young, handsome, and accomplished Baronet.

One of the earliest convictions of Horace Maitland's life had been, that the refining presence of woman was necessary to the perfection of Maitland Park, and when Sir Thomas said to him, "Marry, Horace do not be an old bachelor like your uncle" though he answered nothing, he vowed in the inmost recesses of his heart that it should not be his fault if he did not obey the injunction. Yet to the world it seemed wholly his own fault that at twenty-seven he had not given to Maitland Park a mistress, and even he himself could not attribute his continued celibacy to the coldness or cruelty of woman; for, in truth, though he had "knelt at many a shrine," he had "laid his heart on none." If hardly pressed for his reason, he might have said with Ferdinand,

"For several virtues
Have I liked several women; never any
With so full soul, but some defect in her
Did quarrel with the noblest grace she own'd,
And put it to the foil."

He who after the death of his uncle continued to urge Sir Horace most on the subject of matrimony, was the one of all the world who might have been supposed least desirous to see him enter into its bonds. This was Edward Maitland, a distant cousin, somewhat younger than himself, to whom he had been attached from his boyhood, and who had been saved by his generosity from many of those painful experiences to which a very narrow income would otherwise have subjected him. It had more than once been suggested to Edward Maitland, that should his cousin die unmarried, he might not unreasonably hope to become his heir, as he was supposed to be uncontrolled by any entail in the disposal of his property, and had few nearer relations than himself, and none with whom he maintained such intimate and affectionate intercourse. Nor could Edward Maitland fail to perceive that his own value in society was in an inverse ratio to the chances of the Baronet's marrying, as a report of an actual proposal on the part of the latter had more than once occasioned a visible declension in the number and warmth of his invitations. These considerations appeared, however, only to stimulate the young man's activity in the search of a wife for his cousin. Had he been employed by a marriage broker with a prospect of a liberal commission, he could hardly have been more indefatigable.

"Well, Horace," exclaimed the younger Maitland, as the two sat loitering over a late London breakfast one morning, "how did you like the lady to whom I introduced you last evening?"

A smile lighted the eyes of Sir Horace as he replied, "Very much, Ned she is certainly intelligent, and has read and thought more than most ladies of her age."

"She will make a capital manager, I am sure."

"And an agreeable companion," added Sir Horace.

"And a good wife do you not think so, Horace?"

"She doubtless would be to one who could fancy her, Ned; for me her style is a little too prononce."

"Well, really, Horace, I cannot imagine what you would have. One woman is too frivolous another wants refinement one is too indolent and exacting and when you can make no other objection, why her style is a little too prononce" the last words were given with ludicrous imitation of his cousin's tone. "If an angel were to descend from heaven for you, I doubt if you would be suited."

"So do I," replied Horace, with a gay laugh at his cousin's evident vexation.

And thus did he meet all Edward's well-intended efforts. The power of choice had made him fastidious, and his life of luxury and freedom had brought him no experiences of the need of another and gentler self as a consoler. But that lesson was approaching.

A call from his lawyer for some papers necessary to complete an arrangement in which he was much interested, had sent Sir Horace to Maitland Park, in the midst of the London season, to explore the yet unfathomed recesses of an old escritoire of Sir Thomas. He had been gone but two days when Edward received the following note from him, written, as it seemed, both in haste and agitation:

"Come to me immediately on the receipt of this, dear Edward. I have found here a paper of the utmost importance to you as well as to me. Come quickly take the chariot and travel post.

"Yours, H. D. MAITLAND."

In less than an hour after the reception of this note Edward Maitland was on the road: and travelling with the utmost expedition, he arrived at Maitland Park just as the day was fading into dusky eve.

"How is Sir Horace?" he asked of the man who admitted him.

"I do not think he seems very well, sir. You will find him in the library, Mr. Edward shall I announce you, sir?"

"No;" and with hurried steps and anxious heart Edward Maitland trod the well-known passages leading to the library.

When he entered that room, Sir Horace was standing at one of its windows gazing upon the landscape without, and so absorbed was he that he did not move at the opening of the door. Edward spoke, and starting, he turned towards him a face haggard with some yet untold suffering. He advanced to meet his cousin, and with an almost convulsive grasp of the hand, said, "I am glad you have come, Edward," then, without heeding the anxious inquiries addressed to him by Edward, he rang the bell, and ordered lights in a tone which caused them to be brought without a moment's delay. As soon as the servant who had brought them had left the room, Horace resumed: "Now, Edward, here is the paper of which I wrote to you; read it at once."

Agitated by his cousin's manner, Edward took the old stained paper from him without a word, and seating himself near the lights, began to read, while Sir Horace stood just opposite him, eyeing him intently. In a very few minutes Edward looked up with a puzzled air and said, "I do not understand one word of it. What does it all mean, Horace?"

"It means that you are Sir Edward Maitland that you are master here and that I am a beggar."

"Horace, you are mad!" exclaimed the young man, starting from his chair, with quivering limbs and a face from which every trace of color had departed.

Hitherto the tone in which Sir Horace had spoken, the alternate flush and pallor on his face, and the shiver that occasionally passed over his frame, had shown him to be fearfully excited; but as Edward became agitated, all these signs of emotion passed away, and with wonderful calmness taking the paper in his hand, he commenced reading that part of it which explained its purpose. This was to secure the descent of the baronetcy of Maitland and the property attached to it in the male line. Having made Edward Maitland comprehend this purpose, Sir Horace drew towards him a genealogical table of their family, and showed him that he was himself the only living descendant in a direct line through an unbroken succession of males from the period at which this entail was made.

"And now, Edward," he said in conclusion, "I am prepared to give up every thing to you. That you have so long been defrauded of your rights has been through ignorance on my part, and equal ignorance, I am convinced, on the part of my uncle. You know he paid little attention to business, leaving it wholly to his agents. I have often heard him express a wish to examine the papers in the old escritoire in which I found this deed, saying that they had been sent home by old Harris when he gave up his business to his nephew the old man writing to my uncle, that as they consisted of leases that had fallen in, or of antiquated deeds, they were no longer of any value except as family records. It was a just Providence that led me to that escritoire, to search for the missing title-deeds of the farm I was about to sell."

Edward Maitland had sunk into his chair from sheer inability to stand, and for several minutes after his cousin had ceased speaking, he still sat, with his elbows resting on the table before him, and his face buried in his clasped hands. At length looking up, he said, "Horace, let us burn this paper and forget it."

"Forget! that is impossible, Edward."

"Why? why not live as we have done? You speak of defrauding me, but what have I wanted that you had? Has not your purse been as my own? Your home has it not been mine? It shall be so still. We shall share the fortune, and as to the title, you will wear it more gracefully than I."

"Dear Edward! Such proof of your generous affection ought to console me for all changes, and it shall. I will confess to you that I have suffered, but it is past. My people " his voice faltered, his chest heaved, and turning away he walked more than once across the room before he resumed "they are mine no longer but you will be kind to them, Edward, I know."

"Horace, you will drive me mad!" cried Edward Maitland. "Promise, I conjure you, promise me to say nothing more of this."

He threw himself as he spoke into his cousin's arms with an agitation which Horace vainly sought to soothe, until he promised "to speak" no further on this subject at present to any one. Satisfied with this promise, and exhausted by the emotions of the last hour, Edward soon retired to his own room. It was long before he slept, and had he not been in a distant part of the house, he would have heard the hurried steps with which, for many an hour after he was left alone, Sir Horace Maitland continued to pace the floor of the dimly lighted library. The clock was on the stroke of three when he seated himself and began the following letter:

DEAR EDWARD: I must go, and at once. I cannot without the loss of self-respect continue to play the master here another day, neither can I live as a dependent within these walls no, not for an hour. Do not attempt to follow me, for I will not see you. I will write to you as soon as I arrive at my point of destination I know not yet where that will be. Feel no anxiety about me. I shall take with me a thousand pounds, and will leave an order for Decker to receive from you and hold subject to my draft whatever sum may accrue from the sale, at a fair valuation, of Sir Thomas Maitland's personal property, which he had an undoubted right to will as he pleased, the amount of the mesne rents expended by me during the last three years having been deducted therefrom. Do not attempt to force favors upon me, Edward I cannot bear them now. Such attempts would only compel me to cut myself loose from you and your affection the one blessing that earth still holds for me.

My trunks have been packed two days, for my first resolve was to go from this place and from England. I shall take the chariot in which you came down and fresh horses, but I will send them back to you from London.

God bless you, Edward. I dare not speak of my feelings to you now, lest I should lose the strength and self-command I need so much. God bless you.

H. D. MAITLAND.

Stealthily did Sir Horace move through the wide halls and ascend the lofty stairs of this home of his life, feeling at every step the rushing tide of memory conflicting with the sad thought that he was treading them for the last time. Having reached his sleeping apartments, he rang a bell which he knew would summon his own man. Rapidly as the man moved, the time seemed long to him ere the summons was obeyed, and he had given the necessary orders to have the carriage prepared and the trunks brought down as soon as possible, "and as quietly," he added, "as he did not wish to disturb Mr. Edward, who had retired to bed late."

"Will you not take breakfast, sir, before you set out?" asked the man.

"No, John. Let the carriage follow me. I shall walk on. Be quick, and make no noise."

A faint streak of light was just beginning to appear in the east, when the heretofore master of that lordly mansion went out into a world which held for him no other home. ACCIDENT, as short-sighted mortals name events controlled by no human will, decided whither he should direct his course from London. He had called at his lawyer's the already mentioned "nephew of old Harris" determined to communicate his discovery to him, perhaps with some faint hope of learning that the entail had been in some way set aside, before Sir Thomas had ventured to make his sister's son his heir. Mr. Decker was not in his rooms, and sitting down to wait for him he took up mechanically the morning paper that lay on his table. The first thing on which his eye rested was the advertisement of a steam packet about to sail from Liverpool for America.

"America; the very place for me. I shall meet no acquaintances there," was the thought which flashed through his mind. Another glance at the paper of the day and hour of the packet's sailing, an examination of his watch, an impatient look from the window up and down the street, and again he mused, "I have not a moment to spare, and if I wait for Decker I may be kept for hours, and so lose the packet; and why should I wait? Have I not seen the deed? This indecision is folly."

The result of these reflections was a note rapidly written to Mr. Decker, stating his discovery of the deed of entail, his consequent surrender of all claim to the property to Edward Maitland, and his determination to quit England immediately. All arrangements respecting the settlement of his claims on the estate, and the claims of the present proprietor upon him, he left to Sir Edward and Mr. Decker, empowering the latter to receive and retain for his use and subject to his order, whatever, on such a settlement, should appertain to him.

This note was left on Mr. Decker's table, and in one hour after leaving his office Horace Maitland was advancing to Liverpool with the rapidity of steam. The packet waited but the arrival of the train in which he was a passenger, to leave the shores of England. With what bitterness he watched those receding shores, while memory wrote upon his bare and bleeding heart the record of joys identified with them, and fading like them for ever from his life, let each imagine for himself, for to such emotions no language can do justice.

A voyage across the Atlantic is now too common an event to stay, even for a moment, the pen of a narrator. From Boston, Horace no longer Sir Horace wrote to his cousin as follows

DEAR EDWARD Here I am among the republicans, with whom I may flatter myself I have lost nothing by sinking Sir Horace Maitland into plain Mr. Danforth. Such is now my address, assumed not from fear that in this distant quarter of the world I shall meet any to whom the name of Maitland is familiar but because much of which I do not desire to be reminded is associated with that came. I said to you when leaving my home, dear Edward, "Do not fear for me." I can now repeat this with better reason. The first stunning shock of the change to which I was so suddenly subjected has been borne. My past life already seems to me as a dream from which I have been rudely but effectually awakened. I am now first to begin life in reality.

The accident which determined me to seek these shores was a happy one. I cannot well dream here where all around me is active, vigorous life. We are accustomed in England to think of the American shores as the Ultima Thule in a western direction, but when we reach these shores we find that the movement is still west. The daily papers are filled with accounts of persons migrating west, and thither am I going. "The world is all before me where to choose" the theatre of my new life my life of work — —and I would have it far from the blue sea, out of hearing of the murmur of the waves that lave my island home. I will go where the wide prairies sweep away on every side of the horizon where every link with other lands will be severed, and America below and Heaven above constitute my universe. "You will find no society at the West," has been said to me. This is another attraction to that region. I would work out my destiny in solitude. I desire to travel without company, and have made my arrangements accordingly. I have purchased three substantial horses for a little more than one hundred pounds, and have engaged a shrewd, active lad as groom, valet, and he seems to think, companion, at about two pounds per month. A very light carriage, sometimes driven by my servant and sometimes by myself, will transport the moderate wardrobe which I shall deem it necessary to take with me to the outermost verge of civilization and good roads, where leaving carriage and wardrobe, or at least all of the latter which may not be borne by a led-horse, I shall penetrate still further into the old forests of this New World. I long to be alone with "Nature's full, free heart" perchance, there, my own may beat as of yore.

Farewell, dear Edward. You may hear of me next among the Sacs and Foxes; at present address H. Danforth, care of G & D , Merchants, street, Boston.

Yours ever, H. DANFORTH.

A new external life had indeed opened upon this child of luxury and conventional refinement. He whose movements had been chronicled as matter of interest to the public, for whose presence the "world" had postponed its fêtes, might now travel hundreds of miles without observation or inquiry. He upon whose steps had waited a crowd of obsequious attendants, now found himself with one follower, whose tone of independence hardly permitted him to call him servant. In cities, where he would still have been surrounded by those conventional distinctions of which he had himself been deprived, the sense of a great loss would have been ever present with him, and the contrast with the past would have made the fairest present to which he could now attain, desolate. But there could be no comparison, and therefore no painful contrast, between the wild life of the prairies and the ultra-civilization of English aristocratic society. In the excitement and adventure of the one, he hoped to forget the other. He sought to forget not to be resigned, to acquiesce. His inner life was unchanged. He had been a dreamer a pleasure-seeker and a dreamer and pleasure-seeker he continued, though the dreams and the pleasures must be wrought from new materials. To sketch the progress of such a character through the shifting scenes of his new existence to observe him in his association with the strong, daring, acute, but uncultivated denizens of our frontier States to stand with sympathizing heart beside him as he first entered upon those unpeopled solitudes in whose silence God speaks to the soul, is not permitted us at present. This may be the work of another day; but now we must pass at once with him from Boston to a scene within the confines of Iowa. His carriage had been left behind, and for two days he had been riding over a rolling country, whose grassy knolls, dotted here and there with clumps of trees, brought occasionally to his mind the park scenery of his own land. Early in this day he had passed a farm with a comfortable house and substantial out-buildings, but no dwelling of man had since presented itself to him, though the sun was now low in the western sky. Under ordinary circumstances this would have been of little consequence, for he had already spent more than one night in the open air without discomfort; but his attendant had heard a distant muttering of thunder, and John Stacy was not the lad to encounter without murmuring a night of storm unsheltered. John's anxiety made him keen-sighted, and he was the first to perceive and announce the approach of a rider. We use the neutral term rider not without consideration, for he was one in whom a certain ease of manner, and even an air of command, contradicted the testimony of habiliments made and worn after a fashion recognized nowhere as characteristic of the genus gentleman. A courteous inquiry from Horace Danforth respecting the nearest place at which a night's shelter might be obtained, led to a cordial invitation to him to return with him to his own house. It was an invitation not to be disregarded under existing circumstances, and it was accepted with evident pleasure both by master and man.

  Mr. Grahame, for so the new-comer had announced himself, led the way back for a short distance over the route just pursued by our travellers, and then striking off to the left, rode briskly forward for several miles. The light gray clouds which had long been gathering in the western sky had deepened into blackness as they proceeded, and flashes of lightning were darting across their path, and large drops of rain were falling upon them when they neared a house constructed of logs, yet bearing some evidence of taste in the grounds around it, as well as in its position, which was on the side of a gently sloping hill, looking out upon a landscape through which wound a clear and rapid, though narrow stream.

"Like good cavaliers, we will see our horses housed first," said Mr. Grahame, riding past the main building to one of the out-houses, built also of logs, which served as a stable. Here Horace Danforth relinquished his tired steed to the care of John Stacy, and Mr. Grahame having himself rubbed down his own beautiful animal, and thrown a bundle of hay before him, with a slight apology to his visitor for the detention, led the way into the house. As they entered the vacant parlor a shade of something like dissatisfaction passed over the master's countenance, and having seen his guest seated by a huge fireplace, whose cheerful blaze of wood a chilly evening made by no means unwelcome, he left him alone. He soon returned, however, with a brighter expression, which was explained by his saying, "I feared, on finding this room empty, that my daughter had been sent for to a sick woman with whom she has lately spent several days and nights, and that I could offer you only the discomforts of a bachelor's establishment; but I find she is at home, and will soon give us supper."

During the absence of his host, our Englishman had looked around with increasing surprise at the contents of the parlor. The furniture was of the most simple description, yet marked by a certain neatness and gracefulness of arrangement, indicative, as he could not but think, of a cultivated taste. The same mingling of even rude simplicity of material and tasteful arrangement prevailed in the chamber to which his host now conducted him, and where the luxury, for such he had learned to regard it, of abundance of clear water and clean napkins awaited him. In a few minutes after his return to the parlor a door was opened, through which he obtained a view of an inner apartment, well lighted, and containing a table so spread as to present no slight temptation to a traveller who had not broken his fast since the morning meal. At the head of this table stood a young woman of graceful form, whom his host introduced to him as his daughter, Miss Grahame.

Mary Grahame's clear complexion, glowing with the hue of health, her large and soft and dark gray eyes, her abundant glossy black hair, might have won from the most fastidious some of that admiration given to personal beauty; but in truth Horace Danforth had grown indifferent as well as fastidious, and it was not until in after days he had seen the complexion glow and the dark eyes kindle with feeling, that he said to himself, "She is beautiful!" To the fascination of a peculiarly graceful, gentle, yet earnest manner, he was, however, more quickly susceptible. During this first evening, the chief emotion excited in his mind was surprise at the style of conversation and manner, the acquaintance with books and with les bien-séances which marked these inhabitants of a log cabin in the western wilds these denizens of a half-savage life.

A day of hard riding had induced such fatigue, that even the rare and unexpected pleasure of communication with refined and cultivated minds, could not keep Horace Danforth long from his pillow. As he expected to set out in the morning very early, he would have made his adieus in parting for the night, mingling with them courteous expressions of the enjoyment which such society had afforded him after his long abstinence from all intellectual converse.

"Believe me," said Mr. Graham, and the sentiment was corroborated by his daughter's eyes, "the pleasure has been mutual. Society is the great want of our western life. I have been wishing to ask whether your business were too urgent to permit you to afford us more of this coveted good?"

"I am ashamed to confess," said Horace Danforth, with some embarrassment, "that I have no business at present that I am an idler I verily believe the only one in your country."

"Then will you not give us the pleasure of your company for a longer time? A little rest will be no disadvantage either to your horses or yourself, and on us you will be conferring a favor which you cannot appreciate till you have lived five hundred miles away from civilization."

The invitation was accepted as cordially as it was given, to the great satisfaction of John Stacy, who had been much pleased with the appearance of land in this neighborhood, and wanted time to look about him preparatory to purchasing.

Horace Danforth awoke early next morning, and throwing open the shutters of the only window in his room, found that a stormy night had been succeeded by an unusually brilliant morning. "To brush the dews from off the upland lawn" had not been a habit of his past life; but the cool fresh air, the spicy perfumes which it wafted to him, and the brightness and verdure of the whole landscape, proved now more inviting than his pillow; and dressing himself hastily, he descended the clean but rude and uncarpeted stairs as gently as possible, lest he should arouse Miss Grahame from her slumbers. He found the front door open, showing that he was not the first of the household to go abroad that day. As he stepped out upon the lawn, he discovered that the parlor windows were also open, and a familiar air, hummed in low, suppressed tones, caused him to look through them as he passed. Could he believe his eyes? Was that neatest and prettiest of all housemaids, who, moving with light and even graceful steps, was yet busied in the very homely task of dusting and arranging the furniture in the parlor was she indeed the same Miss Grahame who had last evening charmed him by her lady-like deportment and intelligent conversation? Yes, the very same; for though the glossy black braids were covered by a gay colored handkerchief wound around her head a la Turque, there was the same wide forehead and well-defined brows; the same soft dark gray eyes; the same slightly aquiline nose and smiling mouth. Nor was the conversation of last evening more opposed, in his imagination, to her present employment, than the evident taste and feeling with which she was now singing that most beautiful hymn of the Irish poet:

"O God! Thou art the life and light
Of all this wondrous world I see."

Listening and gazing, wondering and comparing, he had well nigh forgotten himself, when the lady of the mansion turning suddenly to the window, raised her head. Their eyes met! The color which rushed quickly to her very temples, recalled him to himself, and bowing with certainly not less embarrassment than she evinced, he walked rapidly on. He had not proceeded far, however, when he saw his host approaching from an opposite direction. As Mr. Grahame had already spent more than an hour in his fields, sharing as well as directing the labors of his men, he expressed no surprise at meeting his guest abroad. After a cordial greeting, and a few general observations on the weather and scenery had been exchanged, Mr. Grahame, glancing up at the sun, which had now risen considerably above a distant wood, said, "I am sorry to interrupt your walk, but my morning's work has made me by no means indifferent to my breakfast, and I think that Mary's coffee and biscuits are about this time done to a turn."

A few minutes brought them back to the house, and into the parlor from which Mary Grahame had disappeared, leaving behind her, in its neat and tasteful arrangement, and in the fresh flowers that adorned the table and mantelpiece, evidence of her early presence. The gentlemen were soon summoned to breakfast.

It may have been that his early rising had given to Horace Danforth an unusual appetite; but certain it is that no breakfast of which he had ever partaken seemed to him half so inviting as this. And yet, in truth, it was simple enough; toast, crisp and brown, warm, light biscuits, fresh eggs, good butter, excellent coffee, and rich cream were all it offered. Mary Grahame presided, and speaking little herself, listened to her father and Horace, while they discussed the different characteristics of English or European and American society, with a pleased and intelligent countenance. Some observations from him drew from Mr. Grahame the following reply:

"There is one feature of American society upon which I think no foreigner has remarked, or if he have, it has been so cursorily as plainly to show that he was far from appreciating its importance: I mean the fact that here the thinker is also the worker. In England and the European States, the working class is distinct from the consumers, and there must be almost as great a contrast in the intellectual as in the physical condition of the two. All the refinement, the cultivation, must remain with those who have leisure and fortune as a class, I mean, for individuals will of course be found, who, in spite of all disadvantages, will rise to the highest position. But here, in America, there are no idlers. Here, with few if any exceptions, all must be, in some way, workers, and all may be thinkers. We attain thus to a republic of mind."

"Do you not fear that the result of this will be to check the development of individual greatness; that as you have no king in the State, so you will have no king in literature?"

"Even were this so, it would remain a question whether the great increase of general intelligence would not more than compensate the evil."

"Can many Polloks repay us for one Milton many Drydens for one Shakspeare?"

"You take extreme cases; besides, I only admitted your supposition to show that I could produce a set-off to the disadvantage. I do not believe that the necessity for labor of some sort will prevent a truly great mind from achieving for itself the highest distinction. I think the history of such minds proves that it will rather serve as a stimulus to their powers."

Horace Danforth was silent, and after a moment's pause, Mr. Grahame resumed.

"In this union of the working and the thinking classes, the refinements of life, those things which adorn, and beautify it, take their true place as consolers and soothers of the care-worn and toil-wearied mind. No Italian opera can give such delight to the sated man of pleasure as the tired laborer feels in listening to the evening song with which some loved one, in his home, sings him to repose."

"You speak con amore" said Horace Danforth, smiling at his host's fervor.

"I do. Had I been excluded from the refinements of social life, I should long since have fainted and grown weary of my toil here. I felt this when compelled to relinquish my daughter's society for two years, that she might have the advantage of instruction in those branches of a womanly education in which I could give her no aid."

"And having spent two years in the more cultivated East, did Miss Grahame return willingly to her home in the wilderness?"

This question was addressed to Mary Grahame herself, and she answered simply, "My father was here."

"You acknowledge, then, that could your father have been with you, you would have preferred remaining at the East?"

"Oh no! I was fifteen when my father sent me from home, and they who have enjoyed the free life of the prairies so long, seldom love cities."

"But the ease, the freedom from labor, which is enjoyed in a more advanced stage of society, the power to devote yourself to pursuits agreeable to your taste did you not regret these?"

"Permit me to put your question into plainer language," interposed Mr. Grahame. "Mr. Danforth would ask, Mary, whether you would not prefer to live where you would not be compelled to degrade your mind "

"No, no, I protest against the degradation," exclaimed Mr. Danforth.

"To degrade your mind," pursued Mr. Grahame, answering the interruption only by a smile, "by exercising it on such homely things as brewing coffee and baking cakes, or to soil your fair hands with brooms and dusters."

"For the soil of the hands we have sparkling rills, and for the degradation of the mind, I, like Mr. Danforth, protest against it."

"But how can you make your protest good?"

"You have taught me that there is no degradation in labor, pursued for fair and right ends, and that where the end is noble, the labor becomes ennobling."

"But what noble ends can be alleged for the drudgery of domestic life? I am translating your looks into language," said Mr. Grahame, turning playfully to his guest; "correct me if I do not read them rightly."

"If I say you do, I fear Miss Grahame will think them very impertinent looks."

"I shall not complain of them while I can reply to them so easily," said Mary gayly. "He who knows how much a well-ordered household contributes to the cultivation of domestic virtues and family affections, will not think a woman degraded who sacrifices somewhat of her tastes and pleasures to the deeper happiness of procuring such advantages for those she loves."

"But is not that state of society preferable, in which, without her personal interference, by the employment of those who have no higher tastes, she may accomplish the same object?"

"That question proves that you do not, like my father, desire to see the working and the thinking classes united. You seem to propose that the first shall ever remain our hewers of wood and drawers of water."

"Is it not a fact that there have been, are, and always will be those in the world who are fitted for no other position?"

"That there are and always have been such persons, I acknowledge; but when labor ceases to be degrading, because it is partaken by all, may we not hope that new aspirations will be awakened in the laborer that he will elevate himself in the scale of being when he feels elevation possible?"

Mary Grahame spoke with generous enthusiasm, yet with a modest gentleness which made Horace Danforth desire to continue the argument.

"Admitting all this," he said, "it does not answer my question, which was, whether you did not prefer that state of society in which you were able to avail yourself of the services of such a class?"

"There are moments, doubtless, when indolence would plead for such self-indulgence; but I should be mortified, indeed, where this the prevailing temper of my mind."

"Pardon me if I say that I do not see how it can be otherwise how a lady of Miss Grahame's refinement and taste can be pleased with the employments, for instance, to which Mr. Grahame just now referred."

"Not pleased with them in themselves, but she may accept them, may she not, as a necessary part of a great object to which she has devoted herself?"

"And this object? but, forgive me. The interest you have awakened in the subject, and your kindness in answering my questions, make me an encroacher, I fear," he added, as he marked the heightened color with which Mary glanced at her father as he paused for her answer.

"Not at all; but I speak in presence of my master, and will refer you to him," she replied, with another smiling glance at her father.

"You see," said Mr. Grahame, "that even in these wilds, 'the world's dread laugh' retains its power. Mary, I see, is afraid of being called a female Quixote, and even I find myself disposed to win you to some interest in my object, before I avow it. This I think I can best do by a sketch of the circumstances which led to its adoption. I will give you such a sketch, therefore, if you will promise to acquit me of egotism in doing so."

"That I will readily do. I shall be delighted to hear it."

"You shall have it, but not now; for I see, by certain cabalistic signs, known only to the initiated, that Mary is about to leave us for some of those same degrading employments, and if you will take a ride with me, I will relieve you from all danger of contact with them, and will, at the same time, show you something of our neighborhood."

The proposal was of course accepted. The ride embraced a circuit of ten miles, in which they passed only two houses. The first of these was built with an apparent regard to convenience and comfort, and even some effort at adornment, as manifested in the climbing plants with which the windows were draperied, and the flowers which adorned the little court in front. Mr. Grahame stopped before the gateway of this court, and a woman of coarse, rough exterior, though scrupulously clean, came out to speak to him, and to urge his alighting and entering the house with his friend. This Mr. Grahame declined; he had stopped only to inquire after a sick child, and to express a hope that her husband's hay had turned out well.

"Dreadful fine," was her reply to the last. "I'm sure we be much obleeged to you for the seed, and for tellin' Jim how to plant it He never had sich hay before."

"I'm glad to hear it. Where is Lucy?"

"Oh, she's off to school. Tell Miss Mary she's gittin' to be 'most as grand a reader as she be. And yet the child's willin' enough to work, for all."

As the gentlemen rode on, after this interview, Mr. Grahame said, "That last speech expressed one of the greatest difficulties against which we had to contend in our efforts to induce our neighbors to give to their children some of the advantages of education. They were afraid 'larnin'' would make them lazy.' They were of your opinion, that the thinker and the worker must remain of different classes."

"I was much surprised to hear that woman speak of a school. I should not think the teacher could find his situation very profitable."

"He is one who has regard to a higher reward than any earthly one. He is a self-denying Christian missionary, whom I induced to settle in our neighborhood. He preaches on the Sabbath, in a little church about two miles from my house, to a congregation of about twenty adults, and twice that number of children; and during the week, he keeps a school which is well attended in the summer. Some of his earlier pupils are already showing, by their more useful and more happy lives, the importance of the schoolmaster's work in the elevation of a people."

The next dwelling they approached was very small and mean-looking. It seemed to Horace Danforth to contain only one apartment, warmed by an ill-constructed clay chimney, and lighted by one small, square window. That window, however, was not only sashed and glazed, but shaded by a plain muslin curtain.

"Here," said Mr. Grahame, "lives one of those pupils of whom I spoke just now. He has commenced life with nothing but the plot of ground you see, and having a wife to support, he must work hard, yet already he is aiming at something more than the supply of merely physical wants; and I doubt not he will, should he live long enough, become the intelligent and wealthy father of a well-educated family."

They were approaching the house as Mr. Grahame spoke. Near it was a small field, in which a man was hoeing.

"How is your wife, Martin?" asked Mr. Grahame.

"Oh, thank you, sir, she is quite smart. She's been getting better ever since the night Miss Mary sat up with her last. We say she always brings good luck."

"And how are your potatoes?"

"How could they help but be good, sir, with such grand seed as you gave me? Tell Miss Mary, if you please, sir, that the rose-tree is growing finely, and that as soon as I can get time to put up the fence, Sally is to have the flower-garden she talked about."

"I am glad to hear it, Martin; if you are brisk you may have some flowers yet before frost. I will bring you some seeds the next time I come."

"Do you procure your seeds from the East, or is it the result of your superior cultivation, that you are able thus to supply your neighbors?" asked Horace Danforth of Mr. Grahame, as they rode on.

"The potatoes were from my own field, raised from the seed two years ago. The grass and flower seeds were from my agent at the East. These little favors win for my daughter and myself considerable influence over our neighbors, and thus facilitate our attainment of the object for which we have pitched our tent in the wilderness, and accepted those labors which you justly regard as distasteful in themselves."

The return home of Mr. Grahame and his visitor, their dinner and afternoon engagements, offer nothing worthy of our notice. It was not till the labors of the day had been concluded, and the little party were gathered again before a cheerful fire in the parlor, that the subject of the morning's conversation was resumed. As Mary entered from the supper-room, bringing with her a little basket of needle-work, Horace Danforth asked if he might not now hope to receive the promised sketch.

"I will give it you with pleasure when I have had my evening song from Mary," said Mr. Grahame.

Opening the piano for his young hostess, Horace Danforth stood beside her as she sang, but he forgot to turn the leaves of the music before her as he listened once again to a rich and cultivated voice, accompanied by a fine instrument, touched by a skilful hand. As the sweet and well-remembered strains fell on his ear, he closed his eyes and gave the reins to fancy. The loved and lost gathered around him, and it was with a strange, dream-like feeling that, as the sweet sound ceased, and Mary arose from the piano, he opened his eyes and looked upon the rough walls and simple furniture of his present abode.

"It is now nearly nineteen years," began Mr. Grahame, when his daughter and guest had resumed their seats near him, "since, crushed in spirit, I turned from the grave in which I had laid my chief earthly blessing, to wander 'any where, any where out of that world' which had a few weeks before been bright and joyous to me, but which I was now ready to pronounce a desolate waste. The desire to avoid society made me turn westward, and nearly one hundred miles east of our present residence I found myself in the midst of a people without churches, without schools, rude in appearance and in manners. Absorbed in the destruction of my own selfish happiness, I might have passed from among them without knowing that disease was adding its pangs to those inflicted by want, ignorance, and superstition, had not a mother in the agony of parting from her first-born, looking hither and thither for help, turned her eyes entreatingly upon the stranger. I had once studied medicine, though regarding the profession, as our young men too often do, merely as a means of personal aggrandizement, and having received just at the completion of my studies an accession of fortune, which removed all pecuniary necessity to exertion on my part, I had never practised it, nor indeed obtained the diploma necessary to its practice. Now, however, I endeavored to make myself master of the peculiar features of the epidemic under which the child was suffering, and with the aid of a small store of medicines which my good sister had insisted on my taking with me, and a rigid enforcement of some of the simplest rules of diet and regimen, I had the happiness of seeing the child in a few days out of danger, and of receiving the mother's rapturous thanks. That moment, gave me the first gleam of happiness I had known for months, and disposed me to listen to the entreaties of the poor creatures who came from far and near to entreat the aid of the Doctor, as they persisted in calling me, notwithstanding my repeated assurances that I had no right to the title. I spent weeks in that neighborhood, and there I was born to a new life. Till that time I had lived to myself, and when that in which I had centered my earthly joy was snatched from me by death, I had felt that life had nothing left for me; but now I saw that while there were sentient beings in the universe to serve, and a glorious and ever blessed Father presiding over that universe and smiling on such service, life could not be divested of joy. Under the influence of such views my plans for the future were formed, nor have I ever seen reason to change or to regret them. Every where the Christian religion teaches the same precepts, but not every where is it equally easy to see the way in which those precepts may be obeyed; every where it is true, as a distinguished writer of your own land has said, 'Blessed is the man who has found his work let him seek no other blessedness;' but not every where is it equally easy to see where our work lies. Here, in America, the partition-walls which stand elsewhere as a remnant of the old feudalism, have been broken down; every man is irresistibly pressed into contact with his neighbors he cannot shut his eyes to their wants he cannot stop his ears against their cries. In America, too, every man, as I have already said, must be a worker or, if he live an idler, it must be on that which his father gained by the sweat of his brow, and he leaves his children to enslaving toil, or more enslaving dependence. Here the man of pleasure, the idler of either sex, is a foreign exotic which finds no nourishment in our soil, no shelter from our institutions which is out of harmony with our social life, and must ever be marked by the innate vulgarity of unsustained pretension. Therefore it is comparatively easy for us to hold out the hand of love to our brethren, sinking and suffering at our very side, and to teach them that there is no natural inalienable connection between labor and coarseness, ignorance and servility; that man, though compelled to win his bread by the sweat of his brow, may still enjoy all those graceful amenities of which woman was the type in Paradise and is the promoter here; that the light of knowledge and the divine light of faith may still cheer him in his pursuits and guide him to his rest. It seems to me that to bring out these principles fairly to the world's perception, is the mission to which America has been especially appointed is that for which Americans should live; and to this I have accordingly devoted myself. For this I purchased my present property for this I determined, while allowing myself and my daughter all the comforts of life, to dispense with many of those luxuries to which my fortune might have seemed to entitle us, lest I should separate myself too far from those I would aid. Here I have spent seventeen years of life, happy in my work, and happier in the conviction that it has not been in vain."

As Mr. Grahame paused, Horace Danforth turned to Mary Grahame. Her eyes were fixed upon him. They seemed to challenge his admiration for her father, in whose hand her own was clasped, as though she would thus intimate the perfect accordance of her feelings with his.

"And this, then," he said to her, "is your object?"

"It is."

"An object to which you were devoted by your father in your infancy?"

"And which I have since adopted on my own intelligent conviction," said Mary, earnestly, losing all timidity in a glow of that generous enthusiasm which sits so gracefully on a gentle woman.

There was silence in the little circle silence with all; with one, thought was rapidly passing down the long vista of the past, and pointing the awakened mind to the fact that elsewhere than in America was there ignorance to be enlightened and want to be relieved that not here only did Christianity teach that man should live not unto himself alone, and that he should love his neighbor as himself.

The thoughts and feelings aroused on that evening colored the whole future destiny of Horace Danforth. Ere another day had passed, he had confided to his host so much of his history as proved him to be an aimless and almost unconnected wanderer on the earth, with a prospect of a fortune which, unequal to the demands of a man of fashion in England, would give to a worker in America great influence for good or for evil as the personal property of Sir Thomas Maitland could not, as Horace Danforth was well aware, be valued at less than 50,000 dollars. With that rapid decision which had ever marked his movements, the young Englishman determined to purchase land in the neighborhood of Mr. Grahame, there to rear his future hope, and to devote his life to the like noble purposes.

The land was purchased, the site for the house was selected and marked out but the house was never built for ere that had been accomplished Horace Danforth discovered that the companionship of a cultivated woman was essential to his views of "Life in America," and that Mary Grahame was exactly the embodiment of that youthful vision which he had sought in vain elsewhere; for she united the delicacy and refined grace, with the intelligent mind, the active affections and energetic will, which were necessary at once to please his fancy and satisfy his heart Mary Grahame could not consent to leave her father to a lonely home, but yet she could not deny that it would be a sad home to her if deprived of the society of him whose intelligent and varied converse and manly tenderness had lately formed the chief charm of her existence. There was only one way of reconciling these conflicting claims. Horace Danforth must live with Mr. Grahame; and so he did, having first obtained that gentleman's permission to enlarge his house, and to furnish it with some of those inventions by which art has so greatly lightened domestic occupation, and which had been made familiar to him by his life abroad.

Six months had been spent in this abode six months of an existence of joy and love, untroubled as it could be to those who were yet dwellers upon earth six months in which the fastidious and world-wearied man learned the secret of true peace in a life devoted to useful and benevolent objects when a most unexpected visitor arrived in the person of Sir Edward Maitland no, not Sir Edward. He came to announce that to this title he had no right. That he had remained himself, and suffered his cousin to remain so long in ignorance on this point, had been the result of no want of effort to arrive at the truth, still less of any lingering love of the honors forced upon him. He had never assumed the title, nor suffered the secret of his supposed change of circumstances to be known beyond himself and the lawyer to whom his cousin Horace had revealed it. This lawyer, it may be remembered, had lately succeeded in the care of the Maitland estate to an uncle, who had been compelled by the infirmities of advancing age to retire from business. The old man was absent from England when Horace Danforth left it, and it was not till his return that full satisfaction on the subject had been obtained, as it was judged unwise by Mr. Decker to awaken public attention by investigations which his uncle's return would probably render unnecessary. When he did return, and the subject was cautiously unfolded to him, he spent many minutes in pishing and pshawing at the folly and impetuosity of young Baronets, who, knowing nothing of the tenure on which they hold their estates, cannot at least wait till they consult wiser people before they throw them away. The entail of nearly two centuries ago had, it seems, been set aside in little more than one, by an improvident father and son, who had in fact greatly diminished the very fine property so entailed, though most of it had been since recovered by the care of their successors. The intelligence thus conveyed to him who was now once more Sir Horace Danforth Maitland, was of mingled sweet and bitter. He could not be insensible to the joy of returning to the home of his childhood and the people among whom he had grown to manhood, yet neither could he leave, without tender regrets, that in which he had first learned to love, and to live a true, a noble, and a happy life.

When Mary was first saluted as Lady Maitland by Edward, she turned a glance of inquiry upon her husband, and then upon her father, for both were present by previous arrangement; and as she read a confirmation of the fact in their smiling faces, the color faded from hers, and after a moment's vain effort to contend against her painful emotion, she burst into tears.

"Your father has promised to spend his life with us, dearest," said Sir Horace Maitland, as he threw his arm around her and drew her to his side.

"But this dear home," sobbed Mary; "this people, for whom and with whom we have lived so happily."

"All that made this home dear, my daughter, you will take with you to another home."

"And there, too," interposed Sir Horace, "my Mary will find a people to enlighten and to bless, over whom her influence will be unbounded, and to whom she will prove an angel of consolation."

"And can you carry your American life to your English home?" she asked of her husband, smiling through her tears.

"As much of it as is independent of outward circumstances, Mary its spirit, its aims; for they belong to a Christian life, and that I hope, by God's blessing, to live henceforth, wherever I may be."

"And what will become of all our projected improvements here?" she inquired of her father.

"I shall not leave this place myself, Mary, till I can find some one like-minded, who will take our place and do our work. To such a man I will sell the property on such terms as he can afford, or if he cannot buy, he shall farm it for me."

This last was the arrangement made with one whom Mr. Grahame had known in early life, and who had always been distinguished by true Christian uprightness and benevolence The terms offered by Mr. Grahame to this gentleman were such, that the conscientious and excellent agent became in a few years the proprietor and under his fostering care, all those plans for the intellectual and moral improvement of the neighborhood which had been so happily commenced, were matured and perfected.

It was nearly a year after the departure of his children before Mr. Grahame was able to join them at Maitland Park. With his arrival Mary felt that her cup of joy was full. It had been with a trembling heart that she assumed the brilliant position to which Providence had conducted her; not that she feared the judgment of man: her fear had been lest in the midst of abundance she should forget the hand that fed her lest amidst the fascinations of an intellectual and polished society, she should forget the thick darkness which covered so many immortal minds around her. But already she had cast aside this unworthy fear, unworthy of Him in whom is the Christian's strength.

The early dream of the Proprietor of Maitland Park is fulfilled. The softening and refining presence of woman diffuses a new charm over its social life, and while his Mary is to his tenantry what he himself predicted, an angel of consolation, she is to him a faithful co-worker in all that may advance the reign of peace and righteousness, of intelligence and joy, throughout the world.

CHAPTER VII

A Sabbath in the country, with a Sabbath quiet in the air, and a cheerful sunlight beaming like the smile of Heaven on the earth how beautiful it is! Donaldson Manor is only a short walk from the church whose white spire gleams up amidst the dark grove of pines on our left; at least, it is only a short walk in summer, when we can approach it through the flowery lanes which separate Col. Donaldson's fields from those of his next neighbor, Mr. Manly. Now, however, the walk is impracticable, and all the sleighs were yesterday morning in requisition, to transport the family and their visitors to their place of worship. I was a little afraid that the merry music of the sleigh-bells and the rapid drive through the clear air might make our young people's blood dance too briskly that they would be unable to preserve that sobriety of manner becoming those who are about professedly to engage in the worship of Him who inhabiteth Eternity. I was gratified, however, to perceive that they all had good feeling or good taste enough to preserve, throughout their drive and the services which followed it, a quiet and reverent demeanor. It may seem strange to some, that I should characterize this as a possible effect of "good taste;" but in my opinion, he who does not pay the tribute at least of outward respect to this holy day, is incapable not only of that high, spiritual communion which brings man near to his Creator, but of that tender sympathy which binds him to his fellow-creatures, or even of that poetic taste which would place his soul in harmony with external nature. Let it not be thought that I would have this day of blessing to the world regarded with a cynical severity, or that the quietness and the reverence of which I speak are at all akin to sadness. Were not cheerfulness, in my opinion, a part of godliness, I should say of it as some one has said of cleanliness, that it is next to godliness. Like my favorite, Mrs. Elizabeth Barrett Browning,

"I think we are too ready with complaint
In this fair world of God's;"

and like her, I would utter to all the exhortation,

"Let us leave the shame and sin
Of taking vainly, in a plaintive mood,
The holy name of Grief! holy herein,
That, by the grief of One, came all our good."

But cheerfulness, so far from being incompatible with, seems to me inseparable from that true worship which is the best source of the Sabbath seriousness I am advocating.

The remarks of the preacher were quite in unison with these thoughts, and pleased me so much that, were it admissible, I should be delighted to dignify my pages with them. By a few vivid touches, in language simple, yet beautiful, he sketched for us the first Sabbath amidst the living springs and fadeless bloom and verdant shades of Paradise, when sinless man communed with his Maker and his Father, not through the poor symbols of a ceremonial worship, but face to face, as a man talketh with his friend. But all I would say of the Sabbath has been said a thousand times better than I could say it, by good George Herbert, whose words I am sure I need not apologize for introducing here.

SUNDAY

O day most calm, most bright!
The fruit of this, the next world's bud;
Th' indorsement of supreme delight,
Writ by a Friend, and with His blood;
The couch of time; care's balm and bay:
The week were dark, but for thy light;
Thy torch doth show the way.

The other days and thou
Make up one man; whose face thou art,
Knocking at heaven with thy brow;
The worky days are the back-part;
The burden of the week lies there,
Making the whole to stoop and bow,
Till thy release appear.

Man hath straight forward gone
To endless death. But thou dost pull
And turn us round, to look on One,
Whom, if we were not very dull,
We could not choose but look on still;
Since there is no place so alone,
The which He doth not fill.

Sundays the pillars are
On which heaven's palace arched lies:
The other days fill up the spare
And hollow room with vanities.
They are the fruitful bed and borders,
In God's rich garden; that is bare,
Which parts their ranks and orders.

The Sundays of man's life,
Threaded together on time's string,
Make bracelets to adorn the wife
Of the eternal, glorious King.
On Sunday, heaven's gate stands ope;
Blessings are plentiful and rife!

More plentiful than hope.
This day my Saviour rose,
And did inclose this light for His:
That, as each beast his manger knows,
Man might not of his fodder miss.
Christ hath took in this piece of ground,
And made a garden there, for those
Who want herbs for their wound.
The Rest of our creation,
Our great Redeemer did remove,
With the same shake which, at his passion,
Did th' earth, and all things with it, move.
As Samson bore the doors away,
Christ's hand's, though nailed, wrought our salvation,
And did unhinge that day.
The brightness of that day
We sullied, by our foul offence;
Wherefore that robe we cast away,
Having a new at His expense,
Whose drops of blood paid the full price
That was required, to make us gay,
And fit for paradise.
Thou art a day of mirth:
And, where the week-days trail on ground,
Thy flight is higher, as thy birth.
Oh, let me take thee at the bound,
Leaping with thee from seven to seven;
Till that we both, being toss'd from earth,
Fly hand in hand to Heaven!

It is the custom at Donaldson Manor to close the Sabbath evening with sacred music. Annie, at her father's request, played while we all sang his favorite evening hymn, which I here transcribe.

EVENING HYMN

Father! by Thy love and power,
Comes again the evening hour;
Light hath vanish'd, labors cease,
Weary creatures rest, in peace.
Those, whose genial dews distil
On the lowliest weed that grows
Father! guard our couch from ill,
Lull thy creatures to repose.
We to Thee ourselves resign,
Let our latest thoughts be Thine.
Saviour! to thy Father bear
This our feeble evening prayer;

Thou hast seen how oft to-day
We, like sheep, have gone astray;
Worldly thoughts and thoughts of pride,
Wishes to Thy cross untrue,
Secret faults and undescried
Meet Thy spirit-piercing view.
Blessed Saviour! yet, through Thee,
Pray that these may pardon'd be.
Holy Spirit! Breath of Balm!
Breathe on us in evening's calm.
Yet awhile before we sleep,
We with Thee will vigils keep.
Lead us on our sins to muse,
Give us truest penitence,
Then the love of God infuse,
Kindling humblest confidence.
Melt our spirits, mould our will,
Soften, strengthen, comfort, still.
Blessed Trinity! be near
Through the hours of darkness drear.
When the help of man is far
Ye more clearly present are.
Father, Son, and Holy Ghost!
Watch o'er our defenceless heads,
Let your angels' guardian host
Keep all evil from our beds,
Till the flood of morning rays
Wake as to a song of praise.

CHAPTER VIII

Mr. Arlington is a gem of the first water. He reveals every day some new trait of interest or agreeableness. I saw immediately that he was a man of fine taste; I have since learned to respect him as a man of enlarged intellect and earnest feeling; and now I am just beginning to discover that he is master of all those agremens which constitute the charm of general society, and that he might become the "glass of fashion," if he had not a mind elevated too far above such a petty ambition. This last observation has been called forth by mere trifles, yet trifles so prettily shown, with such ease and grace, as to justify the conclusion. He is apt at illustration and application, and has a fine memory, stored brimfull of entertaining anecdotes, snatches of poetry, and those thousand nothings which tell for so much in society, and which it is so pleasant to find combined with much else that is valuable. A few evenings since, he kept Annie and me in the library, with his agreeable chat, till so late an hour, that Col. Donaldson, who is the least bit of a martinet in his own family, gave some very intelligible hints to us the next morning, at breakfast, on the value of early hours. With a readiness and grace which I never saw surpassed, Mr. Arlington turned to us with the exquisite apology of the poet for a like fault,

> "I stay'd too late; forgive the crime;
> Unheeded flew the hours.
> Unnoted falls the foot of time,
> Which only treads on flowers."

This evening again, as he placed a candle-screen before Annie, who, having a headache, found the light oppressive, he said with a graceful mixture of play and earnest, impossible to describe,

> "Ah, lady! if that taper's blaze
> Requires a screen to blunt its rays,
> What screen, not form'd by art divine,
> Shall shield us from those orbs of thine?
> "But oh! let nothing intervene
> Our hearts and those bright suns between;
> 'Tis bliss, like the bewilder'd fly
> To flutter round, though sure to die."

As the others were engaged in very earnest conversation at the time, and I was reading, he probably expected to be heard only by her to whom he addressed himself; but a little romance, such as that of Annie and Mr. Arlington, acted before me, interests me far more than any book, and I brought a bright blush to Annie's cheek and a conscious smile to his lip, by asking, "Where did you find those very apposite lines? I do not remember to have seen them."

"Probably not, as they have never been published. They were addressed by Anthony Bleecker, of New-York, to a belle of his day, and the lady for whose sake, it is whispered, he lived and died a bachelor."

Our colloquy was here interrupted by Robert Dudley, who wanted to know if we were to have no story this evening. Robert was a great lover of stories. "Ask Mr. Arlington, Robert," said I, "I have given three stories to his one already."

"Aunt Nancy," said Mr. Arlington, who had already begun to give me the affectionate cognomen by which I was always addressed at Donaldson Manor, "Aunt Nancy has stories without number, written and ready for demand, but my portfolio furnishes only rude pencilings, or at best a crayon sketch."

"Will you show them to us, Mr. Arlington?" asked the persevering Robert, who stood beside him, portfolio in hand. "May I draw one out, as Aunt Annie did the other evening; and will you tell us about it?"

Mr. Arlington, with good-humored playfulness, consented, and

Robert drew from the portfolio one of his drawings, representing a fisherman's family.

"That man," said I, as I looked at the honest face of the rude, weather-beaten fisherman, "looks as though he had passed through adventurous scenes, and might have many a history to tell."

"He did not tell his histories to me," said Mr. Arlington. "I know nothing more of them than that paper reveals. It seemed to me that the woman and child were visiting, for the first time, the ocean, whose booming sound was to the fisherman as the voice of home. He was probably introducing them to its wonders revealing to them the mysteries which awaken the superstition of the vulgar and the poetry of the cultivated imagination. He has given her, you may observe, a sea-shell, and she is listening for the first time to its low, strange music."

"And is that all?" asked Robert, when Mr. Arlington ceased speaking.

"All I know, Robert," he answered, with a smile at the boy's earnestness.

"But did you never go fishing yourself, Mr. Arlington?"

"Not often, Robert; I like more active sports better hunting "

"Ah! do tell us about your hunting, Mr. Arlington; you must have had some adventures in hunting in those great Western forests I have heard you speak of."

"The greatest adventure I ever had, Robert," said Mr. Arlington, "was in an Eastern forest, and when I was the hunted, not the hunter."

"Indians, Mr. Arlington were they Indians that hunted you?"

"No, Robert; my hunters were wolves."

"Oh! pray tell us about it, Mr. Arlington, will you not?"

"Certainly, with the ladies' permission."

The ladies' permission was soon obtained, and our little party listened with the deepest interest to the thrilling recital which I have called

THE WOLF CHASE

During the winter of 1844, being engaged in the northern part of Maine, I had much leisure to devote to the wild sports of a new country. To none of these was I more passionately addicted than to skating. The deep and sequestered lakes of this State, frozen by the intense cold of a northern winter, present a wide field to the lovers of this pastime. Often would I bind on my skates, and glide away up the glittering river, and wind each mazy streamlet that flowed beneath its fetters on towards the parent ocean, forgetting all the while time and distance in the luxurious sense of the gliding motion thinking of nothing in the easy flight, but rather dreaming, as I looked through the transparent ice at the long weeds and cresses that nodded in the current beneath, and seemed wrestling with the waves to let them go; or I would follow on the track of some fox or otter, and run my skate along the mark he had left with his dragging tail until the trail would enter the woods. Sometimes these excursions were made by moonlight, and it was on one of these occasions that I had a rencontre, which even now, with kind faces around me, I cannot recall without a nervous looking-over-my-shoulder feeling.

I had left my friend's house one evening just before dusk, with the intention of skating a short distance up the noble Kennebec, which glided directly before the door. The night was beautifully clear. A peerless moon rode through an occasional fleecy cloud, and stars twinkled from the sky and from every frost-covered tree in millions. Your mind would wonder at the light that came glinting from ice, and snow-wreath, and incrusted branches, as the eye followed for miles the broad gleam of the Kennebec, that like a jewelled zone swept between the mighty forests on its banks. And yet all was still. The cold seemed to have frozen tree, and air, and water, and every living thing that moved. Even the ringing of my skates on the ice echoed back from the Moccason Hill with a startling clearness, and the crackle of the ice as I passed over it in my course seemed to follow the tide of the river with lightning speed.

I had gone up the river nearly two miles when, coming to a little stream which empties into the larger, I turned in to explore its course. Fir and hemlock of a century's growth met overhead, and formed an archway radiant with frost-work. All was dark within, but I was young and fearless, and as I peered into an unbroken forest that reared itself on the borders of the stream, I laughed with very joyousness: my wild hurrah rang through the silent woods, and I stood listening to the echo that reverberated again and again, until all was hushed. I thought how often the Indian hunter had concealed himself behind these very trees how often his arrow had pierced the deer by this very stream, and his wild halloo had here rung for his victory. And then, turning from fancy to reality, I watched a couple of white owls, that sat in their hooded state, with ruffled pantalettes and long ear-tabs, debating in silent conclave the affairs of their frozen realm, and was wondering if they, "for all their feathers, were a-cold," when suddenly a sound arose it seemed to me to come from beneath the ice; it sounded low and tremulous at first, until it ended in one wild yell. I was appalled. Never before had such a noise met my ears. I thought it more than mortal so fierce, and amidst such an unbroken solitude, it seemed as though a fiend had blown a blast from an infernal trumpet. Presently I heard the twigs on shore snap, as though from the tread of some brute animal, and the blood rushed back to my forehead with a bound that made my skin burn, and I felt relieved that I had to contend with things earthly, and not of spiritual nature my energies returned, and I looked around me for some means of escape. The moon shone through the opening at the mouth of the creek by which I had entered the forest, and considering this the best channel of escape, I darted towards it like an arrow. 'Twas scarcely a hundred yards distant, and the swallow could hardly excel my desperate flight; yet, as I turned my head to the shore, I could see two dark objects dashing through the underbrush at a pace nearly double in speed to my own. By this rapidity, and the short yells which they occasionally gave, I knew at once that these were the much dreaded gray wolf.

I had never met with these animals, but from the description given of them I had very little pleasure in making their acquaintance. Their untameable fierceness, and the untiring strength which seems part of their nature, render them objects of dread to every benighted traveller.

"With their long gallop, which can tire
The deer-hound's haste, the hunter's fire,"

they pursue their prey never straying from the track of their victim and as the wearied hunter thinks he has at last outstripped them, he finds that they but waited for the evening to seize their prey, and falls a prize to the tireless pursuers.

The bushes that skirted the shore flew past with the velocity of lightning as I dashed on in my flight to pass the narrow opening. The outlet was nearly gained; one second more and I should be comparatively safe, when the fierce brutes appeared on the bank directly above me, which here rose to the height of ten feet. There was no time for thought, so I bent my head and dashed madly forward. The wolves sprang, but miscalculating my speed, sprang behind, while their intended prey glided out upon the river.

Nature turned me towards home. The light flakes of snow spun from the iron of my skates, and I was some distance from my pursuers, when their fierce howl told me I was still their fugitive. I did not look back, I did not feel afraid, or sorry, or glad; one thought of home, of the bright faces awaiting my return, of their tears if they never should see me, and then every energy of body and mind was exerted for escape. I was perfectly at home on the ice. Many were the days that I had spent on my good skates, never thinking that at one time they would be my only means of safety. Every half minute an alternate yelp from my ferocious followers made me only too certain that they were in close pursuit. Nearer and nearer they came; I heard their feet pattering on the ice nearer still, until I could feel their breath and hear their snuffing scent. Every nerve and muscle in my frame were stretched to the utmost tension.

The trees along the shore seemed to dance in the uncertain light, and my brain turned with my own breathless speed, yet still they seemed to hiss forth their breath with a sound truly horrible, when an involuntary motion on my part turned me out of my course. The wolves close behind, unable to stop, and as unable to turn on the smooth ice, slipped and fell, still going on far ahead; their tongues were lolling out, their white tusks glaring from their bloody mouths, their dark, shaggy breasts were fleeced with foam, and as they passed me their eyes glared, and they howled with fury. The thought flashed on my mind, that by this means I could avoid them, viz., by turning aside whenever they came too near; for they, by the formation of their feet, are unable to run on ice except on a straight line.

I immediately acted upon this plan. The wolves, having regained their feet, sprang directly towards me. The race was renewed for twenty yards up the stream; they were already close on my back, when I glided round and dashed directly past my pursuers. A wild yell greeted my evolution, and the wolves, slipping upon their haunches, sailed onward, presenting a perfect picture of helplessness and baffled rage. Thus I gained nearly a hundred yards at each turning. This was repeated two or three times, every moment the animals getting more excited and baffled.

At one time, by delaying my turning too long, my sanguinary antagonists came so near, that they threw the white foam over my dress as they sprang to seize me, and their teeth clashed together, like the spring of a fox-trap. Had my skates failed for one instant, had I tripped on a stick, or caught my foot in a fissure in the ice, the story I am now telling would never have been told. I thought all the chances over; I knew where they would first take hold of me if I fell; I thought how long it would be before I died, and then there would be a search for the body that would already have its tomb; for oh! how fast man's mind traces out all the dread colors of Death's picture, only those who have been near the grim original can tell.

But soon I came opposite the house, and my hounds I knew their deep voices roused by the noise, bayed furiously from the kennels. I heard their chains rattle; how I wished they would break them! and then I should have protectors that would be peers to the fiercest denizens of the forest. The wolves, taking the hint conveyed by the dogs, stopped in their mad career, and after a moment's consideration, turned and fled. I watched them until their dusky forms disappeared over a neighboring hill. Then, taking off my skates, wended my way to the house, with feelings which may be better imagined than described.

But even yet, I never see a broad sheet of ice in the moonshine, without thinking of that snuffling breath and those fearful things that followed me so closely down the frozen Kennebec.

CHAPTER IX

"What a noble forest!" cried Annie, as she gazed with rapturous admiration on a noble specimen of the engraver's art so noble, indeed, that the absence of color seemed hardly to be felt. It was a richly-wooded scene, with interesting figures forming a procession in the centre and foreground of the landscape. The original might have been painted by Ruysdael. "Those old oaks," she exclaimed, "with their gnarled and crooked branches, look as though they might have formed part of the Druidical groves whose solemn mysteries inspired even the arrogant Roman with awe. This picture, however, belongs to a later period that of the Crusades, perhaps, for here is a procession in which appear figures in the long robe of the monk, and I think I can discern a cross on that banner borne at their head. But what, dear Aunt Nancy, could you possibly find in our land of yesterday, to associate with such a scene?"

"Our people may be of yesterday, Annie, but our land bears no marks of recent origin. The most arrogant boaster of the Old World may feel himself humbled as he stands within the shadow of our forests, and looks up to trees which we might almost fancy to have waved over the heads of 'the patriarchs of an infant world?'"

"And you have seen some such forests, and on the branches of these old trees 'hangs a tale' which you will tell us. Is it not so, Aunt Nancy?"

"I have seen such a forest, and I have a sketch of certain events occurring within its circle. The narrative was given me by my friend, Mrs. H., who was acquainted with the parties. You will find it in her handwriting in the compartment of my desk from which you took the engraving."

Annie found the paper, and I saw a quiet smile pass around as she read aloud its title. Mr. Arlington, at my request, took the reader's place, and we spent our evening in listening to

THE HISTORY OF AN OLD MAID

It is an almost universal belief among those who have faith in man's immortality, that when his spiritual nature has been divested of its present veil the bodily organization by which it at pleasure reveals or conceals itself it shall be manifested to all at a glance in the unsullied beauty of holiness, or the dark deformity of vice. Shall our vision extend further? Shall we read the soul's past history? Shall we know the struggles which have given strength to its powers? The fears which have shadowed, and the hopes which have lighted, its earthly path? Shall we learn the unspoken sacrifices which have been laid on the altar of its affections or its duty? Shall we see how a single generous impulse has shaped the whole course of its being, and been as a heavenly flame, to which every selfish desire and feeling have been committed in noiseless devotion? If this be so, how many such records shall be furnished by the life of woman? How often shall it be found, that from such a flame has risen the light with which she has brightened the existence of others!

Meeta Werner was the daughter of industrious, honest Germans, who had emigrated to the western part of Pennsylvania when she was a child of only seven years old. Only a quarter of a mile from the spot on which Carl Werner had fixed his residence lived a brother German, Franz Rainer. Franz was a widower, with one child, a son, named Ernest. He was a hard, stern man, and the first smiles which had lighted the existence of the young Ernest were caught from the sprightly Meeta and her kind-hearted mother. The children became playfellows and friends. It was a wild country in which they lived. A very short walk from their own doors brought them into a forest which seemed to their young imaginations endless; where gigantic trees interlaced their branches, and with their green foliage shut out the sun in summer, or in winter reflected it in dazzling brightness, and a thousand gorgeous colors, from the icicles which cased their leafless branches and pendent twigs. There was not a footpath, a sunny hill or flowery dell, for miles around their homes, which had not been trodden together by Meeta Werner and Ernest Rainer before their acquaintance was a year old. Now they would come home laden with wood-flowers, and now they might be seen treading wearily back from some distant spot, with baskets filled with blackberries, or with the dark-blue whortleberries. There were no schools in the neighborhood, but they had been taught by their fathers to read and write their own language, and Ernest afterwards acquired some knowledge of English from the good pastor who had accompanied the emigrants from Germany, and who acted as their interpreter when they required one. Having access to few books, they seemed likely to grow up with little more learning than might be gathered from their own observation of the world around them; but when Ernest was eighteen and Meeta fifteen years of age, circumstances occurred which gave an entirely new coloring to their lives.

Franz Rainer had not always been so stern and hard as he now seemed. He had married imprudently, in the world's acceptation of that term; that is, he had made a portionless but lovely girl his wife, and in doing so had incurred his father's lasting displeasure. He had been banished from a home of plenty with a small sum, "to keep him from starving," he was told. With that sum and a young delicate wife he sailed for America, and found a home for himself and his boy, and a grave for his wife, in the forests of Pennsylvania. Too proud to seek a reconciliation with those who had cast him off, he had held no communication with his own family after leaving Germany; and it was not till Ernest was, as we have said, eighteen, that the silence of his home was broken by what seemed a voice from the past. After many hindrances and delays, and passing through many hands for which it had not been intended, a letter reached him from a merchant in Philadelphia, who had been requested to institute a search for Franz by his only brother. The old Rainer was dead, and the family estate had descended to this brother, a scholar and a man of solitary habits. Finding himself growing old in a lonely home, and retaining some kindly memory of the brother in whose companionship his childhood had been passed, he wished him to return to Germany, and again dwell with them in the house of their fathers. To this Franz would by no means consent. His nature was cast in too stern a mould to re-knit at a word the ties which had been so violently sundered. He consented, however, after some correspondence with his brother, to send Ernest to Germany, to be educated there; at least, to receive such an education as could be gained in four years; for he insisted that at the end of that time he should return to America, and remain there while his father lived. "After my death, if he choose to return to the home from which his father was banished, he may," wrote the still resentful Franz.

And how was this change in all the prospects of his life received by the young Ernest and his companion Meeta? By him with mingled feelings; regret, joy, fear, hope, by turns ruled his soul. The regret was all for Meeta and her mother; they were the sources of all his pleasant memories; and as he gazed upon Meeta's hitherto bright face, now clouded with sorrow, and kissed from her cheek the first tears he had ever known her to shed for herself, he was ready to give up all his fair prospects abroad and live with her for ever. Meeta herself, however, gave a new direction to his thoughts, by generously turning from the subject of her grief in parting, to dwell on the idea of the delight with which they would meet again, and especially on her peculiar pleasure in seeing Ernest come back "riding in a grand coach, with servants following him on horseback, as she remembered to have seen in Germany, and knowing enough to teach Parson Schmidt himself!" After listening to such prophecies, Ernest no longer expressed any desire to remain with Meeta; he contented himself, instead, with promising to return as soon as he could, and with winning from her a promise that, come when he might, she would be his wife. This was not a new thought or a new word to either. They could scarcely tell themselves when the idea had first arisen in their minds that they would one day live together, and be what Carl Werner and his wife were to each other. They had even chosen a site for their house; and Ernest had more than once of late expressed the opinion that they were old enough to inform their parents of their intentions; but the more timid Meeta objected. Now, however, she could refuse Ernest nothing, and before the day of parting came they had made a confidante of Meeta's mother, and from her the two fathers had learned the desires of their children. Carl Werner heard the story with a smile; but a denser shadow gathered on the dark brow of Franz. For a moment something of his father's pride was in his heart; but his own blighted life arose before him, and he said, "The boy may do as he pleases. No man has a right to control another on such a subject."

The sun had not yet risen, though its rays were gilding the few light clouds that flecked the eastern sky, when Meeta and Ernest stood together beneath an old oak which had long been their favorite "trysting-tree," to say those words and give and receive those last looks which are among life's most sacred treasures. Smiles and blushes mingled with tears on Meeta's cheek as Ernest pressed her to his bosom, kissed her again and again, and promised that his first letter from Germany should be addressed to her, and that in exactly four years from that date he would be again beneath that tree, to claim her promise to be his for ever. The voice of Carl Werner, who was to accompany Ernest the first stage of his journey, startled them in the midst of their adieus; and bursting from the arms of her companion, Meeta plunged deeper into the woods to escape her father's eye. When Carl returned in the evening he handed her a small parcel, saying, "There's some foolery that Ernest bought for you, Meeta. Silly boy! I hope they'll teach him in Germany to take better care of his money!"

The parcel contained a very plain locket, with one of Ernest's dark curls inclosed in it. Plain as it was, it seemed to Meeta, as it probably had seemed to Ernest, a magnificent present; yet she valued more the few simple words written on the paper which enveloped it: "For Meeta, my promised wife." Four months passed away before Meeta heard again of her lover. Then there came a letter to her, which was full of the great cities through which Ernest had passed, the home to which he had come, and the new life which was opening to him there. In his descriptions his uncle seemed a very grand gentleman, and his uncle's housekeeper almost as grand a lady. He told of the new wardrobe which had been provided for him, the acquaintances to whom he had been introduced, and the studies he had commenced. And in all this Meeta saw but the first step towards that grandeur which she had predicted for him, and she rejoiced.

Four or five such letters were received by Meeta, each full of her lover himself; but they came at lengthening intervals, and during the third year she received from him only messages sent through his father, though every message still conveyed a promise to write soon. The letters of Ernest showed that he had made great advances in scholarship during his residence in Germany, and to all but Meeta herself, and perhaps her mother, they gave equal evidence that his heart was not with the home or the friends he had left in America. But no shadow ever passed over the transparent face of Meeta. Ernest was to her still the frank, ardent, simple-hearted boy whom she had loved so long and so truly. She was still his promised wife. Her quick sensibility to all which touched him made her feel that there was a change in the tone with which her father named him, and an expression, half of anger, half of pity, on his face when she alluded to him. It was an expression which gave her pain, though she did not understand its meaning; and she ceased to speak of Ernest, lest she should call it up; but his locket lay next her heart, his letters were well-nigh worn away with frequent reading, and no day passed in which she did not visit the oak beneath which they had parted, and beneath which she fondly believed they were to meet again.

During the fourth year of Ernest's absence his letters to his father became more frequent, and sometimes inclosed a few lines to Meeta. To both he expressed a strong desire to stay one more year abroad, alleging that to interrupt his studies now would be to render all his past labors unavailing. There was hardly a struggle in Meeta's mind in yielding her almost matured hopes to what seemed so reasonable a wish of Ernest; but the elder Rainer was not so easily won to compliance. Urgent representations from his brother as well as Ernest, did at length, however, induce him to consent to the absence of his son for another year.

This was an important year to Meeta. It brought her an acquaintance through whom her dormant intellect was aroused, and her manners fitted for something more than the rude life by which she had been hitherto surrounded. This was Mrs. Schwartz, the wife of a young pastor, who had come to assist Mr. Schmidt in those duties to which his advancing years rendered him unequal. Mrs. Schwartz was a woman of no ordinary stamp. Highly educated, with an intense enjoyment of every form of beauty and grace, she saw something of them embellishing the homeliest employments and most common life with which a sentiment of duty was connected. Severe illness had confined her to her bed for many weeks soon after her arrival, and before she had been able to establish that perfect domestic economy, which renders the daily and hourly inspection and interference of the mistress of a mansion needless to the comfort of its inmates. During this period, Meeta, whose sympathies had been deeply interested in the stranger, nursed her, and planned for her, and worked for her, until she made herself a place in her heart among her life-friends. As

Mrs. Schwartz saw her moving around her with such busy kindness, the thought often arose in her mind, "What can I do for her?" This is a question we seldom ask ourselves of any one sincerely without finding an answer to it.

We have said that Meeta had access to few books in early life; we might have added that she had little opportunity of hearing the conversation of persons more cultivated than herself. Thus were the two great sources of intellectual development sealed to her. She had a thoughtful, earnest mind. She loved the beautiful world around her, and the GREAT BEING who made and sustained that world. But if the contemplation of these things awakened thoughts of a higher character than the daily baking and brewing, milking and scrubbing in her father's house, she had no language in which to clothe them, and vague and undefined, they fleeted away like the morning mists, leaving no impress of their presence. Her acquaintance with Mrs. Schwartz, and the conversation she sometimes heard between her and her husband, gave to these shadows substance and form, and awakened a new want in Meeta's soul the want of knowledge. As in all else, Ernest was present in this. He would doubtless be intelligent, wise, like Mr. Schwartz, and how could she be his companion? Something of these new experiences in Meeta was divined by Mrs. Schwartz, and with a true womanly tact she became her teacher without wounding her self-love. The road to knowledge once opened to Meeta, her advance on it was rapid. How could it be otherwise, when every step was bringing her nearer to Earnest! The elevation and refinement of mind which Meeta thus acquired impressed themselves on her agreeable features. Her dark eyes became bright with the soul's light, and her whole aspect so attractive, that her old friends exclaimed, as they looked upon her, "How handsome Meeta Werner grows, she who used to be so plain!"

After a time these superficial observers thought they had found the cause of this change in Meeta's change of costume, for a new sense of beauty had been awakened in her, under whose guidance her dark hair was brought in soft silken braids upon her cheeks, wound gracefully around her well-shaped head, and sometimes ornamented with a ribbon or a cluster of wild flowers: while her dresses where remodelled so as to resemble less the fashion which her mother and her sister emigrants had imported thirteen years before from Germany, and to give a more natural air to her really fine figure.

"How wonderfully Meeta has improved," said Mr. Schwartz, one evening to his wife, as he looked after the retreating form of her friend.

"Yes, and I am truly rejoiced that she has so improved before her lover returns to claim her."

"I wish he could have taken away with him such an impression as our handsome and intelligent Meeta would now make. He would have been much more likely to remain constant to her. There must be a painful contrast between the cultivated and graceful women he has known in Germany, and his memory of his early love."

"Love is a great embellisher," said Mrs. Schwartz, with a gay smile, and the conversation passed to more general topics.

The fifth year of Ernest's absence was gone, and still he came not; but he was coming soon, at least so his father said, though he did not show Meeta the letters on which he founded his assertion. It was the first time he had withheld them; a circumstance the more remarkable, because of late he seemed to regard Meeta with greater affection and confidence than he had ever done before. He now sought her society, and seemed pleased and even proud of the connection to which he had at first consented with some reluctance. It was very soon after the reception of the letter from Ernest to which we have alluded, that Franz Rainer's health began to fail, and that so rapidly, that Meeta feared Ernest could not arrive in time to see him. She was to the old man an angel of consolation, and he clung to her as to his last hope. In pity to his lonely condition, her own parents were willing to spare her for a time, and Meeta, that she might take care of him by night as well as by day, had removed to his house a week before Ernest's arrival. He came not wholly unwarned of the sorrow that awaited him, for he had found a letter from Meeta at the house of the merchant in Philadelphia through whom he had corresponded with his father, tenderly yet plainly revealing her fears, and urging him to hurry homeward without delay. He travelled with little rest or refreshment for two days and nights, and arrived late on the third day at his father's house. It was a still summer evening, and while the old man slept, Meeta sat near him in the only parlor the house afforded, reading by a shaded night lamp. She heard the sound of carriage wheels, and paused to listen; the sound ceased; a shadow darkened the moonlight which had been streaming through an open window, and then Ernest, the playfellow of her childhood, the lover of her youth, stood before her; but how changed, how gloriously changed thought Meeta, even in that hour of hurry and agitation. They gazed on each other in silence for a moment, and then Meeta with a bright smile, yet in a whisper, for even then she forgot not the dying man, asked:

"Do you not know me, Ernest?"

"Meeta!" he ejaculated, as he took the hand she extended to him, but dropping it almost immediately, he said anxiously: "My father! he lives, Meeta?"

"He does, Ernest, and may live, I think will live, for many days yet."

"Thank GOD! then I shall see him again!"

The conversation had till now been in whispers, but Ernest uttered his ejaculation of thankfulness aloud. There was a movement in the old man's room, a sound, and Meeta glided to his side.

"Who were you talking with, my daughter?" he murmured feebly. For many days Franz Rainer had called Meeta daughter, as though he found pleasure in recalling the tie between them.

"With one who tells me Ernest has arrived, and will see you soon," said Meeta.

"It is Ernest himself. I knew his voice: Ernest, my son!" And the old man's tones were loud and strong, as Meeta had heard them for days. In another moment, Ernest was bending over his father, and they were gazing on each other with a tenderness whose very existence they had not before suspected. Tears were rolling down the face of the once stern old man, as he pressed his son's hand again and again, and murmured blessings on him, and thanks to GOD for his safe return; and Ernest, as he marked the death-shadow on his father's brow, felt that a tie was tearing away which had been woven more intimately than he had supposed with his heart's fibres. The weeping Meeta composed herself that she might soothe them.

"Ernest, I cannot let you stay longer here; I am your father's nurse."

"My nurse, my daughter, my all, Ernest; your gift to me, my son, which, thank GOD! you have come in time to receive again from my hands. Take her to you, Ernest."

The old man held Meeta's hand clasped in his own towards his son, and Ernest touched it, but so slightly and with a hand so cold, that Meeta looked up in alarm. There was a beseeching expression in the eyes that met hers; a look which she did not understand, and yet on which she acted.

"Ernest," she said, "you are fatigued to death, and your father has been too much agitated already. Go, I pray you, for the present; I cannot leave your father, but you will find coffee and biscuits by the kitchen fire, and there is a bed prepared in your own room. Good-night; we shall meet again to-morrow," she added with a smile to the old man.

Ernest gave her a more cordial glance and pressure of the hand than she had yet received from him; told his father that he would only snatch an hour's sleep and be with him again, and left the room.

"Go with him, Meeta; you must have much to say."

"Nothing that we cannot say as well to-morrow. And now you must take another sleeping draught, for I see Ernest has carried off all the effect of your last."

Meeta spoke cheerfully, yet her heart was sad, she scarcely knew why. She would not think Ernest unkind, yet how different had been their meeting from that which fancy had so often sketched for her!

Franz Rainer fell asleep, and again Meeta returned to the parlor. A lamp was still burning there, and by its dim light she saw the form of Ernest extended on a settee with his cloak and valise for his bed and pillow. At first she drew timidly back into the chamber, but as the slight noise she had made before perceiving him, had failed to disturb him, she felt assured that he slept soundly, and an irresistible desire arose in her heart to draw near him, and look at him more closely than she had yet ventured to do. She stood beside him; her heart bounded against the locket, his gift, which lay in its accustomed place, as she marked with a quick eye how the handsome but uncouth stripling had expanded into the man of noble proportions, whose features had, like her own, acquired a new character under the refining touch of intellect. Meeta looked on him till her eyes grew dim with tears pressed from a heart full of emotion, compounded of happy memories and glad hopes, shadowed by disappointment and saddened by doubt. Above all other feelings, however, rose the undying love which had "grown with her growth, and strengthened with her strength." Suddenly, by an irrepressible impulse, she laid her hand softly on the dark locks of waving hair which clustered over his broad brow, and breathed in low, tender accents, "My Ernest!"

On leaving his father's room, Ernest had thrown himself on his hard couch, not to sleep, but to rest; and when slumber overpowered him, he had yielded to it unwillingly, and with the determination to be on the alert and ready to arise on the first summons. Sleep that comes thus, howsoever it may continue through other disturbing causes, rarely resists a touch, or the sound of our own name, and light as was Meeta's touch, and low as were her tones, Ernest was partially aroused by them. He stirred, and she would have retreated noiselessly from his side, but as his eyes unclosed, they fell upon her with an expression of such rapturous love as she had never seen in them before, and in an instant he had encircled her form with his arm, and drawn her to his bosom. In glad surprise she rested there a moment; it was but a moment.

"Sophie my Sophie!" were the murmured words that met her ear, and gave her strength to burst from his embraces and glide rapidly, noiselessly back into the darkened chamber. There, sheltered by the darkness, she could see Ernest raise himself slowly up from his couch, look almost wildly around him, and then seemingly satisfied that he had only dreamed, sink back again to rest.

A dream it had indeed been to him; a shadow of the night; to Meeta a dark cloud, in whose gloom she was henceforth to walk for ever. Hours of conversation could not so fully have revealed the truth to Meeta as those simple words: "Sophie my Sophie!" uttered by Ernest in such a tone of heart-worship. Ernest loved with all the fond idolatry which she had thought of late belonged not to man's affections; but he loved another. Jealousy; the bitter consciousness of her own slighted love; the memory of his vows; the crushing thought that she was nothing to him now; that while he had been the life of her life, another had filled his thoughts and ruled his being, created a wild tempest in her soul. All was still around her. The sick man, the tired Ernest slept; and without, not even the rustling of a leaf disturbed the repose of Nature. She seemed to herself the only living thing in the universe; and to her, life was torture. An hour passed in this still concentrated agony, and she could endure it no longer; she must be up and doing; she would wake Ernest; she would tell him the revelation she had made; upbraid him with her blighted life, and leave him. Let him send for his Sophie; what did she, the outcast, the rejected, there in his house? why should she nurse his father? She arose and approached again the couch of Ernest; she was about to call to him, but she was arrested by the expression of agony in his face. His brow was contracted, and as she continued to gaze, low moans issued from his quivering lips. Ernest too was a sufferer; how that thought softened the hard, cold, icy crust that had been gathering around her heart! The bitterness of pride and jealousy gave place to tenderer emotions. Tears gathered in her eyes, and stealing softly back to her sheltered seat, she wept long and silently.

"In sorrow the angels are near;" and Meeta's heart was now full of sorrow, not of anger. Sad must her life ever be, but what of that, if Ernest could be happy? Perhaps he suffered for her; the good, true Ernest. It might be that only in dreams he had told his love to Sophie, bound to silence, painful silence, by his vows to her. She then could make him happy, and was not that her first desire? If it were not, her love was a low, selfish, unworthy love, and she would pray that it might be purified. She did pray, not as she would have done an hour before, to be taken out of the world, but that she might be made meet to do the will of her FATHER while in the world. She prayed for herself, for Ernest; and sweet peace stole into her heart, and before the morning light came, she had resolved not to leave the old man who loved her, during his few remaining days, yet not to keep Ernest in doubt of his own freedom. She was impatient that he should awake, and fell asleep imagining various modes of making her communication to him. Exhausted by mental agitation even more than by watching, she slept long and heavily. When she awoke, Ernest was shading the window at her side, through which the sun was shining brightly into the room. As she moved he looked at her kindly, and said:

"I am afraid I awoke you, Meeta, when I meant only to prolong your sleep by shutting out this light."

"I have slept long enough," was all that Meeta could say. The old Rainer was awake, and dreading above all things some allusions from him to the supposed relations of Ernest and herself, she hastened from the room and busied herself in the preparation of breakfast. Having seen that meal placed upon the table, she returned to the sick room and begged that Ernest would pour out his own coffee, while she did some things that were essential to his father's comfort. She lingered till Ernest came to see whether he could take her place, and then, as the old man slept peacefully, and she could make no further excuse, she accompanied him back to the table. The breakfast, a mere form to Meeta at least, proceeded in silence, or with only a casual remark from Ernest, scarcely heard by her, on the weather, the rapidity with which he had travelled, or his father's condition. Suddenly Meeta seemed to arouse herself as from a deep reverie:

"Why do you not talk to me of Sophie?" she said, attempting to speak gayly, though one less embarrassed than Ernest could not have failed to note the tremulousness of her voice, and the quivering of the pallid lip which vainly strove to smile.

But Meeta's agitation was as nothing to that of Ernest. For a moment he gazed upon her as though spell-bound, then dropping his face into his clasped hands, sat actually shivering before her. It was plain that Ernest had not lightly estimated his obligations to her. If he had sinned against them he had not despised them, and this conviction gave new strength to Meeta. She rose for the hour superior to every selfish emotion. Laying her hand upon his arm, she said, gently:

"Be not so agitated, Ernest; can you not regard me as your friend, and talk to me as you did in old days of all that disturbs you; and why should you be disturbed at my speaking of of your Sophie? You do not suppose that you know that in short, Ernest, we cannot be expected to feel now as we did five years ago; but surely that need not prevent our being friends."

Meeta had been herself too much confused of late, to remark her companion. When she now ventured with great effort to meet his eyes, she found them fixed upon her with an expression of lively admiration and grateful joy.

"Meeta, dear Meeta!" he exclaimed, seizing her hand and kissing it. "You give me new life. I have been a miserable man for weeks past, torn by conflicting claims upon my heart and my honor. You had claims on both, Meeta; sacred claims, which I could never have asked you to forego; and so had Sophie, for though I resisted long, there came a moment of mad passion, of madder forgetfulness, in which, abandoning myself to the present, I sought and obtained an avowal of her love. It was scarcely over ere I felt the wrong I had done. I revealed that wrong to her; pity me, Meeta! I told her all your claims, your worth. To you I resolved to be equally frank, and my only hope was in your generosity. But my father had never suffered me to doubt that your heart was still mine, and though I was assured that you would enable me to fulfil my obligations to Sophie, I feared, I mean, I could not hope, that it would be without any sacrifice; I mean without any regrets on your part."

Ernest paused in some embarrassment; but Meeta could not speak, and he resumed:

"You have made me perfectly happy, Meeta, which even Sophie could not have done, had I been compelled in devoting myself to her to relinquish the friend and sister of my childhood."

"Always regard me thus, Ernest, as your friend and sister, and I shall be satisfied."

Meeta had risen to return to the sick room, but Ernest caught her hand and held her back, while he said:

"But you must see my Sophie, Meeta; you must know her and then you will love her too. She will be here soon with her sister, Mrs. Schwartz."

"Mrs. Schwartz her sister? Then my last doubt is removed Ernest. She is worthy of you."

"Worthy of me!" And Ernest would have run into all a lover's rhapsodies on this text, but Meeta had escaped from him.

Hitherto Meeta's life had been one of quietness, of inaction, and now in a few short weeks ages of active existence seemed crowded. One object she had set before her as the great aim of her life; it was to secure Ernest's happiness and preserve his honor. She understood now the coldness with which her father had of late named him. It was essential to her peace that this coldness should not deepen into anger. Not even in her own family then must she have rest from the strife between her inner and her outer life. Sympathy she must not have, since sympathy with her was almost inseparably connected with reproach of Ernest. Time had another lesson to teach, and Meeta soon learned it; that in a combat such as she had to sustain, no half-way measures would suffice, that she must not drive her griefs down to the depths of her heart, shutting them there from every human eye, but she must drive them out of her heart. We talk of feigning cheerfulness, of wearing a mask for the world and throwing it off in solitude, and we may do this for a week, a month, a year, but those who have a life-grief to sustain, from whose hearts hope has died out, know that there are only two paths open to them in the universe; to lie down in their despair and breathe out their souls in murmurs against their GOD, and lamentations over their destiny; or, humbly kissing the rod which has smitten them, to go forth out of themselves, where all is darkness and woe, and find a new and happier life in living for and in others. And thus did Meeta.

We may not linger over the details of the next few weeks of her existence. The old Rainer died; died blessing his children, Ernest and Meeta, and praying for their happiness. Often would Ernest have told him all; but Meeta kept back a disclosure which would have given him pain. "Do not disturb him now, Ernest," she said; "he will know all soon, and bless your Sophie from heaven, where there is no sorrow."

Meeta returned home, and exhaustion won for her a few days rest; rest even from her mental struggles; but when the funeral was over, and things returned to their usual routine, she felt that she must prepare her father and mother to receive Ernest in the character in which they were henceforth to regard him. She found strength for this in her lofty purpose and her simple dependence upon Heaven, and her voice did not falter nor her color change as she said to her mother:

"Do you not think Ernest is much altered?"

"Yes, he is greatly improved."

"Improved! Well, he may be so to the eyes of others, but"

"Is he not as tender to you, my daughter?" asked the sensitive mother.

"That is not it," said Meeta, coloring for the first time: "we neither of us feel as we once did; it was a childish folly to suppose that we should. I have told Ernest that I could not fulfil our engagement, and he is satisfied."

Madame Werner looked long at her daughter, but Meeta met the glance firmly.

"And is this all, Meeta?"

"All! What more would you have, dear mother?"

"And are you happy, Meeta?"

"Happier than I should be in marrying Ernest now, dear mother."

Madame Werner explained all this to her husband, at her daughter's request. He was not grieved at it. "Ernest," he said, "had never valued Meeta as she deserved. He was glad she had shown so much spirit."

Meeta had a more difficult task to perform. Mrs. Schwartz's sister has come at last. She came from Germany at the same time with Ernest, but stopped to make a visit to another sister in Philadelphia, and arrived here only last night. "I will go and see her," said Meeta one morning to Madame Werner. She went. As she approached the house, there came through the open windows the sound of an organ, accompanied by a rich and highly cultivated voice. Meeta would not pause for a moment, lest she should grow nervous. It was essential to Ernest's happiness that Sophie should be friendly with her; and the difficulties were of a nature which, if not overcome at once, would not be overcome at all. Meeta entered the small parlor without knocking, and found herself tete-a-tete with the musician; a young, fair girl, delicately formed, with beautiful hands and arms, and pleasing, pretty face. As she saw the visitor, her song ceased. Meeta smiled on her, and extending her hand, said: "You are Sophie Ernest's Sophie?"

"And you," said the fair girl, with wondering eyes, "are "

"Meeta."

This was an introduction which admitted no formality, and when Mrs. Schwartz entered half an hour later, she was surprised to find those so lately strangers conversing in the low and earnest tones which betoken confidence, while the lofty expression on the countenance of the one, and the moist eyes and flushed cheeks of the other, showed that their topic was one of no ordinary interest.

Six months passed rapidly away, and then Ernest felt that he might, without disrespect to his father's memory, bring home his bride. Their engagement had been known for some time, and had excited no little surprise; though perhaps less than the continued and close friendship between them and Meeta. Many improvements in Sophie's future home had been suggested by Meeta's taste, and Ernest had acquired such a habit of consulting her, that no day passed without an interview between them. At length the evening preceding the bridal-day had arrived, and Ernest and Sophie had gone to secure Meeta's promise to officiate as bridesmaid in the simple ceremony of the morrow. They were to be married at the parsonage, in the presence of a few witnesses only, and were immediately to set out on an excursion which would occupy several weeks. They had urged Meeta to accompany them, but she had declined. "But she cannot refuse to stand up with me do you think she can?" said Sophie to her sister, as she prepared to accompany Ernest to Carl Werner's.

"I do not think she will refuse," Mrs. Schwartz replied.

"You do not think she will!" repeated Mr. Schwartz, in an accent of surprise, to his wife, when Ernest and Sophie had left them. "How does that consist with your idea of Meeta's love for Ernest?"

"It perfectly consists with a love like Meeta's; a love without any alloy of selfishness. Dear Meeta! how little is her nobleness appreciated! Even I dare not let her see that she is understood by me, lest I should wound her delicate and generous nature."

There was a pause, and then Mr. Schwartz said, hesitatingly, "If it be as you think, Meeta is a noble being; but "

"If it be!" interrupted Mrs. Schwartz, with warmth. "Can you doubt it? Have you not seen the loftier character which her generous purpose has impressed upon her whole aspect? the elevation I had almost said the inspiration, which beams from her face when Ernest and Sophia are present? Sophie is my sister, and I love her truly; yet I declare to you, at such times I have looked from her to Meeta, and wondered at what seemed to me Ernest's infatuation."

"Sophie is fair, and delicate, and accomplished, the very personification of refinement, natural and acquired, and the antipodes of all which Ernest, ere he saw her, had begun to dread in the untaught Meeta of his memory. I am not surprised at all at his loving Sophie, but I cannot at all understand how the simple and single-hearted Meeta can feign so long and so well, as on your supposition she has done."

"Feign! Meeta feign! I never said or thought such a thing. A course of action lofty as Meeta's must have its foundation deep in the heart, in principles enduring as life itself. Had Meeta's been the commonplace feigned satisfaction with Ernest's conduct to which pride might have given birth, she would have been fitful in her moods; alternately gay or gloomy; generous and kind, or petulant and exacting. The serenity, the composure of countenance and manner which distinguish our Meeta, spring from a higher, purer source. It is the sweet submission of a chastened, loving spirit, which can say to its FATHER in Heaven:

'BECAUSE my portion was assign'd,
Wholesome and bitter, THOU art kind,
And I am blessed to my mind.'"

"A state of feeling to be preferred certainly to the gratification of any earthly affection; but I scarcely see how it can accord with Meeta's continued love of Ernest."

"That is because you do not separate love from the selfish desires with which it is too generally accompanied. Meeta loves Ernest so truly, so entirely, that she cannot be said to yield her happiness to his, but rather to find it in his; his joy, his honor, are hers."

"And can woman feel thus?" asked Mr. Schwartz, as he looked with admiration upon his wife, her cheeks glowing and her eyes lighted with the enthusiasm of a spirit akin to Meeta's.

"There are many mysteries in woman which you have yet to fathom," said Mrs. Schwartz, with a smile.

To the good pastor and his wife, the next day, even Sophie was a less interesting object of contemplation than Meeta, who stood at her side. She was pale, very pale, and dressed with even more than usual simplicity; yet there was in her face so much of the soul's light, that she seemed to them beautiful. Her congratulations were offered in speechless emotion. The brotherly kiss which Ernest pressed upon her cheek called up no color there, nor disturbed the graceful stillness of her manner; and when Sophie, who had really become sincerely attached to her, threw herself into her arms, she returned her embrace with tenderness, whispering as she did so, "Make Ernest happy, Sophie, and I will love you always!"

And now what have we more to tell of Meeta? It cannot be denied that there were hours of darkness, in which the joyous hopes and memories of her youth rose up vividly before her, making her present life seem sad and lonely in contrast. But these visitors from the realm of shadows were neither evoked nor welcomed by Meeta. Resolutely she turned from the dead past, to the active, living present, determined that no shadow from her should darken the declining days of her father and mother. She is the light of their home, and often they bless the Providence which has left her with them. What would they have done without her cheerful voice to inspire them in bearing the burdens of advancing life?

But not only in her home was Meeta a consolation and a blessing. The poor, the sick, the sorrowing, knew ever where to find true sympathy and ready aid. She was the "Lady Bountiful" of her neighborhood. But there was one house where more especially her presence was welcomed; where no important step was taken without her advice; where sorrow was best soothed by her, and joy but half complete till she had shared it. This house was Ernest Rainer's. To him and Sophie she was a cherished sister, to whose upright and self-forgetting nature they looked up with a species of reverence; and to their children she was "Dear Aunt Meeta! the kindest and best friend, except mamma, in the world!"

How many more useful, more noble, or happier persons than our old maid can married life present? Is she not more worthy of imitation than the "Celias" and "Daphnés" whose delicate distresses have formed the staple of circulating libraries, or than those feeble spirits in real life, who, mistaking selfishness for sensibility, turn thanklessly from the blessings and coldly from the duties of life, because they have been denied the gratification of some cherished desire?

CHAPTER X

It is Christmas, merry Christmas, as we have been duly informed this morning by every inhabitant of Donaldson Manor, from Col. Donaldson to the pet and baby Sophy Dudley, who was taught the words but yesterday, for the occasion. Last evening our readings were interrupted, for all were busy in preparing for this important day. Miss Donaldson was superintending jellies and blanc-manges, custards and Charlottes des Russes; Col. and Mrs. Donaldson were preparing gifts for their servants, not one of whom was forgotten, and Annie and I, and, by his own special request, Mr. Arlington, were arranging in proper order the gifts of that most considerate, mirthful and generous of spirits, Santa Claus. This morning the sun rose as clear and bright as though it, too, rejoiced in the joy of humanity; but long before the sun had showed himself, little feet were pattering from room to room, and childish voices shouting in the unchecked exuberance of delight. I sometimes doubt whether the children are so happy as I am, on such occasions. One incident that occurred this morning would have been enough, in my opinion, to repay all the time, the trouble, and the gold, which Santa Claus, or his agents, had expended on their preparations. Aroused by the voices of the children, I threw on a dressing-gown and hastened to the room appropriated to their patron saint, which I entered at one door just as little Eva Dudley appeared at another. Without being in the least a beauty, Eva has the most charming face I know; merry and bright as Puck's, or as her own life, which from its earliest dawn has been joyous as a bird's carol. She gazed now with eager delight on the toys exhibited by her brothers and sisters, without, apparently, one thought of herself, till Robert said, "But see here, Eva, look at your own."

As her eyes rested on the large baby-house, with its folding-doors open to display the furniture of the parlors, and the two dolls, mother and daughter, seated at a table on which stood a neat china breakfasting set, she clasped her dimpled hands in silent ecstasy for half a minute, then rising to her utmost height on her rosy little toes, she exclaimed, "Oh, isn't I a happy little woman!"

Dear Eva! a little girl's heart would not have seemed to her large enough to contain such a rapture.

Our party has been augmented since breakfast by the arrival of several families of Donaldsons some of whom live at too great a distance for visits at any other time than Christmas, when all who stand in any conceivable, or I was about to say inconceivable, degree of relationship to the Donaldsons of Donaldson Manor, are expected to be here. Among this host of uncles and aunts and cousins, I was really grateful for my own prefix of aunt, and I heard Mr. Arlington whisper a request to Robert to call him uncle a title to which I have no doubt he would willingly make good his claim.

In the midst of this general hilarity, the religious character of the day was not forgotten, and all the family and some of the visitors attended the morning services in the church. We know that there are those who, doubting the testimony on which the Christian world has agreed to observe the 25th of December as the birthday into our mortal life of the world's Saviour, and the era from which man may date his hopes of a happy immortality, consider the religious observances of this day a sheer superstition. On such a controversy I could say but little, and I should be very unwilling so say that little here; but I would ask if it can be wrong in the opinion of any nay, if it be not right, very right, in the opinion of all to celebrate once in the year an event so solemn and so joyous to our race; and whether any day can be better for such a purpose, than that which has been for centuries associated with it wherever the Angel's song of "Peace on earth and good will to man" has been heard? Another class of objectors there are who complain that a day so sacred should be desecrated, as they express it, by revelry and mirth. To their objection I should not have a word of reply, if it were limited to a condemnation of that wild uproar and senseless jollity by which men sometimes make fools or brutes of themselves; but when they condemn the cheerfulness that has its home and its birthplace in a grateful heart, when they frown upon the happy family gathering once more within the old walls that had echoed to their childish gambols, calling up by the spells of association, from the dim recesses of the past, the very tones and looks of the mother that watched their cradled sleep, and the father that guided their first tottering steps in the pursuit of truth; tones and looks by which, if by any thing, the cold, selfish spirit of the world to whose dominion they have yielded, may be exorcised, and the loving and generous spirit of their earlier life may again enter within them; when they declare these things inconsistent with the Christian's joyful commemoration of that event to which he owes his earthly blessings as well as his heavenly hopes. I can only pity them for their want of harmony with the Great Spirit of the Universe, the spirit of Love and Joy.

Our Christmas was continued and concluded in the same spirit in which it was commenced the spirit of kindly affection to Man and devout gratitude to Heaven. Those guests whose homes were distant remained for the night, and in the evening, before any of our party had left us, Col. Donaldson called on Robert Dudley to repeat a poem winch he had learned at his request for the occasion. Robert was a little abashed at first at being brought forward so conspicuously; but he is a manly, intelligent boy, and his voice soon gathered strength and firmness, and his eyes lost their downward tendency, and kindled with earnest feeling, as he recited those beautiful lines of Charles Sprague, entitled

THE FAMILY MEETING

We are all here!
Father, mother,
Sister, brother,
All who hold each other dear.
Each chair is fill'd, we're all at home,
To-night let no cold stranger come;
It is not often thus around
Our own familiar hearth we're found.
Bless, then, the meeting and the spot;
For once be every care forgot;
Let gentle Peace assert her power,
And kind affection rule the hour;
We're all all here.
We're NOT all here!
Some are away the dead ones dear,
Who throng'd with us this ancient hearth,
And gave the hour to guiltless mirth.
Fate, with a stern, relentless hand,
Look'd in and thinn'd our little band:
Some like a night-flash pass'd away,
And some sank, lingering, day by day;
The quiet grave-yard some lie there
And cruel Ocean has his share
We're not all here.
We are all here!

Even they the dead though dead so dear.
Fond Memory, to her duty true,
Brings back their faded forms to view.
How life-like, through the mist of years,
Each well-remember'd face appears!
We see them as in times long past,
From each to each kind looks are cast,
We hear their words, their smiles behold,
They're round us as they were of old
We are all here.
We are all here!
Father, mother,
Sister, brother,
You that I love with love so dear.
This may not long of us be said,
Soon must we join the gather'd dead,
And by the hearth we now sit round
Some other circle will be found.
Oh, then, that wisdom may we know,
Which yields a life of peace below!
So, in the world to follow this,
May each repeat, in words of bliss.
We're all all here!

CHAPTER XI

Yesterday we were more than usually still after the enjoyment of Christmas, and a little quiet chit-chat seemed all of which we were capable, but to-day every thing about us and within us began to settle into its usual form, and this evening there was a general call for our accustomed entertainment. I was inexorable to all entreaties, and Mr. Arlington was compelled to open his portfolio for our gratification.

"Select your subject," he said with a smile, as he drew forth sketch after sketch and spread them on the table before us. "I have no story to tell of any of them."

"I select this," said Annie, as she held up a drawing, entitled, "The Exiled Hebrews."

"Ah!" said Mr. Arlington, as he glanced at it, "you have chosen well; the subject is interesting."

"But can you really tell us nothing of these figures, so noble yet so touching in their aspect?"

"No; nothing of them. I could tell you indeed of a dying Hebrew, whose portrait you may imagine you have before you in that turbaned old gentleman."

"Well, let us hear it."

THE DYING HEBREW

A HEBREW knelt in the dying light,
His eye was dim and cold,
The hair on his brow was silver white,
And his blood was thin and old.
He lifted his eye to his latest sun,
For he felt that his pilgrimage was done,
And as he saw God's shadow there,
His spirit pour'd itself in prayer.
"I come unto Death's second birth
Beneath a stranger air,
A pilgrim on a chill, cold earth,
As all my fathers were;
And men have stamp'd me with a curse,
I feel it is not Thine.
Thy mercy, like yon sun, was made
On me, as all to shine;
And therefore dare I lift mine eye
Through that to Thee, before I die.
In this great temple, built by Thee,
Whose altars are divine,
Beneath yon lamp that ceaselessly
Lights up Thine own true shrine,
Take this my latest sacrifice,
Look down and make this sod
Holy as that where long ago
The Hebrew met his God.
I have not caused the widow's tears,
Nor dimm'd the orphan's eye,
I have not stain'd the virgin's years,
Nor mock'd the mourner's cry.
The songs of Zion in my ear
Have ever been most sweet,
And always when I felt Thee near,
My shoes were 'off my feet.'
I have known Thee in the whirlwind,
I have known Thee on the hill,
I have known Thee in the voice of birds,
In the music of the rill.
I dreamt Thee in the shadow,
I saw Thee in the light,
I heard Thee in the thunder-peal,
And worshipp'd in the night.
All beauty, while it spoke of Thee,
Still made my heart rejoice,
And my spirit bow'd within itself

To hear 'Thy still, small voice.'
I have not felt myself a thing
Far from Thy presence driven,
By flaming sword or waving wing
Cut off from Thee and heaven.
Must I the whirlwind reap, because,
My fathers sow'd the storm?
Or shrink because another sinn'd,
Beneath Thy red, right arm?
Oh! much of this we dimly scan,
And much is all unknown,
I will not take my curse from man,
I turn to THEE alone.
Oh! bid my fainting spirit live,
And what is dark, reveal,
And what is evil oh, forgive!
And what is broken heal.
And cleanse my spirit from above,
In the deep Jordan of Thy love!
I know not if the Christian's heaven
Shall be the same as mine,
I only ask to be forgiven,
And taken home to THINE.
I weary on a far, dim strand,
Whose mansions are as tombs,
And long to find the Father-land,
Where there are many homes.
Oh! grant of all yon shining throngs
Some dim and distant star,
Where Judah's lost and scatter'd sons
May worship from afar!
When all earth's myriad harps shall meet
In choral praise and prayer,
Shall Zion's harp, of old so sweet,
Alone be wanting there?
Yet place me in the lowest seat,
Though I, as now, lie there,
The Christian's jest the Christian's scorn,
Still let me see and hear,
From some bright mansion in the sky,
Thy loved ones and their melody."
The sun goes down with sudden gleam,
And beautiful as a lovely dream,
And silently as air,
The vision of a dark-eyed girl
With long and raven hair,
Glides in as guardian spirits glide,

And lo! is standing by his side,
As if her sudden presence there
Was sent in answer to his prayer.
Oh! say they not that angels tread
Around the good man's dying bed?
His child his sweet and sinless child,
And as he gazed on her,
He knew his God was reconciled,
And this the messenger.
As sure as God had hung on high
His promise-bow before his eye,
Earth's purest hopes were o'er him flung,
To point his heaven-ward faith,
And life's most holy feelings strung
To sing him into death.
And on his daughter's stainless breast,
The dying Hebrew sought his rest.

"Have I fulfilled my task?" asked Mr. Arlington, as he touched the picture on which Annie's eyes were still fixed.

"By no means," she answered; "the poem is beautiful; but is the drawing from your own pencil?"

"Oh, no! It is a copy of a copy. The original is by Biederrmanns, and may be seen, I believe, in the Dresden Gallery. This sketch was made from a copy in the possession of my friend, Mr. Michael Grahame. He had it done while he was in Russia. By-the-by if I had Aunt Nancy's powers as a raconteur, I think I could interest you in the history of Mr. and Mrs. Grahame."

"Let us have it," exclaimed Col. Donaldson; "we will be lenient in our criticisms; and should we ever call on you to give it to severer critics, Aunt Nancy will dress it up for you."

Mr. Arlington in vain sought to excuse himself.

"It is of no use," cried Col. Donaldson; "I am a thoroughbred story hunter, and now you have shown me the game, I must have it."

To Mr. Arlington, therefore, the reader is indebted for the following incidents, though I have fulfilled the promise made for me by the Colonel, and dressed it up a little for its present appearance. I have called the narrative thus prepared,

"ONLY A MECHANIC"

With beauty, wealth, an accomplished education, and a home around which clustered all the warm affections and graceful amenities of life, Lilian Devoe was considered by her acquaintances as one of fortune's most favored children. Yet in Lilian's bright sky there was a cloud, though it was perceptible to none but herself. She was the daughter of an Englishman, who, on his arrival in America with a sickly wife and infant child, had esteemed himself fortunate in obtaining the situation of farm-steward, or bailiff, at Mr. Trevanion's country-seat, near New-York.

"This is a pleasant home, Gerald," said Mrs. Devoe, on the day she took possession of her small but neat cottage, as she stood with him beneath a porch embowered with honey-suckle, and looked out upon a scene to which hill and dale and river combined to give enchantment.

"If you can be well and happy in it, love, I will try and forget that I had a right to a better," said Gerald Devoe, with a grave yet tender smile, as he drew his invalid wife close to his side.

Grave, Gerald Devoe always was; and none wondered at it who knew his early history. His family belonged to the gentry of England, and he had been born to an inheritance sufficient to support him respectably in that class. His mother, from whom he derived a sound judgment, and a firm and vigorous mind, died while he was yet a child, leaving his weak and self-indulgent father to the management of a roguish attorney, by whose aid he made the future maintain the present, till, at his death, little was left to Gerald beyond the bare walls of his paternal home and the small park by which it was surrounded. He had been, for two years before this time, married to one who had brought him little wealth, and whose delicate health seemed to demand the luxuries which he could no longer afford. For her sake, far more than for his own even more than for that of his cherished child he shrank from the new condition under which life was presenting itself to him. When at length his resources utterly failed, and he could no longer veil the truth from his wife, her gentle tender smile, her confiding caress, and above all, her ready inquiry into his plans for the future, and her earnest effort to aid him in bringing the chaos of his mind into order, taught him that there lies in woman's affections a source of strength equal to all the requirements of those who have won their way to that hidden fountain. It was by her advice that, instead of wasting his energies in the vain struggle to maintain his present position, he determined to carve out for himself a new life in another land. The first step towards the fulfilment of this resolution was also the most painful. It was the sacrifice of his home, the home of his childhood, his youth, his manhood, with which all that was dear in the present or tender in the past was associated. And yet higher claims it had. It had been the home of his fathers. For three hundred years those walls had owned a Devoe for their master, and now they must pass into a stranger's hands, and he and his must go forth with no right even to a grave in that soil which had seemed ever an inalienable part of himself. It was a stern lesson, but life teaches well, and it was learned. He could not turn to the liberal professions for support, because he had no means of maintaining himself and his family during the preparatory studies. Of farming he knew already something, and spent some months in acquiring yet further information respecting it, before he sailed from England. The determination and energy with which Gerald Devoe had entered on his new career, had won for him friends among practical men, and when he left England it was with recommendations that insured his success.

It was a fortunate circumstance for Mr. and Mrs. Devoe that Mr. Trevanion required a farm-steward on their arrival, for in him and his wife they found liberal employers, and persons of true Christian benevolence, who, having discovered the superiority of their minds and manners to their present station, hesitated not to receive them into their circle of friends, when a knowledge of their past history had acquainted them with their claims on their sympathy. Howsoever valuable the friendship of persons at once so accomplished and so excellent was to Mr. and Mrs. Devoe, for their own sakes, they prized it yet more for their Lilian's. She was their only child, and their poverty lost its last sting when they saw her linked arm in arm with young Anna Trevanion, the companion of her lessons and her sports. They could not have borne to see her, so lovely in outward form, and with a mind so full of intelligence, condemned either to the dreariness of a life without companionship, or to the degradation of association with the rude and uncultivated. That this feeling was wholly unconnected with any false views of their own position, or vain estimation of the claims derived from their birth and former condition, was evident from their readiness to receive into their friendly regards those in their present sphere in whose moral qualities they could confide, and who did not repel their courtesies by a rude and coarse manner. There was one of this latter class who held a place in their esteem not less exalted than that occupied by Mr. Trevanion himself. This was a Scotchman, living within two miles of Mr. Trevanion's seat, who found at once an agreeable occupation and a respectable support in a garden, from which he supplied the markets of New-York with some of their choicest vegetables, and its drawing-rooms with some of their choicest bouquets. Mr. Grahame was one who, in those early ages when physical endowments constituted the chief distinction between men, might have been chosen king of the tribe with which he had chanced to be associated. Even now, in this self-styled enlightened age, his tall and stalwart frame, his erect carriage, his firm and vigorous step, his broad, commanding brow, his bright, keen eye, and the firm, frank expression of his whole face, won from every beholder an involuntary feeling of respect, which further acquaintance only served to deepen. With little of the education of schools, he was a man of reading, and, what schools can never make, he was a man of thought, and of that sober, practical good sense, and those firm, religious principles which are the surest, the only true and safe guides in life. Mrs. Grahame was a gentle and lovely woman, with an eye to see and a heart to feel her husband's excellences. And a worthy son of such a father was Michael Grahame, the only child of this excellent pair. He was six years older than Lilian Devoe, and having no sister of his own, had been her playfellow and protector from her cradle. Even Anna Trevanion could not rival Michael in Lilian's heart, nor all the luxuries of Trevanion Hall compete with the delight of wandering with him through the gardens of Mossgiel, listening to his history of the various plants for Michael had learned from his father where most of them had first been found, and how and by whom they had been introduced to their present abodes and learning from him the chief points of distinction between the different tribes of the vegetable world, and many other things of which older people are often ignorant. But acquainted as Michael was with the inhabitants of the garden, they did not afford him his most vivid enjoyment. Mechanical pursuits were his passion.

Before Lilian was four years old, she had ridden in a carriage of his construction, which he boasted the most unskilful hand on the most unequal road could not, except from malice prepense, upset. To see Michael a clergyman, or, if that might not be, a lawyer, was Mrs. Grahame's dream of life; but when she whispered it to her husband, he shook his head, with a grave smile, and pointed to the boy, who stood near, putting the finishing touch to what he called his "magical glass." This was the case of an old spy-glass, in which he had so disposed several mirrors, made of a toilet-glass long since broken, as to enable the person using the instrument to see objects in a very different direction from that to which it appeared to be directed. The fond parents watched his movements in silence for a few minutes: suddenly he called in a glad voice, "Here, father, come and look through my magical glass."

Mr. Grahame obeyed the summons, saying to his wife, "He'll make a good mechanic better not spoil that, for a poor clergyman or lawyer."

Michael had the advantage of the best schools to which his father could gain access; and his teachers joined in declaring that his father might make what he would of him, but his own inclination for mechanics continued as fixed as ever, and Mr. Grahame was equally fixed in his determination to let his inclination decide his career.

"Let him be what he will, he must be something above the ordinary, or your high people will remember against him that his father was a gardener," said Mr. Grahame to his wife; "and you may be sure he'll rise highest in what he loves."

At sixteen Michael Grahame commenced his apprenticeship to the trade of a mathematical instrument maker, to the perfect satisfaction of himself and his father, the secret annoyance of his mother, and the openly expressed chagrin of Lilian Devoe, who had shared all Mrs. Grahame's ambitious hopes for her friend. From this period Lilian became the inseparable companion of the young Trevanions, their only rival in her heart being removed from her circle. She still considered Michael as greatly superior to them, and indeed to all others, in personal attributes, but she could seldom enjoy his society, since he resided in the city; and as she approached to womanhood, and he exchanged the vivacity of the boy for the man's thoughtful brow and more controlled expression of feeling, their manner in their occasional interviews assumed a formality which made it a poor interpreter of her heart's true emotions.

At seventeen Lilian Devoe was an orphan, left to the guardianship of Mr. Trevanion and Mr. Grahame, with a fortune which secured to her a prospect of all the comforts, and many of the elegancies of life. This fortune was the result of a successful speculation made by Mr. Devoe about a year before his death, with the little sum, which, by judicious management, he had saved from his salary during many years. It was a sum too small to secure to his daughter a maintenance in case of his death, and with a trembling and almost despairing heart he had thrown it on the troubled sea of speculation. From that hour he knew no peace. His life was probably shortened by his anxieties, and when he received the assurance of the successful issue of his experiment, he had but a few days to live. Before his death, Mr. Trevanion had spoken very kindly to him, and both he and Mrs. Trevanion had expressed the most friendly interest in Lilian, and had offered to receive her as a member of their own family, when her "home should be left unto her desolate." Mr. Grahame and his kind-hearted wife had already made the same offer, and Mr. Devoe, with the warmest expression of gratitude, commended his daughter to the guardianship of both his friends. It was winter when Mr. Devoe died the Trevanions were in the city, and, by her own wish, Lilian passed the first few months of her orphanage at the cottage of Mr. Grahame. Never was an orphan more tenderly received, more dearly cherished.

Michael Grahame had now acquired his trade, and had entered into an already established and profitable business with his former master, who predicted that with his application, and his unusual talent and his delight both in the theory of mechanics and the actual development of that theory in practice, he must one day acquire a high reputation. Perhaps this opinion might have been in some degree shaken by the long and frequent holidays of his young partner during this winter. Michael had never been so much at home since he left it, a boy of sixteen, and before the winter had passed, all formality between him and Lilian had vanished. Again they wandered together, as in childhood, through the garden walks; again Lilian learned to regard him, not only as a loved friend, but as a guide and protector.

Mrs. Grahame saw the growth of these feelings with delight. She loved Lilian, and gave the highest proof of her esteem for her, in believing her worthy of her son. Mr. Grahame was less satisfied. He, too, loved Lilian, and would have welcomed her to his heart as a daughter, but her lately acquired fortune, and her connection with the Trevanion family, gave her a right to higher expectations in marriage, than to become the wife of a mechanic of very moderate fortunes, howsoever great was his ability, or howsoever distinguished his personal qualities. No Mr. Grahame was not satisfied, and nothing but his confidence in Michael kept him silent. The confidence was not misplaced.

The news of Lilian's fortune, and of Mr. and Mrs. Trevanion's offer to receive her into their family, had sent a sharp pang through the heart of Michael Grahame, which had taught him the true character of his attachment to her.

"She is removed from my world she can be nothing to me now," was the first stern whisper of his heart, which was modified after two or three interviews into "She can only be a dear friend and sister. I must never think of her in any other light." And, devoted as he had been to her through the winter, no word, no look had told of love less calm or more exacting than this. But there came a time when the quick blush on Lilian's cheek at his approach, the tremor of her little hand as he clasped it, told that she shared his feeling, without his power of self-control. Then came the hour of trial to Michael Grahame's nature. Self-immolation were easy in comparison with the infliction of one pang on her. And wherefore should either suffer? Was it not a false sentiment that denied to her the right to decide for herself, between those shows and fashions which the world most prizes, and the indulgence of the purest and sweetest affections of our nature? Was he not in truth sacrificing her happiness to his own pride? It was a question which he dared not answer for himself, and he applied to his father, in whose high principles and clear judgment he placed implicit confidence. Mr. Grahame was too shrewd, and in this case too interested an observer to be unprepared for his son's avowal of his past feelings and present perplexities.

"You are right, my son," he replied to his appeal; "It is Lilian's right to decide for herself on that which will constitute her own happiness."

"Then I may speak to her I may tell her "

"All you desire that she should know," said Mr. Grahame, gently, "when Lilian has had an opportunity of knowing what she must sacrifice in accepting you."

"True true I will ask no promise from her nay I will accept none I will only assure her that should the world fail to fill her heart, the truest and most devoted love awaits her here."

"And in listening to that assurance, without rebuking it, a delicate woman would feel that she had pledged herself."

Michael Grahame's brow contracted, and his voice faltered slightly as, after a moment's thoughtful pause, he asked, "What then would you have me do?"

"Nothing at present Lilian will soon leave us, and at Mr. Trevanion's she will see quite another kind of life a life which, with her fortune and their friendship, may be hers, but which she must give up should she become the wife of a mechanic and the daughter-in-law of a gardener. Let her see this life, my boy, and then let her choose between you and it."

"And how can I hope that she will continue to regard me with kindness if I suffer her to depart without any expression of interest in her?"

"Any expression of interest! I do not wish you to be colder to her than you have hitherto been, and I am much mistaken if Lilian would exchange your brotherly affection for all the gewgaws in life."

"I will endeavor to take your advice, but I hope I shall not be tried too long," were the concluding words of Michael Grahame, as he turned from his father to seek composure in a solitary walk. When he had returned, he found that his father had gone to the city an unusual circumstance at that season, and one which he could not afterwards avoid connecting with a letter which Lilian received the next day from Anna Trevanion, before she had risen from the breakfast table.

"Papa," wrote Miss Trevanion, "has made me perfectly happy, dear Lilian, by declaring that he cannot consent to leave you longer in the country. I hope you will not find it very difficult to obey his commands in the present instance, which are, that you shall be ready at noon to-morrow to accompany him to the city, where you will find Mamma and your Anna, waiting to receive you with open arms."

"What is the matter, Lilian? Does your letter bring you bad news?" asked Mrs. Grahame, as she saw the dejected countenance with which Lilian sat gazing on these few lines.

Michael said nothing, but, as Lilian looked up to answer Mrs. Grahame, she saw that his eyes were fixed upon her, and the blood rushed to her temples, while she said, "It is only a note from Anna Trevanion, to say that her father is coming for me to-day at noon, and and " Lilian could go no farther her voice faltered, and she burst into tears. Michael Grahame started from his chair, but a movement of his father's arm prevented his approaching Lilian, and unable to endure the scene, he rushed from the room, while his mother, folding the weeping girl in her arms, exclaimed, "Don't cry, Lilian, Mr. Trevanion will not certainly make you go with him, if you do not wish it."

"Hush, hush, good wife," said the kind but firm voice of Mr. Grahame; "Lilian must not be so ungracious to such friends as Mr. and Mrs. Trevanion, as to refuse to go to them when they wish her. Go, my dear child," he continued, laying his hand on her bent head; "and remember that no day will be so happy for us as that in which you come back if indeed," he added, more gayly, "you can come back to such an humble home, after living among great folks."

There was another voice for which Lilian listened, but she listened in vain. Her first feeling on perceiving that Michael Grahame had left the room while she lay weeping in his mother's arms was very bitter, but Mrs. Grahame soothed her by saying, "Michael couldn't bear to see you crying, dear, so when his father wouldn't let him speak to you, he jumped up and ran off. Poor Michael! sadly enough he'll miss you."

In about an hour, Michael again sought Lilian, bringing with him three bouquets of hot-house flowers. Two of these had been arranged by his father for Mrs. and Miss Trevanion, and the other was of flowers which he had himself selected for Lilian. She stood beside him while he first wrapped the stems of the flowers in a wet sponge, and then put them into a box, to defend them from the cold. This was done, and the box handed to Lilian without a word. As she took it, she asked in a low tone, and turning away to hide her embarrassment as she spoke, "When shall I see you in New-York?"

"I shall be in New-York very soon," he replied; "perhaps to-morrow but we move there in such different spheres, Lilian, that I do not know when we shall meet."

"Perhaps never," said Lilian, endeavoring, not very successfully, to steady her voice and speak with nonchalance, "unless you are willing to leave what you call your sphere and seek me in mine."

"I only need your permission to do so with delight," and so charming had her evident emotion made her in his eyes, that Michael could not refrain from pressing her hand to his lips. There was no anger in the flush which this action brought to Lilian's cheek.

Mr. Trevanion was punctual to the hour of his appointment, and descended from his carriage only to hand Lilian into it.

"You will call sometimes to see how your ward does," he said good-humoredly to the elder Mr. Grahame, but to Michael not a word. He had determined to discourage, and, if possible, completely to overthrow any intimacy which Mr. Grahame had acknowledged to him was not unattended with danger. Mr. Trevanion was a man of liberal mind, yet he was not wholly free from the prejudices of his class, which made the highest happiness the result of the highest social position. There is in the mind of man so unconquerable a desire for the unattainable, that it is not wonderful perhaps that this opinion should be entertained by those who do not occupy that position; but to those who do, we should suppose its fallacy would stand out too glaringly to be doubted or denied. We are far from denying the advantages of rank and wealth: but we view them not as an end, but as a means for the attainment of an end, and that end, not happiness, except as happiness is indissolubly connected with the perfection of our own powers, and with the extension of our usefulness to others. He who, like Michael Grahame, can command the means of intellectual cultivation and refinement, and a fair arena for the exercise of his powers, when thus cultivated, need not envy the possessor of larger fortune and higher station with his weightier responsibilities and greater temptations.

Michael Grahame understood Mr. Trevanion's coolness, but he was not one to retreat from an unfought field. Three days had scarcely given to Lilian the feeling of ease in her new home, when he called on her. He had chosen morning, as the hour when others would be the least likely to dispute her attention with him. She was at home Mrs. and Miss Trevanion were out and a long tete-a-tete almost reconciled him to her new abode. He had not forgotten his father's advice, nor taken the seal from his lips. He might not speak to her of love, but the nicest honor did not forbid him to show her the true sympathy and affection of a friend. In a few days he called again, and at the same hour; Miss Devoe was not at home, she had gone out with Mrs. and Miss Trevanion. Again the next day he came at the same hour, and the answer was the same. He called in the afternoon at five o'clock, and she was at dinner; at seven o'clock, she was preparing for an evening party, and begged he would excuse her. "I will seek no more," said Michael Grahame at length, with proud determination, "to enter the charmed circle which shuts her from me in the city. They cannot keep her to themselves always, and if Lilian's heart be what I deem it, it will take more than a few months of absence to efface from it the memories of years."

A few days only after this determination, Lilian was called down at nine o'clock in the morning, to see Mr. Grahame. Early as it was, the furtive glance towards her mirror and the hasty adjustment of her ringlets, might have suggested to an observer, that she hoped to receive in her visitor one who had an eye for beauty; and the sudden change that passed over her countenance as she entered the parlor in which her two guardians sat in earnest talk, would have awakened strong suspicions that she did not see the Mr. Grahame whom she had expected. Mr. Trevanion rose as she entered, and shaking hands with Mr. Grahame, said kindly, "I leave you with Lilian, Mr. Grahame, but I hope to see you again at dinner we dine at five."

"Thank you, sir, but I hope to be taking tea with my good woman at home at that hour."

"Well, I shall hope to see you again soon you must call often and see your friend Lilian."

"Why, I've been thinking, sir, that that would hardly be best for any of us and to tell the truth, I came to-day to talk with Lilian about that very thing, and if you please, I have no objection that you should hear what I have to say."

Mr. Trevanion seated himself again, and Lilian placing herself on the sofa beside him, Mr. Grahame resumed: "It seems to me, sir, that Lilian has to choose between two kinds of life, which, should she try to put them together will only spoil one another, and I want her to have a fair chance to judge between them. Now, you know, sir, I speak the truth when I say that there are many among the fine gay people whom Lilian will meet at your house, who would look down upon her for having such friends as I and my wife, or even my son, though President B says he will be a distinguished man yet."

"I do not care for such people, or for what they think," exclaimed Lilian indignantly.

"I dare say not, my dear child, and yet they are people who are thought a great deal of, and whom, if you are to live amongst them, it would be worth your while to please but that isn't my main point, Lilian. What I want to say, though I seem to be long coming at it, is, that I want you to see this gay life that fine folks in the city lead, at its best without any such drawbacks as it would have for you, if you were suspected of having ungenteel acquaintances, and so we shall none of us come to see you barring you should be sick, or something else happen to make you want us until you make a fair trial, for six months at least, of this life then should the beautiful, rich Miss Devoe like the old gardener and his family well enough to come and see them, she will learn how fondly and truly they love their Lilian."

"I had hoped you loved her too well to give her up so needlessly for six months, or even for one month," said Lilian, tears rushing to her eyes.

"Ask Mr. Trevanion if I am not right in what I have said, my dear child," said Mr. Grahame tenderly.

"I will not dispute the correctness of your principles in the main, Mr. Grahame, but I hope you do not think that all Lilian's fine acquaintances as you call them, would be so unjust in their judgment as to think the less of her for her love of you, or to undervalue you on account of your position in life."

"No sir no sir I don't think so of all but I want Lilian to see this life without even one little cloud upon it such a cloud as the being looked down upon, though it were by people she didn't greatly admire, would make. We have our pride too, sir, and we want Lilian to try for herself whether our friendship, with all its good and its bad, be worth keeping. She is too good and affectionate, we know, to shake off old friends that love her, even if they become troublesome but we will draw ourselves off, and then she will be free to come back to us or not, as she pleases. Now, sir, tell me frankly, if you think me wrong."

"Not wrong in principle, as I said before, Mr. Grahame, but excuse me you required me to be frank would it not have been better to have made this withdrawal gradually and quietly, in such a manner that Lilian would not have noticed it, instead of giving her the pain of this abrupt severance of the ties between you?"

"A great deal better, sir," said Mr. Grahame, coloring with wonderful feeling, and fixing his clear, keen eye full on Mr. Trevanion, "a great deal better if I wished to sever those ties a great deal better if I would have Lilian believe that we had grown cold and indifferent to her. But, my dear child," and he turned to her, and taking both her hands, spoke very earnestly "believe me, when I tell you, that you will find few among those who see you every day, that love you so warmly as the friends who have loved you from your birth, and who now stand away from you only because they will not be in the way of what the world considers higher fortunes for you if you desire them. To leave you free to choose for yourself, is the strongest proof of love we could give you, and I repeat, when you have tried all that this new life has to give you tried it for six months if your heart still turns with its old love to those early friends, you will give them joy indeed."

Mr. Grahame paused, but neither Mr. Trevanion nor Lilian attempted to reply to him for some minutes at length she raised her eyes, and said,

"You did not think of this when I left you what has changed your mind I will not say your heart towards me?"

"You are right not to say our hearts, Lilian; but, indeed, even my mind has not been changed I thought then as I think now but I could not persuade others of our family to think with me. Now, however, they all feel that they cannot keep up their old friendly intercourse with you without mortification to themselves, and pain to you. And, as I said before, we were none of us willing to withdraw from that intercourse without giving you our reasons for it, lest you should think we had grown indifferent to you."

Mr. Grahame soon departed, leaving Lilian saddened and Mr. Trevanion perplexed by his visit. "Singular old man!" this gentleman exclaimed to himself more than once, in reflecting on all that Mr. Grahame had said; so difficult is it for those whose minds have been forced into the strait forms of conventionalism to comprehend the dictates of untrammelled common sense, on points which that conventionalism undertakes to control. One thing at least Mr. Trevanion did comprehend that on the succeeding six months depended Lilian's choice of her position and associates for life.

"So far Mr. Grahame is right Lilian," he said to her, "you cannot have a place at once in two such different spheres as his and ours. I always knew that to be impossible."

"You called my father friend," said Lilian, with unusual boldness.

"Your father was a gentleman by birth and breeding."

"And he has told me," persisted Lilian, "that he has never known more true refinement and even nobility of mind than in Mr. Grahame."

"I agree with him of mind, mark but there is a want of conventional refinement which would make itself felt in society."

"There is no want even of this in his son," said Lilian with a trembling voice, and turning away to hide the blush that burned upon her cheek.

"Probably not, for Michael Grahame has been for years at the best schools, with the sons of our first families but we cannot separate him from his father, and from the associates which his trade has given him."

Neither Mr. Trevanion nor Lilian ever spoke on this subject again; but the former resolved that no effort should be lost on his part to restore one so beautiful and so accomplished as his young ward to what he considered her true place in society, and the latter was as firmly determined that nothing should make her forgetful of the friends of her childhood. In furtherance of this resolve, Mr. Trevanion, instead of retiring to his country-seat with his family on the approach of summer, sent his younger children thither under the care of their faithful and intelligent nurse; and with Mrs. and Miss Trevanion, and Lilian, set out for Saratoga, at that season the great focus of fashion. Mrs. Trevanion, entering fully into his designs, had attended to Lilian's equipments for this important campaign, with no less care than to Anna's, and the result equalled their fondest expectations. Lilian was the beauty, the heiress, the belle of the season. Report exaggerated her fortune, appended all sorts of romantic incidents to her history and her connection with the Trevanions, and thus increased the interest which her own beauty and modest elegance was calculated to awaken. Admirers crowded around her, and to render her triumph complete, one who had hitherto found no charms in America worthy his homage, bowed at her shrine. This was Mr. Derwent, an Englishman of high birth and large fortune, whose elegant exterior, and the perfect savoir faire which marked his manners, made him at Saratoga,

"The observed of all observers,
The glass of fashion and the mould of form."

Mr. Trevanion looked on with scarcely concealed delight.

"Why, father! do you wish to see Lilian leave us for England?" cried Anna Trevanion, to whom he had expressed his satisfaction.

"Certainly, my daughter, if only in that way I can see her take that position which is hers by inheritance, and from which only her father's misfortunes have estranged her."

But Mr. Trevanion's hopes of so desirable a termination of his cares for Lilian faded, as he saw the reserve with which she met the attentions of her admirers not excepting even the admired Mr. Derwent.

"Among the beauties at this place, Miss L D , the ward of Mr. T , stands unrivalled. She is an heiress as well as a beauty, but the report is that both the fortune and the beauty are to be borne to another land, in the possession of the Honorable Mr. D , whose personal qualities, united to his station and fortune, render him, in the opinion of the ladies at least, irresistible."

Such was the paragraph in a New-York daily paper, which Mr. Trevanion one morning handed to Lilian with a smile. She read it silence, and laid it down without a comment, except that which was furnished by the proud erection of her figure, and the almost scornful curl of her lip.

When next she met Mr. Derwent, Mr. Trevanion's eye was on her, for he thought, "She cannot preserve her perfect indifference of manner with the consciousness that their names have been thus associated." He was mistaken. The color on Lilian's cheek deepened not at Mr. Derwent's approach, nor did her hand tremble as she laid it upon the arm he offered in attending her to dinner. "Her heart must be already occupied," said Mr. Trevanion to himself, and perhaps he was right in believing that nothing but a deep and true affection one which was founded on no adventitious circumstances, but on the immovable basis of esteem could have enabled her to resist the blandishments which surrounded her in her present position. But she did resist them, and still, from the luxurious elegancies, the gay entertainments and the flatteries of fashionable life, her heart turned with undiminished tenderness to the tranquil shades of Mossgiel, and still paid there its willing homage to the loftiest intellect and the noblest heart, in her estimation, with which earth was blessed.

September, with its cool, invigorating freshness, had come, when Mr. Trevanion's family returned to the city. To Lilian's great, though unspoken disappointment, the children met them there, and no thought seemed to be entertained of a visit to the country. Carefully she had kept the date of Mr. Grahame's conversation, in which he had demanded that she should make a six months' trial of life, freed from the associations which her early poverty had fastened on her. In a few weeks after her return to New-York, the six months were completed. On the day preceding its exact completion, Lilian expressed to Mr. Trevanion her wish to visit Mossgiel. "It is now six months," she said with a blush and a smile, "since I saw Mr. Grahame."

Whatever might have been Mr. Trevanion's wishes for his ward, he had neither the right nor the will to control her actions, and he not only consented to her going, but went down with her himself to Trevanion Hall, where they arrived late in the evening.

Lilian knew that the inhabitants of Mossgiel kept early hours, and the gay pink and blue and white convolvuluses, which arched the rude gate leading from the more public road into the rural lane by which their house was approached, had just unfolded their petals, when she rode through it on the morning succeeding her arrival at Trevanion Hall. She had declined the attendance of a servant, and set off at a brisk canter, but soon reined in her horse and proceeded at a slower pace. Hope and fear were busy at her heart. Six months! What changes might not have taken place in that time! Again Lilian touched her horse with her light riding-whip, and rode briskly on till she reached the gate of which we have spoken. Here she alighted to open the gate. As she entered the lane she saw, not far in advance of her, a boy who had been hired to assist Mr. Grahame in the garden. She called to him, and giving him her bridle to lead her horse to the stable, walked on herself towards the house, which was little more than a hundred yards distant. After walking a few steps, she turned to ask, "Are Mr. and Mrs. Grahame well?"

Another question trembled on her lips but she could not speak it. "If he love me, he will be here," she whispered to herself, and again passed on. The road wound around the house, and led to the entrance on the river front. There was a side gate leading to the garden, and there, at that hour, Lilian knew she would most probably meet the elder Mr. Grahame, while his wife was almost certain to be found in the dairy, to which the same gate would give her access; but the gate was passed with a light, quick step, and Lilian entered the house at the front. With a fluttering heart, but a steady purpose, she passed on, without meeting any one, or hearing a sound, to the usual morning room. The door was open; she entered, and her heart throbbed exultingly, for he was there. Michael Grahame sat at a table writing. His back was towards the door, and her light step had given no notice of her presence. Agitated by a thousand commingled emotions, wishing, yet dreading to meet his eye, she stood gazing on his face as it was reflected in an opposite mirror. It seemed to her paler and graver than of yore. Manhood had stamped its lines more deeply on the brow since last they parted. But some movement, a sigh, perhaps, from her, has startled him. He raises his head, and in the mirror their eyes meet. In that glance her whole soul has been revealed, and with one glad cry of "Lilian! my Lilian!" he turns, and she is folded in his arms.

There was no more doubt, no more fear, on her part no concealment on his. She had chosen freely and nobly, and she was rewarded by love as deep, as devoted, and as unselfish as ever woman inspired, or man felt.

The marriage of Lilian, which took place in three months after her return to Mossgiel, could not but excite some interest in the world in which she had so lately occupied a conspicuous place. When, however, to the great question "Who is this Mr. Grahame?" the answer, "Nothing but a mechanic," was received the interest soon faded away, and in the winter Lilian found herself in New-York, with scarcely an acquaintance, except the Trevanions, and she could easily perceive that something of pity was mingled with their former kindness. Yet never had Lilian been less an object of pity. Every day increased not only her affection to her husband, but her pride in him, by revealing to her more of his high powers and noble qualities. Those powers had received a new spring from his desire to prove himself worthy of his cherished wife. He had long been occupied with a problem whose solution, he believed, would enable him to increase greatly both the speed and safety of steam navigation. In the early part of the winter succeeding his marriage, with a glad spirit, with which Lilian fully sympathized, he cried "Eureka." Before the winter concluded he had been to Washington, and explaining to the officers of our own government the importance of his invention, sought permission to test it on a government vessel. After many delays, with that short-sighted policy which cannot look beyond the present expense to the overpaying results, the proposition was declined. During his stay in Washington, his object had become noised abroad, and the Russian Minister had opened a correspondence with him and with his own court on the subject. The result of this correspondence was, that in the following spring Michael Grahame sailed for Russia, to test his invention first in the service of its emperor. He was accompanied by Lilian. Their departure and its object were talked of for awhile, but soon ceased to be remembered, except by men of science, and those immediately interested in the result of his experiment.

In the mean time Anna Trevanion married. Her husband, Mr. Walker, was a man of large property, and of social position equal to her own. They spent the first two years of their married life abroad. It was in the second of these two years, and when Lilian had been four years in St. Petersburgh, that Mr. and Mrs. Walker entered that city. One of their first inquiries of the American Minister was, "What Americans are here?" and at the head of the list he presented, stood Mr. and Mrs. Grahame. "And who are Mr. and Mrs. Grahame?" asked Mr. Walker. "You say they are from New-York, and I remember no such names of any consequence in society there."

"I do not know what their consequence was there, but I assure you it is as great here as the partiality of the Emperor, the favor of the Imperial family, and their association with the highest rank, can make it."

"But how did people unknown at home work themselves into such a position?"

"They did not work themselves into it all they took it at once, by the only right which Americans have to any position abroad the right of their own fitness for it. Mr. Grahame, besides his high attainments in science, and his skill in mechanics, which first introduced him to the Emperor, is a man of fine appearance, of very extensive information, and very agreeable manners, and Mrs. Grahame is one of the most beautiful and cultivated women I know. I repeat, you cannot enter society here under better auspices than theirs."

And thus the long-severed friends met in reversed positions; and if something of triumph did flash from Lilian's eyes, as she saw her husband, day after day, procuring from the Emperor's favor, privileges for Mr. and Mrs. Walker, not often enjoyed by strangers, her triumph was for him, and may be excused.

After eight years spent in Russia, during which he had acquired fortune as well as fame, Michael Grahame returned to America, with his wife and three lovely children, and retired to a beautiful country seat within a mile of Mossgiel, purchased and furnished for him during his absence. His father still cultivates his garden, though he has ceased to sell its produce, and through those flowery walks Lilian and her husband still delight to wander, recalling the happy memories with which they are linked, with grateful and adoring hearts.

"I shall never object again to any woman in whom I am interested, marrying the man of her choice, because he is only a mechanic," said Mrs. Trevanion to her husband, as they were returning one day from a visit to Mr. and Mrs. Grahame.

"There, my dear, in those words, only a mechanic, lies our mistake, the world's mistake, in such matters. No man is only what his trade, his profession, or his position in life makes him. Every man is something besides this, something by force of his own inherent personal qualities. By these the true man is formed, and by these he should be judged."

CHAPTER XII

Again we were all assembled in the parlor in which so many of our cheerful evenings had been spent, but a shadow seemed to have fallen on our little circle. The New-Year was now close in its approach, and immediately after the commencement of the New-Year we must separate. Mr. and Mrs. Dudley, with their children, and Mr. and Mrs. Seagrove, with theirs, and Mr. Arlington and I, must all leave within a day or two of each other, and a year, with all its chances and changes, will probably intervene before we meet again. The very thought, as I have said, threw a shadow upon us; but Col. Donaldson, who is a most inveterate foe to sadness, would not suffer us to yield unresistingly to its influence. If our time was short, the greater necessity for crowding enjoyment into its every moment, he said: we could spare none of it for lamentations.

"Now, Aunt Nancy," he continued, "if I am not mistaken, you can match Mr. Arlington's story with one quite as romantic, of an extraordinary marriage in high life. Do you remember Lady Houstoun and her son Edward Houstoun "

"Oh, yes!" I cried, interrupting him, "and the beautiful Lucy Watson too."

"Then I am sure you must have their story somewhere in your bundle of romances."

"I believe I have," I replied, as opening my desk I drew out package after package, the amusement of many an hour, which but for such a resource might have been sad in its loneliness. Some were looking fresh and new, and others yellow from age. Among the latter was that for which I was searching, and which Annie insists that I shall give to the reader, under the title of

LOVE AND PRIDE

A proud and stately dame was Lady Houstoun, as she continued to be called after the independence of America had rendered such titles valueless in our land. Sir Edward Houstoun was an English baronet, whose estates had once been a fit support to his ancient title, but whose family had suffered deeply, both in purse and person, by their loyalty to Charles the First, and yet more by their obstinate adherence to his bigot son, James II. By a marriage with Louisa Vivian, an American heiress possessed of broad lands and a large amount of ready money, Sir Edward acquired the power of supporting his rank with all the splendor that had belonged to his family in the olden time; but circumstances connected with the poverty of his early years had given the young baronet a disgust to his own circle, which was not alleviated by the rapid changes effected by his newly-acquired wealth, and he preferred returning to America with his young bride, and adopting her country as his own. Here wealth sufficient for their most extravagant desires was theirs houses in New-York, and fertile acres stretching far away from the city, now sweeping for many a rood the banks of the fair Hudson, and now reaching back into the rich lands that lie east of that river. When the separation of this country from England came, the representative of her most loyal family, whose motto was "Dieu et mon Roi" was found in the ranks of republican America. "He could not," he said, "recognize a divine right in the House of Hanover to the throne of the Stuarts, or justify by any human reason the blind subservience of Americans to the ruinous enactments of an English parliament, controlled by a rash and headstrong minister and a wayward king." Ten years after the proclamation of peace Sir Edward died, leaving one son who had just entered his twentieth year.

Young as Edward Houstoun was, he had a man's decision of character; and when the question of his assuming his father's title, and claiming the estates attached to it in England, was submitted to him, he replied that "his proudest title was that of an American citizen, and he would not forfeit that title to become a royal duke." He could therefore inherit only his father's personal property, consisting principally of plate, jewels and paintings. The property thus received was all which the young Edward Houstoun could call his own. All else was his mother's, and though it would doubtless be his at her death, the Lady Houstoun was not one to relinquish the reins of government before that inevitable hour should wrest them from her hand. She made her son a very handsome allowance, however, and, with a higher degree of generosity than any pecuniary grant could evince, she never attempted to control his actions, suffering him to enjoy his sports in the country and amusements in the city without constraint. The Lady Houstoun was a wise woman, as well as an affectionate mother. She saw well that her son's independent and proud nature might be attracted by kindness to move whither she would, while the very appearance of constraint would drive him in an opposite direction. On one subject he greatly tried her forbearance the unbecoming levity, as she esteemed it, with which he regarded the big-wigged gentlemen and hooped and farthingaled ladies whose portraits ornamented their picture gallery. For only one of these did Edward profess the slightest consideration. This was that of the simple soldier whose gallantry under William the Conqueror had laid the foundation of his family fortunes and honors.

"Dear mother," said he one day, "what proof have we that those other fine gentlemen and ladies deserved the wealth and station which, through his noble qualities, they obtained?"

"Sir James Houstoun, my son, who devoted life and fortune to his king."

"Pardon me, noble Sir James," interrupted Edward, bowing low and with mock gravity to the portrait, "I will place you and your stern-looking son there at your side next in my veneration to our first ancestor. Yet you showed that, like me, you had little value for wealth or station."

"Edward!" ejaculated Lady Houstoun, in an accent of displeasure, "that we are willing to sacrifice a possession at the call of duty does not prove us insensible of its value."

"Nay, mother mine, speak not so gravely, but acknowledge that you would be prouder of your boy if you saw him by his own energies winning his way to distinction from earth's lowliest station, than you can be of him now idler as he is."

"There is no less merit, Edward, in using aright the gifts which we inherit, than in acquiring them. There is as much energy, I can assure you, demanded in the proper management of large estates, and the right direction of the influence derived from station ay, often more energy, the exercise of higher powers, than those by which a fortunate soldier, in time of war, may often spring in a day from nameless poverty to wealth and rank."

The Lady Houstoun's still fine figure was elevated to its utmost height as she spoke, and her dark eye flashed out from beneath the shadow of the deep borders of her widow's cap. A stranger would have gazed on her with admiration, but her son turned away with a slight shrug of the shoulders and a curling lip, as he said to himself, "My mother may feel all this, for she manages the estates, and she bestows the influence while I amuse myself. Mother," he added aloud, "they say there is fine sport in the neighborhood of the Glen, and I should like to see the place. I will take a party thither next week, if you will write to your farmer to prepare the house for us."

"I will, Edward, certainly, if you desire it, but it has been so long since any of us were there, that I fear you will find the house very uncomfortable."

"So much the better, if it give us a little variety in our smooth lives. I dare say we shall all like it very much. I shall, at least, and if the rest do not, they can return."

The Glen was a wild rural spot among the Highlands, where Sir Edward had delighted occasionally to spend a few weeks with his wife and child and one or two chosen friends, in the enjoyment of country sports. For several years before his father's death, Edward had been too much engaged in his collegiate studies to share these visits. During the three years which had passed since that event, neither Lady Houstoun nor her son had visited the Glen, and it was not without emotion that she heard him name his intention of taking a party thither; but she offered no opposition to the plan, and in a little more than a week he was established in the comfortable dwelling-house there, with Walter Osgood; Philip Van Schaick, and Peter Schuyler, companions who were soon persuaded to leave the somewhat formal circles of the city for a few days of adventure in the country. They had arrived late in the night, and wearied by fifteen hours' confinement on board a small sloop, the visitors slept late the next morning, while Edward Houstoun, haunted by tender memories, was early awake and abroad. Standing in the porch, he looked forth through the gray light of the early dawn on hill and dale and river, endeavoring to recall the feelings with which he had gazed on them seven years before. Then he was a boy of scarcely sixteen, eager only for the holiday sport or the distinction of the school-room now, he stood there a boy still, his heart indignantly pronounced, though he had numbered nearly twenty-three years. Edward Houstoun was beginning to wake to somewhat of noble scorn in viewing his own position beginning to feel that to amuse himself was an object hardly worthy a man's life. Turning forcibly from such thoughts, he sprang down the steps, and pursued a path leading by the orchard and through a flowery lane, towards the dwelling of the farmer to whom the management of the Glen had been intrusted, first by Sir Edward and afterwards by Lady Houstoun. The sun was just touching with a sapphire tint the few clouds that specked the eastern sky; the branches of the wild rose and mountain laurel which skirted the lane on the right were heavy with the dews of night, and the birds seemed caroling their earliest song in the orchard and clover-field on the left, yet the farmer's horses were already harnessed to the wagon, and through the open door of the house Edward Houstoun as he approached caught a glimpse of Farmer Pye himself and his men seated at breakfast. As he was not perceived by them, he passed on, without interrupting them, to the dairy, where the good dame was busy with her white pails and bright pans. A calico bonnet with a very deep front concealed his approach from Mrs. Pye until he stood beside her; but there was one within the dairy who saw him, and whose coquettish movement in snatching from her glossy brown ringlets a bonnet of the same unbecoming shape with that of Mrs. Pye, did not escape his observation.

"Well, now did I ever see the like! Why, Mr. Edward, you've grown clean out of a body's memory but after all, nobody couldn't help knowing you that ever seen your papa, good gentleman how much you are like him!"

Thus ran on Dame Pye, while Edward, except when compelled by a question to attend to her, was wondering who the fair girl could be, who was separated from her companion not less by the tasteful arrangement of her dress simple and even coarse as it was in its material and by a certain grace of movement, than by her delicate beauty. Her form was slender in proportion to its height, yet gave in its graceful outline promise of a development "rich in all woman's loveliness;" and her face, with its dark starry eyes, its clear, transparent skin, and rich, waving curls of glossy brown, recalled so vividly to Edward Houstoun's memory his favorite description of beauty, that he repeated almost audibly:

> "One shade the more, one ray the less,
> Had half impair'd the nameless grace
> That waves in every glossy tress,
> Or softly lightens o'er her face,
> Where thoughts serenely sweet express
> How pure, how dear their dwelling-place."

His admiration, if not audible, was sufficiently evident to its object at least so we interpret her tremulous and uncertain movements, the eloquent blood which glowed in her cheeks, and the mistakes which at length aroused Mrs. Pye's attention.

"Why, Lucy! what under the sun and earth's the matter with you, child? Dear dear to go putting the cream into the new milk, instead of emptying it into the churn! There there child better go in now I'll finish and just tell Mr. Pye that Mr. Edward is here," said Mrs. Pye, fearful of some new accident.

The discarded bonnet was put on with a heightened color, and the young girl moved rapidly yet gracefully toward the house.

"I did not remember you had a daughter, Mrs. Pye," said Edward Houstoun, as she disappeared.

"And I haven't a daughter only the two boys, Sammy and Isaac good big boys they are now, and help their father quite some but this girl's none of mine, though I'm sure I love her 'most as well she's so pretty and nice, and has such handy ways, though what could have tempted her to put the cream in the new milk just now, I'm sure I can't tell."

"But who is she, Mrs. Pye?"

"Who is she? Why, sure, and did you never hear of Lucy Watson? Oh! here's Mr. Pye."

Edward Houstoun was too much interested in learning something more of Lucy Watson, not to find a sufficient reason for lingering behind the farmer, who was impatient to be in his hay-field. Mrs. Pye was communicative, and he soon learned all she knew that Lucy was the daughter of a soldier belonging to a company commanded by Sir Edward Houstoun during the war that this soldier had received his death-wound in defending his commander from a sword-cut, and that Sir Edward had always considered his widow and only child as his especial charge. The widow had soon followed her husband to the grave, and the child had been placed by Sir Edward with the wife of a country clergyman. To Mr. and Mrs. Merton, Lucy had been as an own and only daughter.

"The good old people made quite a lady of her," said Mrs. Pye. "She can read and write equal to the parson himself, and I've hearn folks say that her 'broidery and music playin' was better than Mrs. Merton's own; but, poor thing! Mrs. Merton died, and still the parson begged Sir Edward to let her stay with him she was all that was left now, he said so Sir Edward let her stay. Mr. Merton died a year ago, and when Mr. Pye wrote to the lady that's your mother, Mr. Edward about her, she said she'd better come here and stay with us, and she would pay her board, and give her money for clothes, and five thousand dollars beside, whenever she should get married. I'm sure she's welcome to stay, if it was without pay, for we all love her, but, somehow, it don't seem the right place for her and, as to marrying, I don't think she'll ever marry any body around her, for, kind-spoken as she is, they wouldn't any of them dare to ask her, though they're all in love with her beautiful face."

In a week Edward Houstoun's friends had grown weary of ruralizing they found no longer any music in the crack of a fowling-piece, or any enjoyment in the dying agonies of the feathered tribes, and, having resisted all their persuasions to return with them, he was left alone.

"I shall report you as love-sick, or brain-sick, reclining by purling streams, under shady groves, to read Shakspeare, or Milton, or Spenser, for each of these books I have seen you at different times put in your pocket, and wander forth with a most sentimental air doubtless to make love to some Nymph or Dryad."

"Make love! Ah! there, I take it, you have winged the right bird, Van Schaick."

"If I had seen a decent petticoat since we took leave of Mynheer Van Winkle and his daughter, on board the good sloop St. Nicholas, I should think so too, Osgood."

"At any rate, it would be wise to report our suspicions to his lady mother."

"Your suspicions of what lunacy or love?" asked Edward Houstoun.

"A distinction without a difference they are equivalent terms."

Thus jested his friends, and thus jested Edward Houstoun with them well assured that no gleam of the truth had shined on them that they never supposed his visits at Farmer Pye's possessed any greater attraction than could be derived from the farmer's details of improvements made at the Glen, of the increased value of lands, or the proceeds of the last year's crop. They had never seen Lucy Watson, and how could they suspect that while the farmer smoked his pipe at the door, and the good dame bustled about her household concerns, he sat watching with enamored eyes the changes of a countenance full of intelligence and sensibility, and listening with charmed ears to a soft, musical voice recounting, with all the simple eloquence of genuine feeling, obligations to the father whose memory was with him almost an idolatry. Still less could they divine that Shakspeare, and Milton, and Spenser were indeed often read beside a purling stream, and within the dense shadow of a grove of oak and chestnut-trees not to Nymph or Dryad, but to a "mortal being of earth's mould,"

> "A creature not too bright or good
> For human nature's daily food,
> For simple pleasures, harmless wiles,
> For love, blame, kisses, tears and smiles."

Here, one afternoon, a fortnight after the departure of his friends, sat Edward Houstoun with Lucy at his side. They had lingered till the sunlight, which had fallen here and there in broken and changeful gleams through over-arching boughs, touching with gold the ripples at their feet, had faded into that

"mellow light
Which heaven to gaudy day denies."

Edward Houstoun held a book in his hand, but it had long been closed, while he was engaged in a far more interesting study. He had with a delicate tact won his companion to speak as she had never spoken before of herself not of the few events of her short life, for these were already known to him, but of the influence of those events on feeling and character. Tenderness looked forth without disguise from the earnest eyes which were fastened on her, as he said, "You say, Lucy, that you have found friends every where, have met only kindness, and yet you weep you are sad."

"Do not think me ungrateful," she replied. "I have indeed found friends and kindness but these give exercise only to my gratitude stronger, tenderer affections I have, which no father, or mother, or brother, or sister, will ever call forth."

"Nay, Lucy, were you not adopted by my father, and am I not your brother?"

A glance whose brightness melted into tears was her only answer.

"Fie! fie! tears again? I shall have to scold my sister," said Edward Houstoun. "What complaint can you make now that I have found you a brother?"

Lucy laughed, but soon her face grew grave, and, after a thoughtful pause, she said, "I believe those cannot be quite happy who feel that they have nothing to do in the world. Better be the poorest drudge, with powers fitted to your station, than to be as I am, an idler a mere looker-on at the world."

"Why, Lucy! what else am I?"

"You! You, with fortune to bless, and influence to guide hundreds! What are you? God's representative to your less fortunate fellow-creatures the steward of his bounty. Oh! be sure that you use your gifts faithfully."

Lucy spoke solemnly, and it was with no light accent that Edward Houstoun replied "You mistake, Lucy you mistake I am in truth no less an idler than yourself a looker-on, with no part in the game of life. To the Lady Houstoun belong both the fortune and the influence." A mocking smile had arisen to his lip, but, as he caught her look of surprise, it passed away, leaving a gentle gravity in its place, while he continued "Do not think I mean to complain of my mother, Lucy. She has been ever affectionate and indulgent to me. She leaves me no want that she can perceive. My purse is always full, and my actions unrestrained. I suppose I ought to be happy."

"And are you not happy?"

"No, Lucy, no! There has long been a vague restlessness and dissatisfaction about me and, now, your words have thrown light on its cause. I am weary of the perpetual holiday which life has been to me since I left the walls of a college. I want to be doing I want an object something for which to strive and hope and fear what shall it be, Lucy?"

"I have heard Mr. Merton say that no one could choose for another his aims in life, but were I choosing for myself, it should be something that would connect me with the minds of others something by which I could do service to their spiritual beings. Were I a man, I should like to write books such books as would give counsel and comfort to erring and sad hearts "

Edward Houstoun shook his head "Even had I an author's gifts, Lucy, that would not do for me I must have action in my life "

"What say you to the pulpit?"

"The noblest of all employments, Lucy but it is a heavenly employment and needs a heavenly spirit. I would not dare to think of that. Try again "

"The law? Ah! now I see I have chosen rightly you will be a lawyer a great lawyer, like Mr. Patrick Henry."

"You have spoken, Lucy and I will do my best to fulfil your prophecy. I may not be a Patrick Henry two such men belong not to one age but I may at least hew out for myself a place among men, where I may stand with a man's freedom of thought and action. The very decision has emancipated me has emboldened me to speak what a moment since I scarcely dared to think nay, turn not from me, beloved oh how passionately beloved! Life has now its object for me, Lucy your love for that I will strive hope whisper me that I need not fear that when I have a right to claim my bride "

When Edward Houstoun commenced this passionate apostrophe, he had clasped Lucy's hand, and, overcome by his emotions and her own forgetting all but his love conscious only of a bewildering joy she had suffered it to rest for one instant in his clasp. It was but for one instant the next, struggling from him as he strove to retain her, she started to her feet, and stood leaning against the trunk of the tree that overshadowed them, with her face hidden by her clasped hands. He rose and drew near, saying, in low, tremulous tones "Lucy, what means this?"

"Mr. Houstoun," she exclaimed, removing her hands from her face, and wringing them in passionate sorrow "how could you speak those words?"

"Wherefore should I not speak them are they so terrifying to you, Lucy?"

"Can they be otherwise, since they must separate us for ever? Think you that the Lady Houstoun would endure that the creature of her bounty should become the wife of her son?"

"I asked, Lucy, that you would promise to be mine when I had won a right to act independently of the Lady Houstoun's opinions."

"Has a son ever a right to act independently of a mother?"

"Is the obedience of a child to be exacted from a man? Is his happiness ever to be at the mercy of another's prejudices? Does there never come a period when he may be permitted to judge for himself?"

Edward Houstoun spoke with indignant emphasis.

"Look not so sternly speak not so angrily," exclaimed Lucy. "I cannot answer your questions but my obligations, at least, are irreversible they belong to the irrevocable past, and while I retain their memory I can never "

"Hush hush, Lucy! you will drive me mad. Is my happiness of less value in your eyes than the few paltry dollars my mother expended for you?"

"Shall I, serpent-like, sting the hand that has fed me? No! no! would I had never heard those words. We were so happy you will be happy again but I leave me, I pray you, for we must part now and for ever oh! leave me."

"No, Lucy, we will never part I will never leave you."

He would again have drawn her to his side, but at his touch, Lucy roused herself, and with a wild, half-frenzied effort, breaking from him, she rushed rapidly, blindly forward. He would have followed her, but stumbling against the root of a tree, before he could recover himself she was at the outskirts of the wood, in sight of the farm-house, and though he might overtake he could not detain her. He returned home, not overwhelmed with disappointment, but with joy throbbing at his heart, and hope beaming in his eyes. Lucy loved him of that he felt assured and bucklered by that assurance he could stand against the world. Life was before him a life not of sickly pleasures and ennui breeding indolence but a life of contest and struggle and labor, perhaps even of exhausting labor, yet a life which should awaken and discipline his powers: a life of victory and of repose sweet because won with effort a life to which Lucy's love should give its crowning joy. Such are youth's dreams. In his case these dreams were somewhat rudely dispelled by a summons from his mother's physician. Lady Houstoun was ill very ill he must not delay, said the physician; and he did not; yet a hastily pencilled line told that even at this moment Lucy was not forgotten it was a farewell which breathed love and faith and hope.

On Edward Houstoun's arrival in New-York, he found his mother already recovering from the acute attack which had endangered her life and occasioned his recall. He soon unfolded to her his new views of life, and the career which he had marked out for himself. New views indeed new and incomprehensible to Lady Houstoun! She saw not that the life of indulgence, the perpetual gala-day, which she anticipated for her son, would have condemned him to see his highest powers dwindle away and die in the lethargy of inaction, or to waste in repinings against fate those energies given to command success. Time moderated her astonishment, and quiet perseverance subdued her opposition subdued it the more readily, perhaps, from the knowledge that her son could accomplish his designs without her aid, by turning into money the plate, jewels and pictures received from his father. Edward Houstoun's first act, after securing the execution of his designs, was to inform Lucy of the progress he had made. His own absence from New-York at this time would have excited his mother's surprise, and might have aroused her suspicions; but the haste with which he had left the Glen furnished him with a plausible excuse for sending his own man to look after clothing, books, &c., that had been forgotten, and by him a letter could, he knew, be safely sent.

A few days brought back to him his own letter, with the intelligence that Lucy had left Farmer Pye's family. Whither she had gone, they could not, or would not tell. Setting all fears at defiance, he went himself to the Glen he sounded and examined and cross-examined every member of the farmer's family; but in vain were his efforts. He learned only that she had declared her intention of supporting herself by her own exertions, instead of continuing dependent on the Lady Houstoun that she had returned the lady's last donation, through the farmer, with many expressions of gratitude, and that she had left home for the house of an acquaintance in New-York, from whom she hoped to receive advice and assistance in the accomplishment of her intentions. She had mentioned neither the name nor place of residence of this friend, and though she had written once to the good farmer, she had only informed him that she had found a home and employment, without reference to any person or place. Edward asked to see the letter it was brought, but the post-mark told no secret it was that of the nearest post town, and the farmer, opening the letter, showed that Lucy had said she had requested the bearer to drop it into that office. Who that bearer was, none knew. Bitter was the disappointment of Edward Houstoun. A beautiful vision had crossed his path, had awakened his noblest impulses, kindled his passionate devotion, and then vanished for ever. But she had left ineradicable traces of her presence. His awakened energies, his passionate longings, his altered life, all gave assurance that she had been that the bright ideal of womanly beauty and tenderness, and gentleness and firmness, which lived in his memory, was no dream of fancy. He anticipated little pleasure now from the pursuits on which he had lately determined, but his pride forbade him to relinquish them, and when once they had been commenced, finding in mental occupation his Lethe, he abandoned himself to them with all his accustomed ardor.

Two years passed away with Edward Houstoun in the most intense intellectual action, and in death-like torpor of the affections. From the last his mother might have saved him, had not her want of sympathy with his pursuits occasioned a barrier of reserve and coolness to arise between them fatal to her influence. During this time no token of Lucy's existence had reached him: and it was with such a thrill as might have welcomed a visitant from the dead, that, one morning as he left his own house to proceed to the office in which he pursued his studies, he saw before him at some distance, yet without any intervening object to interrupt his view of her, a form and face resembling hers, though thinner and paler. The lady was approaching him, with slow and languid steps; but as her eyes were fixed upon the ground she did not perceive him, and just as his throbbing heart exclaimed, "It is Lucy," and he sprang forward to greet her, she entered a house and the door closed on her. The inmates of that house were but slightly known to him, as they had only lately moved into the street, yet he hesitated not an instant in ringing the bell, and inquiring of the servant who presented himself at the door, for Miss Watson.

"Miss Watson, sir?" repeated the man, "there is no such person living here."

"She may not live here, but I saw her enter your door, and I wish to speak to her." At this moment Lucy crossed the hall at its further end, and he sprang forward, exclaiming "Lucy Miss Watson thank Heaven I see you once more!"

A slight scream from Lucy, and the tremor which shook her frame, showed her recognition of him. She leaned for an instant against the wall, too faint for speech or action, while he clasped her hand in his; but a voice broke in upon his raptures and her agitation a sharp, angry voice, coming from a lady who, leaning over the balustrade of the stairs, had seen and heard all that was passing below.

"Lucy Lucy come up here I am waiting for you this is certainly very extraordinary conduct very extraordinary indeed."

"You shall not go," said Edward Houstoun, while the red blood flushed to his brow at the thought that his Lucy could be thus ordered. Lucy's face glowed too, and there was a proud flush from her eye, yet she resisted his efforts to detain her, and when he placed himself before her to prevent her leaving him, she opened a door near her, and though he followed her quickly through it, he was just in time to see her rushing up a private staircase. He would not leave the house without an interview, and going into one of the parlors, he rang the bell, and requested to see Mrs. Blakely, the lady of the house. She came, looking very haughty and very angry. He apologized for his intrusion, but expressed a wish to see a young lady, Miss Watson, who was, he perceived, under her care. With a yet haughtier air, Mrs. Blakely replied, "I am not acquainted with any young lady of the name of Watson. Lucy Watson, the girl whom you met in the hall just now is my seamstress. If you wish to see her, I will send her down to you, though I do not generally allow my servants to receive their visitors here."

"I shall be happy to see her wherever you please," was Edward Houstoun's very truthful reply.

Mrs. Blakely left him, and he stationed himself at the door to watch for Lucy. Minutes, which seemed to him hours, passed, and she came not. At length, as he was about to ring again, steps were heard approaching; he turned quickly, but it was not Lucy. The girl who entered handed him a sealed note. He tore it open and read "I dare not see you. When you receive this I shall have left the house, and, as no one knows whither I have gone, questions would be useless."

In an instant he was in the street, looking with eager eyes hither and thither for some trace of the lost one. He looked in vain, yet he went towards his office with happier feelings than he had long known. He knew now where Lucy was, and a thousand expedients suggested themselves, by which he could not fail to see her. If he could only converse with her for a few minutes, he was assured he could prevail on her to leave her present position, of which he could not for a moment bear to think. His heart swelled, his brow flushed, whenever the remembrance of that position flashed upon his mind, yet he never for an instant regarded it as changing his relations with Lucy, or lessening his desire to call her his. He recollected with pleasure two circumstances which had scarcely been remarked at the moment of their occurrence. The man who had opened the door to him, when he saw him spring forward to meet Lucy, had exclaimed, "Oh! it was Miss Lucy you meant, sir;" and the girl who had handed the note had said, "Miss Lucy has gone out, sir." It was evident she was not regarded by the servants as one of themselves she had not been degraded by association with menials. This was true. Lucy had made such separation on her part an indispensable necessity, and Mrs. Blakely had been too sensible of the value of one possessing so much taste and skill in all feminine adornments, to hesitate about complying with her demand. This lady was one of the nouveaux riches, who occupied her life in scheming to attain a position to which neither birth nor education entitled her. The brightest dream connected with her present abode had been that its proximity to Lady Houstoun's residence might lead to an acquaintance with one of the proudest of that charmed circle in which Mrs. Blakely longed to tread. Hitherto this had proved a dream indeed, but Edward Houstoun's incursion into her domain, and the developments made by it, might, she thought, with a little address, render it a reality. It was with this purpose that she sent a note to Lady Houstoun, requesting an interview with her on a subject deeply connected with the honor of her family and the happiness of her son. Immediately on despatching this note, the servants were ordered to uncover the furniture in the drawing-room, while she herself hastened to assume her most becoming morning dress. Her labors were fruitless. "Lady Houstoun would be at home to Mrs. Blakely till noon," was the scarcely courteous reply to her carefully worded note. It was an occasion on which she could not afford to support her pride, and she availed herself of the permission to call.

The interview between Lady Houstoun and Mrs. Blakely would have been an interesting study to the nice observer of character. The efforts on the part of the one lady to be condescending, and on that of the other to be dignified, were almost equally successful. Mrs. Blakely had seldom felt her wealth of so little consequence as in the presence of her commanding yet simply attired hostess, and Lady Houstoun had never been more disposed to assert the privileges of her rank, than when she heard that her son had forgotten his own so far as to visit on terms of equality nay, if Mrs. Blakely were to be believed, positively to address in the style of a lover a seamstress the seamstress of Mrs. Blakely.

"This is very painful intelligence to me, Mrs. Blakely of course you must be aware that Mr. Houstoun could only have contemplated a temporary acquaintance with this girl. I do not fear that in his most reckless moment he could have thought of such a mésalliance but this young woman must be saved she was a protege of Sir Edward Houstoun, and for his sake must not be allowed to come to harm may I trouble you to send her to me?"

The request was given very much in the style of a command. Mrs. Blakely would not confess that she had great doubts of her power to comply with it, but this would have been sufficiently evident to any one who had marked the uncertain air and softened tone with which Lady Houstoun's wishes were made known to Lucy. Indignant as she was at Mrs. Blakely's impertinent interference, Lucy scarcely regretted Lady Houstoun's acquaintance with her son's feelings. We do not know that far below all those acknowledged impulses leading her to comply with the lady's request, there did not lie some romantic hope that influences were astir through which

"Pride might be quell'd and love be free,"
but this she did not whisper even to her own heart.

"Better that the lady should know all she will act both wisely and tenderly perhaps for her son's sake, she will aid me to leave New-York." Such was the only language into which she allowed even her thought silently to form itself.

Arranging her simple dress with as much care as though she were about to meet her lover himself, Lucy set out for her interview with Lady Houstoun. She had but a short distance to traverse, but she lingered on her way, oppressed by a tremulous anxiety. She was apprehensive of she knew not what or wherefore for again and again her heart acquitted her of all blame. At length she is at the door it opens, and, with a courtesy which the servants of Mrs. Blakely never show to a visitor who comes without carriage or attendants, she is ushered into the presence of Lady Houstoun. The lady fixes her eyes upon her as she enters, bows her head slightly in acknowledgment of her courtesy, and says coldly, "You are the young woman, I suppose, whom Mrs. Blakely was to send to me?"

Lucy paused for a moment, to still the throbbing of her heart, before she attempted to reply. The thought flashed through her mind, "I am a woman, and young, and therefore she should pity me" but she answered in a low, sweet, tremulous tone, "I am the Lucy Watson, madam, to whom Sir Edward Houstoun was so kind."

At that name a softer expression stole over the Lady Houstoun's face, and she glanced quickly at a portrait hanging over the ample fireplace, which represented a gentleman of middle age, dressed in the uniform of a colonel of the American army. As she turned her eyes again on Lucy, she saw that hers were fastened on the same object.

"You have seen Sir Edward?" she said in gentle tones.

"Seen him, lady! I loved him oh how dearly!"

"Honored him would be a more appropriate expression."

"I loved him, lady we are permitted to love our God," said Lucy, firmly.

Lady Houstoun's brow grew stern again. "And from this you argue, doubtless, that you have a right to love his son."

Lucy's pale face became crimson, and she bent her eyes to the ground without speaking the lady continued "I scarcely think that you could yourself have believed that Edward Houstoun intended to dishonor his family by a legal connection with you."

The crimson deepened on Lucy's face, but it was now the flush of pride, and raising her head she met Lady Houstoun's eyes fully as she replied "I could not believe that he ever designed to dishonor himself by ruining the orphan child of him who died in his father's defence."

"And you have intended to avail yourself of his infatuation. The menial of Mrs. Blakely would be a worthy daughter, truly, of a house which has counted nobles among its members."

"If I have resisted Mr. Houstoun's wishes separated myself from him, and resigned all hope of even looking on his face again, it has not been from the slightest reverence for the nobility of his descent, but from self-respect, from a regard to the nobleness of my own spirit. I had eaten of your bread, lady, and I could not do that which might grieve you yet the bread which had cost me so much became bitter to me, and I left the home you had provided to seek one by my own honest exertions. I have earned my bread, but not as a menial not in the companionship of the vulgar and this Mrs. Blakely could have told you."

"If your determination were, as you say, to separate yourself from Mr. Houstoun, it is unfortunate that you should have taken up your residence so near us."

"I knew not until this morning that I was near you."

"If you are sincere in what you say, you will have no objection now to leave New-York."

"I have no objection to go to any place in which I can support myself in peace."

"As to supporting yourself, that is of no consequence. I will "

"Pardon me, Lady Houstoun, it is of the utmost consequence to me. I cannot again live a dependent on your bounty."

"What can you do? Has your education been such that you can take the situation of governess?"

"Mr. Merton was a highly educated man, and Mrs. Merton an accomplished woman it was their pleasure to teach me, and mine to learn from them."

"Accomplished! There stands a harp which has just been tuned by a master for a little concert we are to have this evening. Can you play on it?"

Lucy drew the instrument to her and played an overture correctly, yet with less spirit than she would have done had her fingers trembled less.

"Can you sing?"

Elevated above all apprehension by the indignant pride which this cold and haughty questioning aroused, Lucy changed the music of the overture for a touching air, and, sang, with a rich, full voice, a single stanza of an Italian song.

"Italian! Do you understand it?"

"I have read it with Mr. Merton."

"This is fortunate. I have been for weeks in search of a governess for a friend residing in the country. I will order the carriage and take you there instantly or stay return home and put up your clothes. I will send a coach for you."

Again Lucy had vanished from Edward Houstoun's world, nor could his most munificent bribes, nor most active cross-examination win any other information from Mrs. Blakely's household, than that "Miss Lucy went away in a carriage" a carriage whose description presented a fac simile to every hackney-coach. Spite of all her precautions, he suspected his mother; to his consciousness of her want of sympathy with his pursuits, was therefore added a deep sense of injury, and his heart grew sterner, his manner colder and more reserved than ever. Two years more were passed in his studies, and a third in the long delays, the fruitless efforts which mark the entrance on any career of profitable exertion. During all this time, Lady Houstoun was studious to bring around him the loveliest daughters of affluence and rank. Graceful forms flitted through her halls, and the music of sweet voices and the gay laughter of innocent and happy hearts were heard within her rooms, but by all their attractions Edward Houstoun was unmoved. Courteous and bland to all, he never lingered by the side of one no quick flush, no flashing beam told that even for a passing moment his heart was again awake. Could it be that from all this array of loveliness he was guarded by the memory of her who had stamped the impress of herself on his whole altered being? If the gratification of the man's sterner ambition could have atoned for the disappointment of the youth's dream of love, the shadow of that memory would have passed from his life. Step by step he had risen in the opinions of men, and at length one of the most profound lawyers of the day sought his association with himself in a case of the most intense interest, involving the honor of a lovely and much-wronged woman. His reputation out of the halls of justice had already become such that many thronged the court to hear him. Gallant gentlemen and fair ladies looked down on him from the galleries but far apart from these, in a distant corner, sat one whose tall form was enveloped in a cloak, and whose face was closely veiled. Beneath that cloak throbbed a mother's heart, and through that veil a mother's eyes sought the face she loved best on earth. He knew not she was there, for she rarely now asked a question respecting his engagements, or expressed any interest in his movements, yet how her ears drank in the music of his voice, and her eyes flashed back the proud light that shone in his! As she listened to his delineation of woman's claims to the sympathy and the defence of every generous heart, as she heard his biting sarcasm on the cowardly nature that, having wronged, would now crush into deeper ruin his fair client, as she saw kindling eyes fixed upon him, and caught, when he paused for a moment exhausted by the rush of indignant feeling, the low murmur of admiring crowds, how she longed to cry aloud, "My son my son!" He speaks again. Higher and higher rises his lofty strain, bearing along with it the passions of the multitude. He ceases and, as though touched by an electric shock, hundreds spring at once to their feet. The emphatic "Silence!" of the venerable judge hushes the shout upon their lips, but the mother has seen that movement, and, bursting into tears of proud triumphant joy, she finds her way below, and is in the street before the verdict which his eloquence had won was pronounced.

Edward Houstoun had fitted up a room in his mother's house as a study, and over his accustomed seat hung his father's portrait. To that room he went on his return from the scene we have described. Beneath the portrait stood one who seldom entered there. She turned at the opening of the door the lip, usually so firmly compressed, was quivering with emotion, and those stern eyes were full of tears. She advanced to him, drew near, and resting her head upon his shoulder whispered, "I, too, am a woman needing tenderness shut not your heart against me, my son, for without you I am alone in the world."

The proud spirit had bent, the sealed fountain was opened, and as he clasped his arms around her, the tears of mother and son mingled; but amidst the joy of this reunion Edward Houstoun felt more deeply than he had done for long months the desolation that had fallen on his life. His heart had been silent it now spoke again, and sad were its tones.

It is summer. The courts are closed, and all who can are escaping from the city's heat to the cool, refreshing shades of the country. Woe to those who remain! The pestilence has stretched her wings over them. The shadow and the silence of death has fallen on their deserted streets. The yellow-fever is in New-York introduced, it is said, by ships from the West Indies. Before it appeared Edward Houstoun was far away. He was travelling to recruit his exhausted powers to Niagara, perhaps into Canada, and in the then slow progress of news he was little likely to be recalled by any intelligence from the city. His mother was one of the first who had sickened. And where were now the fair forms that had encircled her in health where the servants who had administered with obsequious attention to her lightest wish? All had fled, for no gratified vanity no low cupidity can give courage for attendance on the bed of one in whose breath death is supposed to lurk. The devotedness of love, the self-sacrifice of Christian Charity, are the only impulses for such a deed. Yet over the sufferer is bending one whose form in its perfect development has richly fulfilled its early promise, and whose face is more beautiful in the gentle strength and thoughtfulness of womanhood than it had been in all its early brightness. In her peaceful home, where the reverent love of her young pupils and the confidence of their parents had made her happy, Lucy had heard from one of Lady Houstoun's terrified domestics of the condition in which she had been left, and few hours sufficed to bring her to her side. Days and nights of the most assiduous watchfulness, cheered by no companionship, followed, and then the physician, as he stood beside his patient and marked her regular breathing, her placid sleep, and the moisture on her brow, whispered, "You have saved her."

We will not linger to describe the emotion with which Lady Houstoun, awakening from this long and tranquil slumber, exhausted, but no longer delirious, first recognised her nurse. At first, no doubt, painful recollections were aroused, but with the feebleness of childhood had returned much of its gentleness and susceptibility, and Lucy was at once so tender and so cheerful, that very soon her ministerings were received with unalloyed pleasure.

Sickness is a heavenly teacher to those who will open their hearts to her. Lady Houstoun arose to a new life. She had stood so near to death that she seemed to have looked upon earth in the light of eternity. In that light, rank and title, with all their lofty associations and splendid accompaniments, faded away, while true nobleness, the nobleness which dwells in the Christian precept "Love your enemies do good to those that despitefully use you," stood out in all its beauty and excellence.

As soon as Lady Houstoun could be removed with safety, she went, by the advice of her physician, to her country-seat. Lucy would now have returned to her pupils she feared every day lest Edward Houstoun should appear, and a new contest be necessary with his feelings and her own but Lady Houstoun still pleaded her imperfectly restored health as reason for another week's delay, and Lucy could not resist her pleadings.

It was afternoon, and Lucy sat in the library, which was in the rear of the house, far removed from its public entrance. Spenser's Faery Queen was in her hand, but she had turned from its witching pages to gaze upon the title-page, on which was written, in Edward Houstoun's hand, "June 24th, 18 ." It was the day, as Lucy well remembered, on which he had first revealed his love, and chosen his career in life. She was aroused from her reverie by Lady Houstoun's entrance. As she held the door open, the bright sunlight from an opposite window threw a shadow on the floor which made Lucy's heart throb painfully. She looked eagerly forward a manly form entered and stood before her. She could not turn from the pleading eyes which were fixed with such intense earnestness on hers. With a bewildered half-conscious air she rose from her chair. He came near her and extended his arms. One glance at the smiling Lady Houstoun showed Lucy that her interdict was removed, and the next instant she lay in speechless joy once more upon her lover's bosom.

CHAPTER XIII

We were within three days of the New Year. Mr. Arlington, who was quite learned on the subject, had been amusing us with an account of its various modes of celebration in various countries. He was perfectly brilliant in a description of New-York as seen under the sun of a clear, frosty New-Year's morning, with snow enough to make the sleighing good. The gay, fantastic sleighs, dashing hither and thither, and their exhilarated occupants bowing now on this side and now on that, to acquaintances rushing by almost too rapidly to be distinguished, while the silvery bells ring out their merry peals on the still air. Then the festive array which greets the caller at every house within which he enters. Beauty adorned with smiles and dress, gayly decorated tables, brightly burning fires, and every thing seeming to speak the welcome not of mere form, but of hearty hospitality. There is one aspect in which he presents this day to us, that is peculiarly pleasing. He says, that many a slight estrangement, springing from some one of those "trifles" which "make the sum of human life," has been prevented, by the influence of this day, from becoming a life-long enmity. Thus the New-Year's day becomes a Peace-maker, and has on it the blessing of Heaven. Long live the custom which has made it such!

"And how shall we celebrate our New-Year?" asked Col. Donaldson.

"Let us introduce the New-York custom," suggested one.

"That would not do without some previous agreement with your neighbors," replied Mr. Arlington, "as their ladies would not probably be prepared for your visits, and while you were making them, the ladies of your own family would be left to entertain themselves as they could."

"That will never do," said Col. Donaldson; "better invite all our neighbors to visit us on that day. Suppose we give them a dinner?"

"Oh, papa!" cried Miss Donaldson in dismay. And "My dear husband!" ejaculated the smiling Mrs. Donaldson, "where would you find room to accommodate them all?"

"True true we could not dine them in the open air at this season."

"But there would be no such objection to an evening party," said one of the young Donaldsons. "We have fine sleighing now, and the moon rises only a little after eight on New-Year's evening; why not invite them for the evening."

"What, another such stiff affair as Annie insisted on entertaining her friends the Misses Morrison with the last winter, when I saw one of the poor girls actually clap her hands with delight at the announcement of her carriage?"

"Oh, no! Leave it to me, and it shall not be a stiff affair at all. We will appear in fancy dresses"

"My dear Philip!" remonstrated Mrs. Donaldson.

"Oh! not you, my dear mother, nor my father, unless he should like it indeed, it shall be optional with all but enough, I am sure, will like to make it an entertaining variety."

"But where shall we get fancy dresses, distant as we are from the city?" asked Annie.

"Leave yours to me, Annie, I have it ready for you," said Philip Donaldson, with so significant an air, that I at once suspected this suggestion to have been the result of the arrival on that very day of a box, addressed to him by a ship from Constantinople, of which he had hitherto made a great mystery.

"Thank you, Philip; but you cannot, I suppose, supply all the company, and I had rather not be the only one in fancy costume, if you please."

"If mamma will surrender to me the key of that great wardrobe, up stairs, which contains the brocade dresses, shoe-buckles, knee-buckles, etc., of our great-grandfathers and grandmothers, I will promise to supply dresses for our own party, at least, with a little aid from the needles and scissors."

"I bar scissors," cried Col. Donaldson. "Those venerable heir-looms"

"Shall not lose a shred, sir," said Philip; "the scissors shall only be used to cut the threads, with which the ladies take in a reef here and there, when it is necessary."

"But you have provided only for our party. Are our guests not to be in costume?"

"That may be as they please. We will express the wish, and if they have any ingenuity, they can have no difficulty in getting up some of the staple characters of such a scene, flower-girls and shepherdesses, sailors, sultans, and beggars."

The scheme seemed feasible enough, when thus presented, and had sufficient novelty to please the young people. It was accordingly adopted, and the evening was passed in writing invitations, which were dispatched at an early hour the next morning. The three succeeding days were days of pleasurable excitement, in preparation for the fête. Needles and scissors were both in active use, and the brocade dresses lost, I am afraid, more than one shred in the process of adjusting them to the figures for which they were now designed. Mrs. Dudley and Mrs. Seagrove were thus arranged as rival beauties of the court of Queen Anne. Philip Donaldson, with the aid of a bag-wig, for which Mr. Arlington has written at his request to a friend, in what city I may not say, and with some of his father's youthful finery, and the shoe and knee-buckles aforesaid, will make an excellent beau for these belles. Col. Donaldson, always ready for any harmless mirth, says they must accept him in his father's continental uniform for another. Mr. Arlington makes quite a mystery of his costume, but it is a mystery already revealed, both to Col. Donaldson and Philip, as I can plainly perceive by the significant glances they exchange whenever an allusion is made to it. Robert Dudley is to be a page, Charles Seagrove, a beautiful boy of six years old, an Oberon, and our little Eva a Titania. Mrs. Donaldson and I were permitted to appear in our usual dress, and Miss Donaldson strenuously claimed the same privilege, but it was not allowed. She resisted all entreaties, even from her favorite brother Arthur; but when her father gravely regretted her inability to sympathize with the enjoyments of others, she was overcome. Having yielded, she yielded entirely, and was willing to wear anything her sisters wished. As she is considered by them all, even in her thirty-third year, as the beauty of the family, her dress has been more carefully studied by them than any other. Every book of costumes within their reach was searched for it again and again, without success; one was rich, but unbecoming, another pretty, but it did not suit her style, and a third all they desired, but unattainable at so short a notice. As a last resource, my engravings were resorted to, and there, to my own surprise, they found what satisfied all their demands. One of the historical prints showed the dress worn in her bridal days by Hotspur's Kate. Miss Donaldson accepted it thankfully, as being less bizarre than any yet proposed to her, requiring nothing more than a full skirt of white satin, a jacket not very unlike the modern Polka, and a bridal veil. One condition she insisted on, however, namely, that Arthur should be her Hotspur. To this he consented without difficulty, not without an eye, I suspect, to the appearance of his tall, erect, graceful form and bearing in such a dress as Hotspur's.

The last evening of the Old Year had arrived, our preparations were completed, and our little party were experiencing something of that ennui which results from having nothing to do, when, in putting away the materials lately in use, Annie took up my engraving of Hotspur and Kate. Handing it to me, she said. "I know these engravings are precious, Aunt Nancy, though what can be the association with this one, I am, I acknowledge, at a loss to conceive."

"And yet it is a very simple one. I treasure it in memory of my friend Harry Percy and his bride."

"What! Hotspur?" questioned Annie with dilating eyes.

"Not quite, though he was a lineal descendant of the old Percys, and hot enough on occasion, too."

"You mean Colonel Percy of the British army, who married Miss Sinclair, of Havre de Grace, during our last war with England, or immediately after it, I never quite understood which. There seemed some mystery about the marriage, and I did not like to inquire too closely, but I dare say now, Aunt Nancy, you can tell us all about it."

"I believe I can. See Annie, if among these packages you can find one labelled 'The Test of Love.'"

"What! another story of a proud beauty winning her glove and losing her lover?" asked Mr. Arlington.

"No; my test, or rather my hero's test, was somewhat different," I replied, as I received the package from Annie, and read,

THE TEST OF LOVE:
A STORY OF THE LAST WAR

When Mr. Sinclair, the rector of St John's, in Havre de Grace took possession of his pretty parsonage, and persuaded the fair and gentle Lucy Hillman to preside over his unpretending ménage, and to share the comforts that lay within the compass of his stipend of one thousand dollars per annum, he felt that his largest earthly desires were fulfilled. A daughter was given to him, and with a grateful heart he exclaimed "Surely Thou hast made my cup to overflow."

But he too was a man "born to trouble." He too must be initiated into those "sacred mysteries of sorrow," through which the High-priest of his profession had passed. In the succeeding ten years, three other children opened their soft, loving eyes in his home, made its air musical with their glad voices and ringing laughter, and just as he had learned to listen for the pattering of their dimpled foot, and his heart had throbbed joyously to their call, they were borne from his arms to the grave, and the echoes which they had awakened in his soul were hushed for ever. Still his Lucy and their first-born were spared, and as he drew them closer to his heart he could "lift his trusting eyes" to Him from whom his faith taught him no real evil could come to the loving spirit. The shadow of earth had fallen on his heart, but the light of heaven still beamed brightly there. Years passed with Mr. Sinclair in that deep quiet of the soul which is "the sober certainty of waking bliss." His labors were labors of love, and he was welcomed to repose by all those charms which woman's taste and woman's tenderness can bring clustering around the home of him to whom her heart is devoted. But a darker trial than any he had yet known awaited him.

War is in our borders, and that quiet town in which Mr. Sinclair's life has passed is destined to feel its heaviest curse. Its streets are filled with soldiery. The dark canopy of smoke from which now and then a lurid flame shoots upward, shows that their work is destruction, and that they will do it well. Terrified women flit hither and thither, mingling their shrieks in a wild and fiend-like concert with the crack of musketry, the falling of houses, and the loud huzzas and fierce outcries of excited men. At a distance from that quarter in which the strife commenced, stands a simple village church, within whose shadow many of those who had worshipped in its walls during the last half century, have lain down to rest from the toils of life. No proud mausoleum shuts the sunshine from those lowly graves. Drooping elms and willows bend over them, and the whispering of their long pendent branches, as the summer breeze sweeps them hither and thither, is the only sound that breaks the stillness of that hallowed air. Near the church, on the opposite side from this home of the dead, lies a garden, whose roses and honey-suckles perfume the air, while its bowers of lilac and laburnum, of myrtle and jessamine, almost shut from the view the pretty cottage to which it belongs. All around, all within that cottage, is silent. Have its inmates fled?

The neighboring houses have been long deserted, and those who left them would gladly have persuaded their pastor to accompany them; but when they called to urge his doing so, he could only point to the bed on which, already bereft of sense, and evidently fast passing from life, lay one "all lovely to the last." Mrs. Sinclair's health, delicate for years, had rapidly failed in the last few months, till her anxious husband and child, aware that a moment's acceleration of the pulse, a moment's quickening of the breath from whatever cause, might snatch her from their arms, learned to modulate every tone, to guard every look and movement in her presence. But they could not shut from her ears the boom of the cannon which heralded the approach of the foe they could not hush the startling cries with which others met the announcement of their arrival, and the first evidences of that savage fury which desolated their homes, and left a dark stain on the escutcheon of Britain. Mrs. Sinclair uttered no cry when her terrors were thus excited, she even strove to smile upon her loved ones, to raise their drooping hearts; and in this, woman's holiest task, the springs of her life gave way not with a sudden snap, but slowly, gently so that for hours her husband and daughter stood watching the shadow of death steal over her, hoping yet to catch one glance of love, one whispered farewell ere she should pass for ever from them.

"Fear not, my child," said Mr. Sinclair, when their sad vigils were first interrupted by those who urged their flight "they are enemies, it is true, but they are Englishmen, a peaceful clergyman, a defenceless woman, are safe in their hands they will not harm us."

"I have no fear, no thought of them, father!" said Mary Sinclair, as she turned weeping to the only object of fear, or hope, or thought, at that moment.

But soon others of Mr. Sinclair's parishioners came to warn him that his confidence had been misplaced, that no character, no age, no sex, had proved a protection from the ruthless fury of their assailants. He would now have persuaded his daughter to accompany her friends to a place of safety, and when persuasions proved vain he would have commanded her, but, lifting her calm eyes to his, she said, "Father have you not taught me that, in all God's universe, the only safe place for us is that to which our duty calls us and is not my duty here?"

A colder heart would have argued with her, and might, perhaps, have proved to her that her duty was not there that her father could watch the dying, and that it was her duty to preserve herself for him; but Mr. Sinclair folded her in his arms while his lips moved for an instant in earnest prayer, and then, turning to his waiting friends, he said, "Go, go, my friends I thank you but God has called us to this, and he will care for us."

When the work of desolation had been completed in the quarter first attacked, parties of soldiers straggled off from the main body in search of further prey. Fearful was it to meet these men their faces blackened with smoke, their hands stained with blood, fierce frowns upon their brows, and curses on their lips. The parsonage presented little attraction in its external aspect to men whose object was plunder, and they turned first to larger and more showy buildings. These were soon rifled; the noise of their ribald songs, their blasphemous oaths and drunken revelry penetrating often the chamber of death, yet scarcely awakening an emotion in the presence of the great Destroyer. At length the little gate is flung rudely open, and unsteady but heavy steps ascend from the court-yard to the house. They cross the piazza, they enter the parlor where life's gentlest courtesies and holiest affections have hitherto dwelt, the door of the room beyond is thrown open, and two men stand upon its threshold, sobered for an instant by the scene before them. There, pale, emaciated, the dim eyes closed, and the face wearing that unearthly beauty which seems the token of an adieu too fond, too tender, too sacred for human language, from the parting spirit to its loved ones, the wife and mother, speechless, senseless, yet not quite lifeless, lay propped by pillows. At her side knelt Mr. Sinclair; the pallor of deep, overpowering emotion was on his cheek, yet in his lifted eyes there was an expression of holy faith, and you might almost have fancied that a smile lay upon the lips which were breathing forth the hallowed strains of prayer "Save and deliver us, we humbly beseech Thee, from the hands of our enemies, that we, being armed with thy defence, may be preserved evermore from all perils, to glorify Thee, who art the only giver of all victory, through the merits of thy Son, Jesus Christ our Lord Amen."

Dark, sinful men as they were, fresh from brutal crime, those strains touched a long silent chord in their hearts a chord linked with the memory of a smiling village in their own distant land with a mother's love and the innocence of childhood. Faint faint, alas! were those memories, and Mr. Sinclair's "amen" had scarcely issued from his lips, when the eyes of the leader rested on the beautiful face of Mary Sinclair, as, pressed to the side of her father, she stretched her arms out over her dying mother, and turned her eyes imploringly on their dreaded visitors. The ruffians sprang forward with words whose meaning was happily lost to the failing sense of the terror-stricken girl. Mr. Sinclair started to his feet, and with one arm still clasped around his daughter, stood between her and the worse than murderers before him, prepared to defend her with his life. For the first time he thirsted for blood, and looked around for some weapon of destruction but his was the abode of peace no weapon was there. Unarmed, with that loved burden loved at this moment even to agony, resting upon him he stood opposed to two fierce men armed to the teeth. A father's strength in such a cause, who shall estimate? yet, alas! his adversaries were demons, relentless in purpose, and possessed of that superhuman force which passion gives. Weary of killing, or influenced by that superstition which sometimes rules the soul from which religion is wholly banished, they did not avail themselves of their swords. With fierce threats they unclasped his arm from that senseless form, which sank instantly to the floor at his feet, and drew him across the room. They would have forced him into the parlor, but his resistance was desperate, and ere they could accomplish this, the sound of a drum beating the recall was borne faintly to their ears. Leaving his comrade to hold the wildly struggling father, the bolder ruffian turned back toward the still prostrate Mary. At that moment, before she had been polluted by a touch, the door was thrown violently back, and a tall, manly form strode through it. The gilded épaulettes and drooping feather told his rank, before the step of pride and countenance of stern command had conveyed to the mind the conviction that you stood in the presence of one accustomed to be obeyed. The man who grasped Mr. Sinclair loosened his hold and shrank cowering away. He went unnoticed, for the eye of the officer had fallen upon him who was in the act of stooping to lift Mary Sinclair from the floor. With a single spring he was at his side, and catching him by the collar of his coat, he hurled him from him with such force that he fell stunned against the farther wall. Mr. Sinclair was already bending over his daughter. As he raised her on his arm her head fell back, exposing her face, around which her dark hair swept in dense masses. Her features were of chiselled beauty, and had they been indeed of marble they could not have been more bloodless in their hue, while her jetty lashes lay as still upon her cheek as though the hand of death had sealed her eyes for ever. Mr. Sinclair had no such fear. He knew that she had only fainted, and rejoiced that God in his mercy had spared her the worst horrors of the scene; but as Captain Percy's eyes rested on her, a deeper scowl settled on his brow, and in a hoarse whisper he asked:

"Have they harmed her, sir?"

"Not by a touch, thank God! not by a touch!" exclaimed the father, as he pressed her with passionate joy to his heart ay, joy, even in the presence of her so long the light of his life now passing for ever from earth. For a few minutes the dying had been forgotten, for what was death a death of peace to the long misery into which man's base, brutal passion would have converted the life of that pure and lovely girl? Now, however, she was safe, and still supporting her on his arm, Mr. Sinclair turned to his wife and tenderly moistened her parched lips. What a mockery of all human cares seemed that pale, peaceful brow peaceful, while he whose lightest sorrow had thrown a shadow on her life was suffering anguish inexpressible, and the child who had lain in her bosom, to the lightest throb of whose heart her own had answered, lay senseless from terror in his arms. It was a scene to touch the hardest heart, and Captain Percy's heart was not hard. He looked around for the men whom he had interrupted in their hellish designs they were not there.

"Is this their work?" he asked of Mr. Sinclair, pointing to his scarcely breathing wife.

"No no this is the gentle hand of our Father," said Mr. Sinclair, as he bent his head and touched with his lips the sunken cheek dearer to him now than it had been in all its girlish roundness. The blood had begun to cast a slight tinge of red into the lips of Mary Sinclair before Captain Percy had left the room in search of the men whom he was unwilling to leave behind him, and when he returned, the tremor of her form and the close clasp with which she clung to her father, proved that her consciousness and her memory were awake. His step had startled her, and as he entered he heard Mr. Sinclair say, "Fear not, my daughter, that is the step of your deliverer, and though he is an English soldier "

"I pray you, sir, judge not Englishmen by ruffians like these a disgrace to the name of man. Believe me, every country has within it wretches, who, at moments such as this, when all social restraints are withdrawn, become demons. But I must leave you, in safety, I trust, as I have sent to the ships all the soldiers whom I could discover in your neighborhood."

"Farewell, sir," said Mr. Sinclair, extending his hand "God reward you for the timely aid you have this day brought to the defenceless. Look up, my child, and join your thanks with mine."

Mary Sinclair raised her head from her father's bosom, and lifting her eyes for an instant to the face of Captain Percy, unclosed her lips to speak, but voice and words were denied her.

"God bless you, lady!" he exclaimed, as taking her hand he raised it to his lips, and relinquishing it with one glance of sympathy at the dying, turned away and passed from the room. He returned once more, but it was only to leave his pistols with Mr. Sinclair.

"They are loaded, sir, and in such a cause as you needed them just now, even a Christian minister may use them."

Captain Percy spoke rapidly, only glancing at Mary, who was already bending with self-forgetful devotion above her mother's pillow, and before Mr. Sinclair could answer he was gone.

All was again silent in that deserted suburb, and for long hours nothing disturbed the solemn stillness of the chamber of death, save the low sob or earnest prayer of parting love, though sounds of tumult had not ceased wholly in the village. The invaders had been interrupted in their work of destruction by an alarm from some of their own party of an approaching foe. They hurried to their ships with mad impetuosity, conscious that their acts deserved only war to the knife, and that they were not prepared to cope with any regular force. Only they, who, like Captain Percy, had held themselves aloof from the brutal barbarities which they had striven vainly to prevent, were now composed enough to take any steps for the safety of others. To collect those who had straggled off was the first business, and while the recall was hastily beaten, Captain Percy, selecting a small party of men on whom he could depend, went to patrol the more distant quarters of the town. Having seen no trace of an enemy on his way to the parsonage, he had somewhat hastily concluded the alarm to be false, and therefore did not hesitate, before returning with his pistols to Mr. Sinclair, to send forward his men in charge of those whom he had found, promising to join them before they reached the point of embarcation. Without a thought of danger he traversed the silent and deserted streets on his return, and had arrived where a single turn would bring him within view of the rallying point of his companions in arms, when the sound that met his practised ears told of something more than the hurrying tread and mingling voices of soldiers rapidly embarking. Had his men been opposed? If so, they should not be without a leader and with that thought he sprang forward. He was too late. Already they had fought their way through the band of villagers, who, maddened by the desolation of their homes, had gathered together such weapons as they could, and led on by one gallant and experienced soldier, whom their burning houses had lighted to their aid, were seeking to cut off the retreat of some amongst their invaders, and thus to revenge those whom they had been unable to protect. Captain Percy's men had, as we have said, fought their way through this band not without loss. He now stood alone one against many with only his good sword to aid, for his pistols he had given to Mr. Sinclair. To retreat unobserved was impossible, for his own cry of "Forward forward, my men!" uttered as he rushed to the scene of the just decided contest, had betrayed him to fight against such odds with the faintest hope of success was equally impossible, and to yield was an alternative which there seemed to be no intention of offering him. In an instant twenty swords flashed before his eyes twenty muskets were pointed at his breast. That instant had been his last had not Major Scott, the leader of whom we have spoken, sprang forward and placed himself before him. Himself a brave and generous soldier, he could not tamely witness such butchery;

and pale with the terror for another which he had never felt for himself, he exclaimed, "Yield yourself, sir, quickly a moment's delay, and I cannot protect you."

Captain Percy's sword was in the hand of his noble foe, who, linking his arm in his, turned to face his own band, shouting as he did so, "Back back on your lives he is my prisoner, and who touches him makes me his enemy."

The day had passed with all its exciting incidents. The glow of sunset had faded into twilight's soberer hues, and these had deepened into the darkness of night. With the darkness silence had settled upon the streets of Havre de Grace. They who had trodden, for hours, with burning hearts around the sites of their desecrated homes, retired to the house of some charitable and more fortunate neighbor, to seek such rest as misery may hope. They went with sullen as well as sad brows, and as they passed one house in the village they muttered "curses not loud, but deep." This was the house in which Major Scott had found a refuge for himself and the prisoner, whom all his influence had scarcely been able to protect. To remove him from Havre de Grace in the light of day, and under the eyes of his infuriated enemies, was too hazardous a project to be attempted; and by the advice of some who seemed disposed to second his efforts for his safety, he had delayed his departure till night should veil the obnoxious features of the British officer.

At the parsonage, death had accomplished his work, and the room in which we have already seen Mr. Sinclair, bears the solemn impress of his presence. Beside the bed on which the lifeless limbs have been composed with tender care, the pastor kneels. His prayer is no longer, "Let this cup pass from me" he is struggling for power to say, "Father, not my will, but Thine be done!" In an upper room lies Mary Sinclair. Tears are falling fast as summer rain-drops from her closed eyes; but she utters neither sob nor moan, and by the dim light of the shaded lamp she seems to the two women, who, with well-meant but officious kindness, have insisted on watching with her through the night, to sleep. A slight noise in the street causes one of these women to start, and she whispers to the other, "I am 'feard of every thing to-night the least noise puts me all of a trimble, for I'm thinking of my Jack. He's gone to guard that British soger, and I shouldn't wonder if he had a skrimmage about him before morning."

"And I must say, Miss Dunham, if he did, it would be nothin' more than them deserves us would go for to guard them cruel British."

"But they do say, Miss Caxton, that this Capin for Jack says he is a Capin was better than the rest that he took the part of our people every where when he found there wasn't any fair fight, and that he was drivin' his men to the ships when we caught him."

"Them may believe that that will, but for my part I think that it must be a poor, mean speritted American that will hold guard over one of them British."

"Not so mean speritted as you think perhaps," said Jack's mother with a flushed face.

"Well, I must say, Miss Dunham, I never thought Jack would do such a thing if I had "

Miss Caxton stopped abruptly, but her companion would hear the whole "Well ma'am, if you had what if you had?"

"Why, then, Miss Dunham, I shouldn't have been so well pleased to see him keepin' company with my Sarah but after this, of course, that's at an end."

"May be, Miss Caxton, you may think to-morrow mornin' that it would have been just as well to wait till the night was gone before you said that when you see the British Capin hanging by the neck in his fine regimentals, and hear that his guard were the men that did it as I know they've sworn to do you may think after all they an't so mean speritted."

"Miss Dunham! if they'll do that, I'll unsay every word I've said, and proud enough I would be to call one of 'em my son-in-law but now do tell me all about it she's asleep you see," glancing at Mary Sinclair, "and there an't nobody to hear."

"Why, there an't much to tell. You see the Major wouldn't give way any how at all about this here man so, as they didn't want to fight him, they agreed that some of the real true blues who an't afeard of nothin', should seem to help the Major and persuade him to keep the man here till late in the night, and that they would guard him but they were to take care to have the key of his room, and when the Major goes there he'll find it empty, or at best only a bloody corpse there. They'll hang him if they can get him out of the window without too much noise, but if there's any danger of his waking the Major with his screeching, they'll stop his voice quick enough."

Any further conversation between these discreet watchers was prevented by a sudden movement on the part of Mary Sinclair. Springing from her bed she was hastening to the door when her steps were arrested.

"Dear me, Miss Mary! where are you going? Now do lie down again, my dear young lady! be patient it's the Lord's will, you know." Such were the remonstrances of her officious attendants, while, one on either side, they strove to lead her back again, but Mary persisted.

"I must go to my father, Mrs. Dunham, pray let me go, Mrs. Caxton, I must speak to my father."

"Well, then, my good young lady, just put your wrapping gown around you first, and put your feet in these slippers."

Mary complied silently, and then was suffered to proceed. Rapidly she flew to her father's room it was unoccupied, and a glance at his bed showed her that it had not been disturbed. Mary was at no loss to conjecture where she should find her father but as she approached that room her steps grew slower, lighter she was treading on holy ground. With difficulty she nerved herself to turn the latch of the door, and in an awed whisper she entreated her father to come to her. Mr. Sinclair rose from his knees, but he lingered a moment to cast one look on that still lovely face, to press his lips to that cold brow, and then, reverently veiling it, he approached his daughter.

"Come quickly, papa! not a moment is to be lost if you would save him from death, and such a death oh, papa, papa! it may be even now too late."

Her tale was rapidly told, and before it was concluded Mr. Sinclair was ready for action.

"But the house, Mary, what house is he in?"

This Mary could not tell, but rapidly ascending the stairs to her room, Mr. Sinclair obtained from the two gossips the information he sought. Startled as they were by his appearance, they reverenced the rector too much to question his designs. Leaving his daughter to forget even her own heavy sorrow in the imminent danger of another of one whom, without any very satisfactory reason, she as well as Mr. Sinclair had at once concluded to be her deliverer of the morning let us follow his steps.

The church clock tolled eleven as Mr. Sinclair passed, and the sound made his fleet movements fleeter still. Street after street was traversed without a voice or tread, save his own, breaking the stillness of the night. At length he reached the point of the day's devastations. Dismantled and roofless houses, from which a dull glimmer showed that the fire was not yet wholly extinguished, were seen rising here and there, while in intervening spaces a charred and smouldering heap alone gave evidence that man had had his dwelling there. A rapid glance as he passed without a pause over this ground told its desolation. But see what object meets his eye, and causes every nerve to thrill with apprehension! From the midst of one of those blackened heaps a single post shoots up wildly Mr. Sinclair casts his eyes upward to its summit gracious heaven! is he too late? To that post, about twenty feet from the ground, a cross-piece is attached, to which a rope has been secured, and from that rope a dark object hangs motionless. Sick with horror he stops he gazes no! it is no illusion dimly defined against the star-lit sky, his eye, dilated by terror, traces the form of man, and fancy supplies the traits of him who stood before him but a few hours since in all the flush of manhood every moment replete with energy, every look full of proud resolve and generous feeling. With a searching glance Mr. Sinclair looks around for the murderers but they are gone again, his strangely fascinated eye turns to that object of horror. Is it the agitation of a death struggle which causes it now to swing to and fro in the dusky air? The thought that life may not yet be extinct gives him new strength he runs he flies to Major Scott's lodgings, for from him alone is he secure of aid in his present purpose.

As Mr. Sinclair approached the house in which Major Scott had found accommodations for himself and his prisoner, he found himself no longer in darkness. More than one burning torch threw a lurid light upon the scene, while the men who held them, and perhaps as many as twenty more stood clustered together, near the house, against which some of them were engaged in elevating a ladder. In what service that ladder might have been last used Mr. Sinclair shuddered to think. Perfect stillness reigned in this party. Their few orders were given in whispers.

Keeping cautiously in shadow, and moving with stealthy steps, Mr. Sinclair passed them and reached the house. Even when there, he had little hope of making Major Scott hear him without alarming them, and he could not doubt that they would do every thing in their power to frustrate his object. But Heaven favored his merciful design he touched the door and found it ajar. All was dark as midnight within it, and he had scarcely taken a step when he stumbled against a man whose voice sounded fiercely even in the low whisper in which he ejaculated, "D n you. Do you want to wake the Major? Don't you see you're at his room door?"

"I see now, but it was so dark at first," whispered Mr. Sinclair in reply adding with that quickness of perception and readiness of invention which danger supplies to some minds "I have come to watch him you are wanted."

The man obeyed the intimation, and he had no sooner turned away than Mr. Sinclair laid his hand upon the latch of the door which had been indicated as Major Scott's. It yielded to his touch, and with a quick but cautious movement he entered the room, and closed the door behind him. Cautious as he was, the soldier's light sleep was broken, and he exclaimed hurriedly, "Who's there?"

Mr. Sinclair's communication was made in a hasty whisper, and Major Scott only heard enough to know that his prisoner was in danger. Of Mr. Sinclair's worst suspicions he did not even dream when, starting to his feet, half dressed, as he had thrown himself on the bed, he snatched his pistols from under his pillow, and exclaiming to Mr. Sinclair, "Follow me, sir," hurried to the scene of action, the room of Captain Percy. Mr. Sinclair followed with rapid steps.

In one respect the conspirators had been disappointed they had not obtained the key of Captain Percy's room, for being now a prisoner on parole, he was subject to no confinement. He had, however, locked the door of his room himself, to guard against the incursion of curiosity rather than of hostility; but the lock was none of the strongest a single vigorous application of Major Scott's foot to the door started the screws which held it, and a second burst it off and threw the entrance open before him. As Mr. Sinclair glanced forward, "Thank God!" burst from his lips, to the no small surprise of Major Scott, who saw little cause for gratitude in finding the object of his solicitude retreating, sword in hand, towards the door, while several athletic men, their faces dark with hate, were already pressing dangerously upon him, and others were crowding in at the opened window. The impetuous rush of his friends freed Captain Percy for a moment from his assailants, but they returned fiercely to the charge, too furious now to postpone their revenge even to their deference for Major Scott. Vain were Mr. Sinclair's entreaties to be heard, till their advance was stayed by the sight of Major Scott's firearms weapons with which they had not furnished themselves, considering them useless in an enterprise to whose complete success silence was essential. Then first they listened to him as he exclaimed, "This man is innocent, and if you shed his blood it will call to Heaven for vengeance. I saw him myself this day oppose himself to two of his own countrymen to save a defenceless woman from injury. That woman was my daughter some of you know her well ah, Thompson!

you may well hang your head would you slay the deliverer of her whose good nursing saved the life of your motherless child? Wilson, it was but last week that she sat beside your dying mother, and soothed and comforted her but for this good and brave man she would now have been with her in heaven."

It was only necessary to gain a hearing for such words to produce an influence on the rash, but not cruel men whom Mr. Sinclair addressed, and scarcely half an hour had passed since their entrance into the room, when they offered their hands in pledge of amity to him whose life they had come to seek. As a proof of their sincerity, they advised Major Scott no longer to delay his departure from the town, and some of them volunteered to accompany him as a guard to his country-seat.

"You have saved my life," said Captain Percy, as he shook hands with Mr. Sinclair at parting.

"And you have preserved for me all, except my duties, for which I can now desire to live," answered Mr. Sinclair with emotion: then turning to Major Scott, he added, "as soon as you consider it safe, you will, I hope, bring Captain Percy to visit us. In the mean time, Captain Percy, remember that the stranger and the prisoner are a clergyman's especial care, and suffer yourself to want nothing which I can do for you. By-the-by," and he took Major Scott aside and whispered him.

"Give yourself no concern about that, my dear sir," said Major Scott in reply, "I will attend to it."

He did attend to it, and Captain Percy's drafts on his captor were promptly met, till he was able to open a communication with the British commander.

In as quiet a manner as possible Major Scott and Captain Percy moved off from the hotel, and were met in the suburbs by their volunteer guard, while another party of the men whom he had thus saved from a great crime, attended Mr. Sinclair to his home. As he entered the area of the smouldering ruins his eye sought the object lately viewed with so much horror. He had scarcely glanced at it, when one of his companions stepped up and disengaged a dark cloak from the noose already prepared for its expected victim "I knew no one would steal it from the gallows," said the man, as he threw it over his shoulders. Mr. Sinclair smiled to think how easily imagination had transformed that harmless object into the fair proportions of a man.

Nothing more was heard of Captain Percy for weeks dreary weeks to many in Havre de Grace melancholy weeks to the inmates of the parsonage, who missed at every turn the familiar step and voice which had been life's sweetest music to their hearts. At length Mr. Sinclair received a note from Major Scott, announcing his own approaching departure to the army on our northern frontier, and requesting permission for Captain Percy and himself to call on Mr. and Miss Sinclair. Permission was given the call was made, and they who had met only in scenes of terror and dismay, amidst flushing looks and fierce words, now greeted each other with gentlest courtesy among sounds and sights of peace. The call was succeeded by a visit of some days, and this by one of weeks, till at last it seemed to be understood that the parsonage was to be the home of Captain Percy while awaiting the exchange which Major Scott had promised to do all in his power to expedite. His society was at the present time peculiarly pleasing to Mr. Sinclair, who was diverted from his own sad thoughts by the varied intelligence of the soldier and traveller in many lands. Mary Sinclair had been unable to meet her deliverer without a thrill of emotion which communicated an air of timidity to her manner, whose usual characteristic was modest self-possession. Captain Percy, at thirty-five, had outlived the age of sudden and violent passion, but he had not outlived that of deep feeling. A soldier from boyhood, he had visited almost every clime, and been familiar with the beauties of almost every land, yet in this lovely and gentle girl, whom he had guarded from ill, and whom he now saw in all the pure and tender associations of her home, blessing and blessed, there was something which touched his heart more deeply than he liked to acknowledge even to himself. Again and again when he saw the soft, varying color that arose to her cheek at his sudden entrance, or heard the voice in which she was addressing another, sink into a more subdued tone as she spoke to him, did he take his hat and wander forth, that he might still in solitude his bosom's triumphant throb, and reason with himself on the folly of suffering his affections to be enthralled by one from whom, ere another day passed, he might be separated by orders which would send him thousands of miles away, and detain him, perhaps, for years.

"If I thought her feelings were really interested," he would say to himself at other times "but nonsense how can I be such a coxcomb all she can feel for me is gratitude."

This last sentiment was echoed by Mary Sinclair, who, when self-convicted of unusual emotion in Captain Percy's presence, ever repeated, "It is only gratitude."

One evening Mr. Sinclair retired after tea to his study, leaving his daughter and his guest together. He had not been gone long when a servant entered with the letters and papers just brought by the semi-weekly mail, which conveyed to the inhabitants of Havre de Grace news of the important events then daily transpiring in distant parts of the country. The only letter was a somewhat bulky one for Captain Percy. Mary received the papers and commenced reading them, that she might leave her companion at liberty. Had she been looking at him she would have seen some surprise, and even a little annoyance in his countenance as his eyes rested on the seals of his dispatch. He opened it, and the annoyance deepened. He read it more than once. Minutes passed in perfect silence, and Mary began to wonder what correspondent could so deeply interest him. A heavy sigh made her look up. His letter lay open on the table before him, but he had evidently long ceased to read, for his arm rested upon it, while his eyes were fixed with an expression at once intent and mournful on her. Mary thought only of him as she said, "I hope you have no painful intelligence there, Captain Percy."

"I suppose I ought to consider it very joyful intelligence I am no longer a prisoner I have been exchanged, and" he hesitated, looked away, then added rapidly "I am ordered immediately to join my regiment in Canada."

A quick drawing of the breath, as though from sudden pain, met his ear his heart beat quickly, but he would not embarrass her by a glance. There was a slight rustling of her dress, and turning he saw that she had risen, and with one hand pressed upon the table for support, was advancing to the door. Falteringly, one two three steps were taken, and completely overcome, pale and ready to faint, she sank upon a sofa near her. He sprang forward, but she motioned him away, and covering her face with her hands, burst into tears tears of shame as well as of sorrow. For an instant he stood irresolute but only for an instant, when bending over her, he whispered, "Dare I hope that you sympathize with me, Mary that the feeling which made even liberty painful to me since it separates me from you, is not confined to my own bosom?"

Mary's sobs ceased but she spoke not moved not.

"Answer me, dear Mary remember I have little time to woo, for my orders admit of no delay in their execution I must leave you to-morrow. Rise then above the petty formalities of your sex, and if I may indeed hope ever to call you mine, let me do so this night this hour your father will not, I think, fear to commit you to my tenderness."

Mary uncovered her face, and raised her eyes for an instant to his, with an expression so confiding that he thought his suit was won, and pressing her hand to his lips, he said, "That glance tells me that you are my own, Mary. My life shall prove my gratitude but now I must seek your father our father will you await us here?"

"I have something to say to you sit down and hear me," said Mary, in a voice which she strove in vain to raise above a whisper.

He placed himself beside her on the sofa, still clasping the hand he had taken, and with a voice faltering and low at first, but gathering strength as she proceeded, Mary resumed: "I will not attempt I do not wish to deny that you have read my heart aright that that you who saved me are are " a lover's ear alone could detect the next words "very dear to me but I cannot I think I ought not "

She paused, and Captain Percy said, "You are not willing to intrust your happiness to one so lately known."

"Oh, no! you mistake my meaning I can have no doubt of you no fear for my own happiness but my father who will care for him if I, his daughter, his only child, thus give myself to another at the very time that he needs me most?"

"I will not take you from him at least not now, Mary give me but the right to call you mine, and I will leave you here in your own sweet home not again, I trust, to be visited by war till peace shall leave me at liberty to return to England with my bride my wife."

He would have clasped her to him as he named her thus, but Mary struggled almost wildly to free herself, exclaiming, "Oh! plead not thus lest I forget my father in myself my duty in love the forgetfulness would be but short I should be unhappy even at your side, when I thought of the loneliness of heart and life to which I had condemned him."

"But he should go with us he should have our home. It will be a simple home, Mary for though I come of a lordly race, I inherit not their wealth but it will be large enough for our father."

"Kind and generous!" exclaimed Mary, as she suffered her fingers to clasp the hand in which they had hitherto only rested, "would that it might be so but that were to ask of my father a sacrifice greater even than the surrender of his daughter the sacrifice of his sense of duty to the people who have chosen him as their spiritual father and to whom he considers himself bound for life."

Captain Percy remained silent long after she had ceased to speak, with his eyes resting on her downcast face. At length in low, sad tones, he questioned, "And must we part thus?"

Mary's lips moved, but she could not speak.

"I will not ask you to remember me, Mary," he resumed, "for if forgetfulness be possible to you, it will perhaps be for your happiness to forget yet pardon me if I am selfish I would have some little light amidst the darkness gathering around my heart may I hope that had no duty forbidden you would have been mine?"

She yielded to his clasping arm, and sinking on his bosom, murmured there, "Yours yours ever and only yours wholly if I could be yours holily."

From this interview Mary retired to her chamber, and Captain Percy sought his host in his study. After communicating to Mr. Sinclair the contents of the dispatch he had just received, he continued, "I must in consequence of these orders leave you immediately but before I go I have a confession to make to you. You will not wonder that your lovely daughter should have won my heart; but one hour since, I could have said that I had never yielded for an instant to that heart's suggestions had never consciously revealed my love, or endeavored to excite in her feelings which, in my position and the present relations of our respective countries, could scarcely fail to be productive of pain. I can say so no longer. The moment of parting has torn the veil from the hearts of both she loves me," there was a joyous intonation in Captain Percy's voice as he pronounced these last words. He was silent a moment while Mr. Sinclair continued to look gravely down then suddenly he resumed "Pardon my selfishness I forget all else in the sweet thought that I am loved by one so pure, so gentle, so lovely. But though I have dared without your permission to acknowledge my own tenderness, and to draw from her the dear confession of her regard, there my wrong has ended she has assured me that she could never be happy separated from you, and that you are wedded to your people." Mr. Sinclair shaded with his hand features quivering with emotion. "At present," continued Captain Percy, "these feelings, which are both of them too sacred for me to contest, place a barrier between us, and I have sought from her no promise for the future if she can forget me " Captain Percy paused a moment, then added abruptly "may a happier destiny be hers than I could have commanded but, sir, the time may come when England shall no longer need all her soldiers an orphan and an only child, I have nothing to bind me to her soil should I seek you then, and find your Mary with an unchanged heart, will you give her to me? will you receive me as a son?"

"Under such circumstances I would do so joyfully," Mr. Sinclair replied, "yet I cannot conceal from you now that I grieve to know that my daughter must wear out her youth in a hope long deferred at best, perhaps never to be realized."

Both gentlemen were for a few minutes plunged in silent thought. Captain Percy arose from his seat walked several times across the room, and then stopping before the table at which Mr. Sinclair was seated, resumed the conversation.

"Had I designedly sought the interest with which your daughter has honored me," he said, "your words would inflict on me intolerable self-reproach, but I cannot blame myself for not being silent when silence would have been a reproach to her delicacy and a libel on my own affection. Now, however, sir, I yield myself wholly to your cooler judgment and better knowledge of her nature, and I will do whatever may in your opinion conduce to her happiness, without respect to my own feelings. If you think that she can forget the past, and you desire that she should" his voice lost its firmness and he grasped with violence the chair on which he leaned "I will do nothing to recall it to her memory. It is the only amende I can make for the shadow I have thrown upon her life dark indeed will such a resolve leave my own."

"It would cast no ray of light on hers. Be assured her love is not a thing to be forgotten it is a part of her life."

"And it shall be repaid with all of mine which my duties as a soldier and subject leave at my disposal. Do not think me altogether selfish when I say that your words have left no place in my heart for any thing but happiness I have but one thing more to ask you it is a great favor inexpressibly great but "

"Nay nay," Mr. Sinclair exclaimed, gathering his meaning more from his looks and manner than from the words which fell slowly from his lips "ask me not so soon to put the irrevocable seal upon a bond which may be one of misery."

"If your words be true if her love be a part of her life, the irrevocable seal has been already affixed by Heaven, and I only ask you to give your sanction to it, that by uniting her duty and her love, you may save her gentle spirit all contest with itself, and give her the fairest hope of future joy."

It was now Mr. Sinclair's turn to rise and pace the floor in agitated silence "I know not how to decide so suddenly on so momentous a question," he at length exclaimed.

"Suppose you leave its decision to her whom it most concerns. It is for her happiness we are most anxious so entirely is that my object that I would not influence her determination even by a look. I will not even ask to be present when you place my proposal before her; but I must repeat, sir, if you design to do it, there is no time to be lost, for I must be on my way to Canada to-morrow."

"So be it then she shall choose for herself, and Heaven direct her choice!"

"Amen!" responded Captain Percy, as Mr. Sinclair turned from the door. He heard him ascend the stairs, and ask and receive admission to his daughter's room. Then he counted the seconds as they grew into minutes the minutes as they extended to a quarter of an hour a half-hour and rolled slowly on towards the hour which lacked but little to its completion, when his straining ear caught the sound of an opening door, and then Mr. Sinclair's sedate step was heard slowly descending the stairs and approaching the study. Captain Percy met him at the door, and looked the inquiry which he could not speak. Mr. Sinclair replied to the look, "She is yours!"

"May I not see her and receive such a confirmation of my hopes from her own lips!"

"Not to-night I have persuaded her to retire at once she needs repose, and we must be early astir. Your marriage must for many reasons be kept secret at present, and as I could not, I fear, find witnesses here on whose silence I could rely, we will accompany you in the morning to Major Scott's, and there, in the presence of his wife and sister, your vows shall receive the sanction of the church. You must have some preparation to make, and I will bid you good night, for there are certain legal preliminaries necessary to the validity of a marriage here, to which I must attend this evening unusual as the hour is."

There was a strange mingling of emotion in the hearts of the lovers as they stood side by side within that room in the gray dawn of the next morning. In a few hours they were to part, they knew not for what distance of space or duration of time. It might be that they should never after this morning look upon each other's faces in life; yet, ere they parted, there was to be a bond upon their souls which should make them ever present to each other, should give them the same interests, should, as it were, mould their beings into one. Sacred bond of God's own forming, which thus offers the support of a spiritual and indissoluble union amidst the separations and changes of this ever-varying life! No such strength and peace are to be found in the frail and casual ties for which man in his folly would exchange this bond of Heaven.

Few words were spoken during the burned breakfast at the parsonage, or the drive to Major Scott's, for deep emotion is ever silent. Yet not for them were the coy reserves often evinced by hearts on the verge of a life-union the faltering timidity which hesitates to lift the veil from feelings in whose light existence is thenceforth to pass. They could not forget that they were to part, and even Mary hesitated not to let her lover read in her eyes' shadowy depths the tenderness which might soothe the parting pang, and whose memory might brighten the hours of separation.

Why should we linger on a scene which each heart can depict for itself? With solemn tenderness the father pronounced the words which transferred to another the right to his own earthly sanctuary the heart of his daughter and committed to another's keeping his last and brightest earthly treasure. That treasure was soon, however, returned, for a time, to his care. The vows of the marriage rite had scarcely been uttered, when with one long clasp one whispered word one lingering look the disciplined soldier turned from his newly-found joy to his duties. Never had Mary seemed more lovely in his eyes or her father's than in that moment, when with quivering lips, eyes "heavy with unshed tears," and cheeks white with anguish, she yet smiled upon him to the last. Nor did her heroic self-control cease when he was gone. Her father was still there, and for him she endured and was silent. Only by her languid movements and fading color did he learn the bitterness of her soul through the weary months of her sorrow. Weary months were they indeed!

One letter she received from Captain Percy, written before he had passed beyond the limits of the United States. It breathed the very soul of tenderness. "My wife!" he wrote, "what joy is summed in that little word what faith in the present what promise for the future! I find myself often repeating it again and again with a lingering cadence, while your gentle eyes seem smiling at my folly." Long, long did Mary wear this letter next her heart, and still no other came to take its place.

They had parted in 1813, just as the falling leaves came to herald the approach of winter. That winter passed with Mary in vain longing and vainer hopes. Spring again clothed her home with beauty, but there came no spring to her heart. Summer brought joy and gladness to the earth, but not to her, and another autumn closed over her in anxious suspense. There were moments when she could almost have prayed to have that dread silence broken even by a voice from the tomb other times in which she threw herself on her knees in thankfulness that she could yet hope. From Major Scott she had heard that Captain Percy's regiment had been sent to the South, but of him individually even Major Scott knew nothing. At length came the eighth of January, that day of vain triumph on which thousands fell in the contest for rights already lost and won the treaty of peace having been signed at Ghent on the twenty-fourth of the preceding month. Forgetful of this useless hecatomb at war's relentless shrine, America echoed the gratulations of the victors which fell with scathing power on the heart of the trembling Mary. How could she hope that he, the fearless soldier, had escaped this scene of slaughter! If he had, surely he would now find some way to inform her of his safety, but weeks passed on, and passed still in silence.

During this long period of suspense, no doubt of the tenderness and truth of him she loved had ever sullied Mary's faith. Mr. Sinclair was not always thus confiding, and once, on seeing the deadly pallor that overspread her face on hearing the announcement of "no letters" he uttered words of keen reproach on him who could so wrong her gentle heart.

"Oh, father!" Mary exclaimed, "speak not thus be assured it is not his fault remember that no license could tempt him to wrong the defenceless think how honorable he was in suppressing his own feelings lest their avowal should bring sorrow on us and when my self-betrayal unsealed his lips, how delicate to me, how generous to you was his conduct and who but he could have been so rigid in his observance of a soldier's duty, yet so inexpressibly tender as a man! I loved him because I saw him thus true and noble and having seen him thus how can I doubt him? He may be no longer on earth, but wherever he is, he is my true and noble husband, and you will not again distress me, dear father, by speaking as though you doubted him."

"Never," said Mr. Sinclair emphatically, and he never did, though he saw her form grow thinner, and her cheek paler every day, and before the winter was gone heard that deep, hollow cough from her, which has so often sounded the knell of hope to the anxious heart. With the coming on of summer this cough passed away, but Mary was oppressed by great feebleness and languor scarcely less fatal symptoms. Still she omitted none of those cares essential to her father's comfort while to the poor, the sick, the sorrowing, she was more than ever an angel of mercy. With feeble steps and slow she still walked her accustomed round of charity, and thus living for duty she lived for God, and had His peace shed abroad in her heart, even while sorrow was wearing away the springs of her life. She loved to sit alone and send her thoughts forward to the future not of this life, but of that higher life in which there shall be no shadow on the brightness of our joy where love shall be without fear no war shall desolate no opposing duty shall separate no death shall place its stony barrier between loving hearts. With a mind thus occupied, she wandered one day, in the latter part of August, through the garden of the parsonage and the yard immediately surrounding the church into the little inclosure beyond, within which was the green and flowery knoll that marked her mother's last resting-place. As she turned again towards her home the sound of a carriage driven rapidly by caused her to look towards the road which lay about a hundred yards distant. The carriage rushed by, and she caught but a glimpse of a gentleman leaning from its window. In another moment a grove of trees had hidden both the carriage and its occupant from her sight yet that glimpse had sent a thrill through her whole frame a mist passed over her eyes, and with eager, trembling steps, she proceeded on her way. As she reached the garden, she thought she saw her father approaching it from the house, but her path led through a summer-house, and when she had passed through it he was no longer visible. Every thing in the house wore its usual air of quietness on her entrance, and with a feeling of disappointment, for which she could not rationally account, she turned her steps towards her father's study. As she drew near the door she heard his voice the words, "I dread to tell her," met her ear and made her heart stand still. One step more and she was at the door she looked eagerly forward, and with a glad cry sprang into the extended arms of her husband.

It was long before any of the party were sufficiently composed for conversation. When that time came, Captain or rather Colonel Percy heard with surprise that no letters had been received from him since his joining the army in Canada. He had written often, but had been obliged to send his letters to some distant post-town by his own servant. As he had declined accompanying Colonel Percy to America, there was reason to suppose that he had suspected the character of the correspondence, perhaps had acquainted himself fully with the contents of the letters, and had taken effectual means to prevent their reaching their destination, with the hope of thus completely removing from Colonel Percy's mind every inducement to return to this country. Having received a disabling though not dangerous wound at the battle of New Orleans, Colonel then Major Percy was sent home with despatches, and was immediately ordered to join the army under Lord Wellington, then rapidly hastening to repel the attempt of the prisoner of Elba to re-establish himself on the throne of France. From this period till the battle of Waterloo all private concerns were merged in the interest and the hurry of great public events. In that battle Major Percy was again slightly wounded. His distinguished bravery was rewarded by his being made again the bearer of despatches to England. As it was evident to all that the struggle which had called the whole force of Britain into the field was now at an end, he had no hesitation in asking and no difficulty in obtaining leave of absence from the commander-in-chief, and had lost no time in embarking for America.

"As a consequence of peace," said Colonel Percy in conclusion, "a large part of our force will be disbanded, and many officers put on half-pay. A friend who is very influential at head quarters has undertaken to secure me a place on the list of the latter and henceforth, dear Mary, your home is mine!"

"And did you never doubt me during all this long silence?" he asked of his happy wife a few days after his return.

"Never," said Mary firmly, and then added in a more playful manner "if I should step into the confessor's chair, could you answer as boldly?"

"I can, Mary though I never received a line from you, it never occurred to me to fear any change in your affection. Our marriage had placed on it the seal of duty, and your conduct in relation to your father had shown me that that seal you could not easily break."

"Then you did not love me less for not yielding every other consideration to the gratification of your wishes?" said Mary, endeavoring to speak lightly, but betraying deeper feeling by the slight tremor in her voice, and the quick blush mantling in her cheek.

"Love you less!" exclaimed Colonel Percy warmly "my love had been little worthy of your acceptance, dearest, had it been lessened by seeing that your principles were paramount even to your affections. Happy would it be for all your sex, Mary, did they recognize as the only test of a true and noble love, that it increases with the increase of esteem, and finds more pleasure in the excellence of its object than in its own selfish triumphs."

Ere the winter of 1815 had set in, Mary's rounded form and blooming cheek relieved all Mr. Sinclair's apprehension of her consumptive tendencies, and proved that her love was indeed, as he had said, "a part of her life."

CHAPTER XIV

The New-Year's day the day after which the year is no longer new is come and gone; and while sitting here to record its events before I sleep, I look back at it with pleasure, chastened by such thoughts as the young seldom have. I believe of all such eras the aged may say as the poet says of his birthday:

"What a different sound
That word had in my younger years!
And every time the chain comes round,
Less and less bright the link appears."

To all, these eras mark their progress on the journey of life; but to the young they are bright with the promise of a happier future; the aged, they direct to the grave of the buried past, and they read on them the inscription so often found on the Roman monumental stones, "Siste, Viator." Travellers are we from time to eternity, and it is well that we should meet with these imperative calls to stand and consider. Cheered by the Christian's hope, we can stand; we can look steadily on the past, count the lengthening line of these memorials of our dead years, and feel that but few more probably lie between us and the river of death, yet, strong in the might of Death's great Conqueror, "bate no jot of heart or hope."

These are grave though not sad thoughts; too grave to mingle readily with the record of mirthful scenes, howsoever innocent may have been the mirth. I must, therefore, lay aside my pen, and reserve the description of our New-Year for tomorrow.

Our New-Year opened with a cold and cloudless morning, and our party met at breakfast with faces as bright as the sun. Gifts were exchanged between the parents and children, the brothers and sisters gifts, trifling in themselves, but dear from their association with the cherished givers. It was an endearing sight to see the venerable parents receiving from their children testimonies of that affectionate consideration which the care and tenderness of years had so well deserved. Tears were on Mrs. Donaldson's cheeks, and even the Colonel's eyes glistened as they clasped one after another of their children to their hearts, and invoked on them the blessing of Heaven. From this scene Mr. Arlington and I had stood aloof, silent, but not uninterested spectators. As the excitement of the principal actors subsided, we approached and tendered our hearty congratulations, and received equally hearty congratulations in return. Neither had Aunt Nancy been altogether forgotten in the mementos of affection provided for the day; and I thought Mr. Arlington looked a little envious as Annie, with a kiss, threw around my neck a chain woven of her own hair, and suspended to it the eye-glass which I always wore. I do not know but his envy may have been somewhat allayed by a very handsomely decorated copy of an English work on sporting, with which Col. Donaldson presented him. He had scarcely found time, however, to admire it, when all attention was attracted to Philip Donaldson, who entered with a servant bearing the mysterious box to which I have before alluded.

"There is my New-Year present to you, Annie," he said, as he began to open it. All drew near and looked on with interest, yet few felt much surprise when, the cover being removed, a Greek dress was disclosed. From the rich head-dress of silvered muslin to the embroidered slipper, all was complete. Annie looked on with a smile as he displayed piece after piece yet her smile wore some appearance of constraint; and when Philip, drawing her to him, kissed her cheek and said, "Not a word for me, Annie!" with her thanks were mingled some hesitating expressions of apprehension that this dress would be very conspicuous, concluding with the timid question, "Do you really wish me to wear it this evening, Philip?"

"Certainly, Annie. It was in order to show you in this dress that I proposed fancy dresses for this evening; you will not disappoint me?"

"Certainly not at least not willingly I will wear it. If I wear it ungracefully you will forgive me?"

"I am not afraid of that," said Philip, as he glanced at her glowing face with a brother's gratified pride.

Miss Donaldson advised that Annie should try on the dress at once, as she prudently suggested it might require some alteration.

"Come with me, Aunt Nancy," said Annie as she left the room to comply with this advice.

"Come back here and let us see you, Annie, when you have put it on," said Col. Donaldson.

Annie would have passed from the room without an answer, evading the compliance which she could not refuse, but the Colonel called her back and did not dismiss her till assured that the request, which he knew would be regarded as a command, had been heard.

The dress needed no alteration. We afterwards found that Philip had sent his friend a measure procured from Annie's maid, and the fit was perfect. I am not quite sure that Annie, as she saw the beautiful figure reflected in her glass, regretted the command which compelled her to show herself to the party awaiting her in the library, to which we had withdrawn from the breakfasting room, that we might not interfere with the household operations, of which the latter was, at this hour, the scene. Yet it was with a little coy delay and blushing timidity that she, at length, suffered me to lead her thither.

"Beautiful!" "I never saw her look so well!" "I knew it would become her!" were the exclamations that greeted her, on her entrance, deepening the flush upon her cheek, and calling up a brighter smile to her lips. Mr. Arlington alone was silent, but his soul was in his eyes, and they spoke an admiration compared to which the words of others were tame.

"My dear Annie," said her mother, as she gazed delightedly upon her, "how I wish I had a likeness of you in that dress! you do look so remarkably well in it."

Mr. Arlington stepped forward. "Would you permit me " to Mrs.

Donaldson "Would you do me the favor " to Annie "Might I be allowed " with a glance at the Colonel, "to gratify Mrs. Donaldson's wish. It should be my New-Year's offering. I would ask only an hour of your time " deprecatingly to Annie. "That would give me an outline which I could fill up without troubling you."

Mr. Arlington was so earnest, and Mrs. Donaldson so gratefully pleased, that if Annie had any objections, they were completely overborne. Mr. Arlington produced his sketching materials, and disposed his subject and his light, and then intimated so plainly that the consciousness of the observation of others would be fatal to his success, that we withdrew, leaving only Philip with a book in a distant corner "to play propriety," as he whispered to me on passing, with a mischievous glance at the blushing Annie.

And now the reader doubtless thinks, that in the engraving prefixed to this volume, he has a copy of the sketch made on this New-Year's morning. In this, however, he deceives himself, for the work of this morning amounted to the merest and most unfinished outline, which would have stood for Zuleika as well as for Annie Donaldson. Yet instead of one hour, Annie generously allowed Mr. Arlington nearly to triple the time. How he was occupied during all this time, I cannot tell, though that he did not spend all of it in drawing I had ocular demonstration.

Nearly three hours, as I have said, had passed since we left the library, when, looking from my window, I saw Philip, returning to the house on horseback. Having left in the library a book in which I was much interested, I had been waiting somewhat impatiently for Annie's appearance, to satisfy me that I might without intrusion return thither for it. I now concluded, somewhat too hastily, as it afterwards proved, from seeing Philip abroad, that the sitting was at an end, and accordingly went for my book. I entered noiselessly, I suppose I am usually quiet in my movements by a door directly opposite to the seat which Mr. Arlington had arranged for himself, and behind the sofa on which, at his desire, Annie had been seated when I left her. There still was Mr. Arlington's seat, and before it a table with the drawing materials and unfinished sketch, but Mr. Arlington was on the sofa beside Annie. He was speaking, but in tones so low, that even had I wished it, I could not have heard him; but the few seconds for which surprise kept me chained to the spot, were sufficient to suggest the subject of those murmured words. The reader will probably conjecture that subject without aid from me, when I tell him what I saw. Of Annie, as she sat with her back to me, I could only see the drooping head and one crimson ear and cheek; Mr. Arlington's face was turned to her, and was glowing with joy, and as it seemed to me with triumph. Before I had turned away, he raised her hand to his lips. I saw that it rested unresistingly in his clasp; and gliding through the door by which I stood, I closed it softly and left them unconscious of my presence.

The invitations had been given for the early hour of half-past seven, and at seven, by previous arrangement, our own party collected in the library dressed for the evening. There stood Col. Donaldson in the uniform of a continental major, gallantly attending a lady whose fine dark eyes and sweet smile revealed Mrs. Seagrove, notwithstanding the crimped and powdered hair, patched face, hoop, furbelows, and farthingale, which would have carried us back to the days of Queen Anne. Mrs. Dudley, in similar costume, was attended by Philip Donaldson, who looked a perfect gentleman of the Sir Charles Grandison style in his full dress, with bag-wig and sword. Arthur Donaldson, in the graceful and becoming costume of the gallant Hotspur, was seated with his Kate by his side, and if Kate Percy looked but half as lovely in her bridal array as did her present representative, she was well worthy a hero's homage. But in the background, evidently shrinking from observation, stood a figure more interesting to me than all these it was our "sweet Annie" as Zuleika our Bride, not of Abydos leaning on the arm of a Selim habited in a costume as correct and as magnificent as her own, yet who could scarcely be said to look the character well; the open brow of Mr. Arlington, where lofty and serene thought seemed to have fixed its throne, and his eyes bright with present enjoyment and future hope, bearing little resemblance to our imaginations of the wronged and desperate Selim, whose very joy seemed but a lightning flash, lending intenser darkness to the night of his despair. I was the last to enter the room, and as I approached Mr. Arlington, he presented me with a very beautiful bouquet. I found afterwards that he had made the same graceful offering to each of the ladies at the Manor, having received them from the city, to which he had sent for his Greek dress and Philip's wig. Put up in the ingenious cases now used for this purpose, the flowers had come looking as freshly as though they had that moment been plucked. The bouquet appropriated to Annie differed from all the others. It was composed of white camélias, moss-rose buds, and violets. As I was admiring it, Annie pointed to one of the rose-buds as being eminently lovely in its formation and beautiful in its delicate shading. It was beautiful, but my attention was more attracted by the sparkling of a diamond ring I had never before seen upon her finger. The diamond was unusually large, the antique setting tasteful. With an inconsideration of which I flatter myself I am not often guilty, I exclaimed in surprised admiration, "Why, Annie, where did you get that beautiful ring?"

The sudden withdrawing of the little hand, the quick flushing of cheek, neck, brow, told the tale at once; a tale corroborated by the smiling glance which met mine as it was turned for a moment on Mr. Arlington. Her confusion was beautiful, but he was too generous to enjoy it, and strove to bring me back to the flowers.

"Have you ever seen some beautiful verses, translated from the German, by Edward Everett I believe, entitled 'The Flower Angels?'" he asked.

"I never did; can you repeat them?"

He answered by immediately reciting the verses which I here give to the reader.

THE FLOWER ANGELS

As delicate forms as is thine, my love,
And beauty like thine, have the angels above;
Yet men cannot see them, though often they come
On visits to earth from their native home.
Thou ne'er wilt behold them, but if thou wouldst know
The houses in which, when they wander below,
The Angels are fondest of passing their hours,
I'll tell thee, fair lady they dwell in the flowers.
Each flower, as it blossoms, expands to a tent
For the house of a visiting angel meant;
From his flight o'er the earth he may there find repose,
Till again to the vast tent of heaven he goes.
And this angel his dwelling-place keeps in repair,
As every good man of his dwelling takes care;
All around he adorns it, and paints it well,
And much he's delighted within it to dwell.
True sunshine of gold, from the orb of day,
He borrows, his roof with its light to inlay;
All the lines of each season to him he calls,
And with them he tinges his chamber walls.
The bread angels eat, from the flower's fine meal,
He bakes, so that hunger he never can feel;
He brews from the dew-drop a drink fresh and good,
And every thing does which a good angel should.
And greatly the flowers, as they blossom, rejoice
That they are the home of the angel's choice;
And again when to heaven the angel ascends,
The flower falls asunder, the stalk droops and bends.
If thou, my dear lady, in truth art inclined,
The spirits of heaven beside thee to find,
Reflect on the flowers and love them moreover,
And angels will always around thee hover.
A flower do but plant near thy window-glass,
And through it no spirit of evil can pass;
When thou goest abroad, on thy bosom wear
A nosegay, and trust me an angel is near.
Do but water the lilies at break of day,
For the hours of the morn thou'lt be whiter than they;
Let a rose round thy bed night-sentry keep,
And angels will rock thee on roses to sleep.
No frightful dreams can approach thy bed,
For around thee an angel his watch will have spread;
And whatever visions thy Guardian, to thee,
Permits to come in, very good ones will be.
When thus thou art kept by a heavenly spell,

Shouldst thou now and then dream that I love thee right well;
Be sure that with fervor and truth I adore thee,
Or an angel had ne'er set mine image before thee.

The visitors soon began to arrive. There were among them some amusing characters, so well supported as to give rise during the evening to many entertaining scenes; but to me this was the group and this the incident of the evening. Not a group or an incident for prurient curiosity or frivolous jest, but for an earnest and reverent recognition of that beautiful law imposed on Nature by her Great Author, by which the feeble delight in receiving, and the strong in giving support that law by which a pure and self-abnegating affection is made the source of life in all its commingling relations of its duties and its sympathies its joys and its sorrows of its severest probation and its loftiest development.

It was in the solemnity of spirit, engendered by thoughts like these, that I stood at the window of my room, looking forth upon the still and moonlit night, long after our friends had left us. My door opened softly and Annie glided in, and ere I was aware of her presence, was standing beside me with her head resting on my shoulder. A tear was on the cheek to which I pressed my lips. A few whispered words told me whence the ring came but not for the public are the pure, guileless confidences of that hour.

Our holiday festivities were over, and the next day the Christmas Guests departed. They had stepped aside awhile from the dusty thoroughfares on which they were accustomed to pursue their several avocations, for the interchange of friendly sympathy with each other, and the offering of grateful hearts to Heaven, and now they were returning, cheered and strengthened to their allotted work. Reader, go thou and do likewise

"Like a star
That maketh not haste,
That taketh no rest,
Let each be fulfilling
His God-given best."

THE END

www.ingramcontent.com/pod-product-compliance
Lightning Source LLC
Chambersburg PA
CBHW011255040426
42453CB00015B/2414